GOING
UNDER

LOUISIANA STATE
UNIVERSITY PRESS
Baton Rouge
and London

◎◎◎◎◎◎◎

GOING UNDER

Melville's

Short Fiction

and the

American

1850s

MARVIN FISHER

Copyright © 1977 by Louisiana State University Press
All rights reserved
Manufactured in the United States of America
Designer: Albert Crochet
Type face: VIP Caledonia
Typesetter: Graphic World, Inc., St. Louis, Missouri
Printer and Binder: Kingsport Press, Kingsport, Tennessee

LIBRARY OF CONGRESS CATALOGING IN PUBLICATION DATA

Fisher, Marvin, 1927–
    Going under.
    Includes bibliographical references and index.
    1.   Melville, Herman, 1819–1891—Criticism and
interpretation.   I.   Title.
PS2387.F54   813'.3   77–2986
ISBN 0–8071–0267–9

CONTENTS

ABBREVIATIONS

ATT   "The Apple-Tree Table" (1856)

BC   "Benito Cereno" (1855)

BS   "Bartleby, the Scrivener" (1853)

BT   "The Bell-Tower" (1855)

CDD   "Cock-A-Doodle-Doo!" (1853)

Enc.   "The Encantadas" (1854)

Fid.   "The Fiddler" (1854)

HF   "The Happy Failure" (1854)

HHM   "Hawthorne and His Mosses" (1850)

IMC   "I and My Chimney" (1856)

JR   "Jimmy Rose" (1855)

LRM   "The Lightning-Rod Man" (1856)

PBTM   "The Paradise of Bachelors and the Tartarus of Maids" (1855)

Piaz.   "The Piazza" (1856)

PMP   "Poor Man's Pudding and Rich Man's Crumbs" (1854)

TT   "The Two Temples" (submitted in 1854 but not published in Melville's lifetime)

All of the fifteen stories appear in Jay Leyda (ed.), *The Complete Stories of Herman Melville* (New York: Random House, 1949).

The essay "Hawthorne and His Mosses" appears in *Billy Budd and Other Prose Pieces*, ed. Raymond W. Weaver (New York: Russell & Russell, 1963).

PREFACE

A good prefatory statement should justify and explain the work that follows. These purposes are especially important here because any informed readers would naturally ask whether we really need another study of Herman Melville's short fiction, whether this work, like much of the literary criticism emanating from university faculties, might be another laborious effort to mine a nearly exhausted vein of medium-yield ore. For many years these stories seemed to mark the period of Melville's growing disappointment and, subsequently, the decline of his talent and his reputation. But it would be a serious mistake to read *Going Under* as an analysis or a description of Melville's decline. I clearly do not feel that way, and I hope that no reader who is stimulated to return to Melville's short fiction will feel that way.

Despite the number of analyses and commentaries on individual stories—particularly "Bartleby" and "Benito Cereno"—and despite the existence of a useful book like R. H. Fogle's *Melville's Shorter Tales* or R. Bruce Bickley's recent study, *The Method of Melville's Short Fiction*, I have found that some important things have not yet been said about these stories, their place in the context of Melville's work, and especially their relation to mid–nineteenth-century American culture. Obviously I cannot agree with any easy dismissal of these stories as second-rate efforts of an important, if erratic, writer. While there exists considerable variation in conception and execution (few would want to argue the uniform excellence and profundity of any collection of short fiction), there are notable examples of advanced or experimental narrative, attempts at innovative symbolism, and frequently penetrating efforts to define and evaluate American manners, institutions, and ways of thought.

This concern with the crucial aspects of American experience, often in contrast to the Old World, links the fifteen short stories that Melville wrote between 1853 and 1856. I do not know whether he intended to collect them or publish them as a cycle of short fiction; indeed there is evidence that no publisher would have been willing to gamble on there being an audience for such a collection. There is also evidence that many of these stories were grossly misunderstood. In *The Profession of Authorship in America, 1800–1870*, the late William Charvat wrote that Melville "masks his rejections of public values and slogans so skillfully that, although twelve out of fifteen of his magazine pieces deal essentially and unsentimentally with some kind of loss, poverty, loneliness, or defeat, some of the blackest of these were praised as 'quaint,' 'fanciful,' 'lifelike,' 'genial,' and 'thoroughly magazinish'" (279).

He did, however, bring together the lengthy "Benito Cereno" and "The Encantadas" as well as the shorter "Bartleby," "The Lighting-Rod Man," "The Bell-Tower," and "The Piazza" in a collection which he finally entitled *The Piazza Tales* (1856), after initially considering *"Benito Cereno" and Other Sketches*. No one would argue that "The Piazza" is as significant a story as "Benito Cereno," nor would any admirer of Melville like to think that the author's choice of title for the collection and assignment of primacy to "The Piazza" indicated his estimation of the relative value or importance of the two stories. In my opinion, the choice of the titles and introductory position reveals Melville's attempt to stress a thematic link in the stories and not the superiority of "The Piazza" to "Benito Cereno." The point of "The Piazza"—and a motif in all of these stories—is that where one stands determines his view of truth and reality, and shapes his values. In fact, the concept of point of view is technique as well as theme in these stories and constitutes a good part of Melville's modernity. I think, further, that these six stories were not written with the intent of fitting them together later, but that Melville was aware of his own recurrent concerns in life and in art, and knew quite definitely what he was working toward. The result was a short story cycle with ascertainable lines of connection and integration.

The larger collection—*The Complete Stories of Herman Melville*, edited by Jay Leyda—impresses me as having similar thematic interrelationships. Although lacking the specific focus of a collection like James Joyce's *Dubliners* or Sherwood Anderson's *Winesburg, Ohio, The Complete Stories* seems to have much in common with these later works. Melville, no less than Joyce, was concerned with the moral and spiritual paralysis of his time and place, and the fifteen stories which he wrote in the space of a few years—after the major undertakings of *Moby Dick* (1851) and *Pierre* (1852)—like the fifteen stories of *Dubliners*, explore a series of social, intellectual, and spiritual crises. Despite their markedly different settings, Melville's stories reflect several very grave and distinctively American cultural dilemmas, and in the depths of their disillusionment suggest that mid–nineteenth-century America had betrayed the promises of its inception and fallen victim to its moral faults. They suggest apocalyptically that the social and political ideas of American life and the uniqueness and optimism of the American dream—rather than Melville's talent or intellect—were going under.

My approach to these stories is not strictly chronological but rather thematic, though I have kept chronological development in mind and discussed it when it seemed relevant. I hesitate to list these themes for fear of seeming to pigeonhole the stories when in fact the stories frequently contain overlapping themes. But having justified this exercise in cultural history and literary criticism, I should offer some further explanation. In brief, I have found the following themes instrumental in organization and analysis: (1) innocence and experience; (2) contrasts between America and Europe; (3) freedom and servitude, and class and caste in American society; (4) the condition of Christianity; (5) the interrelatedness of political community, spiritual communion, and artistic communication; (6) the dilemma of the artist in America; and (7) irreconcilable differences and irrepressible conflicts in American attitudes and values.

In the first sketch of "The Encantadas," an overview entitled "The Isles at Large," Melville's assertion that "in no world but a fallen one could such lands exist" expands in meaning as it washes upon distant shores. More skillfully than in *Mardi* (1849), a crude but ambitious allegorical survey of the ways of the world, Melville creates "The Isles at Large" as "the world in small," and the inferno-like physical conditions become a metaphor for the trials of human existence, even in a socially advanced, politically progressive, intellectually enlightened, and technologically impressive New World. To write such things openly would dismay publishers and offend the majority of potential readers; thus, Melville devised a strategy that might provide him a measure of safety as well as an opportunity to publish some unpopular truths through the indirection of symbolism, allusion, and analogy. Although he had tried all these techniques previously, he had not attempted so consciously and thoroughly to practice "the great Art of Telling the Truth" in what he had come to recognize as "this world of lies." He chose to *go under* as a literary strategy, to become our first major underground writer at a time when he could not even ascertain that there existed any significant readership capable of understanding or response.

I am indebted to Melville scholars whose contributions have been variously bibliographical, biographical and historical, critical, and analytic, and I regret that my citations could not include them all. My students have frequently rekindled my interests and occasionally succeeded in freshening my approach. The Arizona State University Grants Committee has generously assisted at several stages. And I should like to thank the editors of the following journals for permission to reprint material that first appeared in their pages: *Southern Review, American Quarterly, Criticism, Studies in Short Fiction, American Transcendental Quarterly, Forum,* and also the Southern Illinois University Press for a segment that appeared in *American Dreams, American Nightmares,* edited by David Madden.

GOING
UNDER

1

◎◎◎

PORTRAIT OF
THE ARTIST IN
AMERICA

"Hawthorne and His Mosses"

Herman Melville's effusive review of Nathaniel Hawthorne's *Mosses from an Old Manse*, published in two parts in the August 17 and 24 issues of *Literary World* for 1850, a full four years after the first publication of Hawthorne's book, must be one of the strangest pieces of literary criticism by an American in the nineteenth century. Like Poe's earlier reviews of Hawthorne's tales, Melville's review is ultimately self-serving and far more revealing of the tastes, ambitions, and anxieties of the reviewer than of his subject. Poe had combined theory and analysis, tonally permeated by sophisticated condescension, in two logical and authoritative essays; Melville's effort, on the other hand, is the antithesis of logical exposition. He applies the devices of fiction to the appraisal of a collection of sketches and short fiction, and the result is far more narrative than expository in form. It is, in this sense, his first published work of short fiction; it predates his other short fiction by three years and falls between the publication of *White-Jacket* in 1850 and *Moby Dick* in 1851.

Occasionally this narrative form becomes markedly dramatic, or even melodramatic, as reviewer and author become protagonists in an elaborately staged, highly imaginative account of intellectual and emotional encounter. The act of a reviewer's intellectual grappling with the work he is considering is a familiar cliché, but Melville finds the metaphor so intriguing that he fashions a fictitious setting, a more appropriately pseudonymous persona for himself, and a cast of

1

lesser characters that includes two minor American writers and two superstars as well. The pseudonym and the fictitious setting enable him to include himself as a quasi-fictitious narrator—to place himself in the work—discussing Herman Melville and Nathaniel Hawthorne as figures in history, participants in a sacramental conception of literary creativity, and characters in a dramatic version of cultural mythology.

The opening sentence of the review provides a set of stage directions for the ensuing drama: "a papered chamber in a fine old farmhouse—a mile from any other dwelling, and dipped to the eaves in foliage—surrounded by mountains, old woods, and Indian ponds—this, surely, is the place to write of Hawthorne."[1] The second sentence compounds the reviewer's attitude and commitment to art: "Love and duty seem both impelling to the task." And the third sentence announces the central dramatic strategy: "A man of a deep and noble nature has seized me in this seclusion"—a strategy of seduction, intellectual impregnation, and creative germination.[2] Elaboration of this strategy not only enables Melville to dramatize Hawthorne's impact on a receptive reader and the anticipated result of this experience, it also enables him to treat in a novel way the familiar idea of an authentic American culture. Melville's approach to this idea leads him to define the task of the American artist and to suggest the obstacles in his way. The intertwined themes of the review are those of American literary nationalism, Hawthorne's impressive contribution to that cause, and Melville's emergent role in the same campaign. It is ostensibly a portrait of Hawthorne as the first literary genius in America, the writer who fills the archetypal role of the artist; but Melville scarcely conceals his hope that his portrait of the artist will be in significant details a self-portrait also. As a

1. Herman Melville, "Hawthorne and His Mosses," *Billy Budd and Other Prose Pieces*, ed. Raymond W. Weaver (New York: Russell & Russell, 1963), 123. Subsequent references to Melville's review are in parentheses.

2. In a lively essay that was regrettably too short to do much more than suggest the underlying pattern and deeper importance of Melville's review, John Seelye has examined these symbolic implications: "The Structure of Encounter," in Howard P. Vincent (ed.), *Melville and Hawthorne in the Berkshires* (Kent, Ohio: Kent State University Press, 1968), 63–69. See also Edgar A. Dryden, *Melville's Thematics of Form: The Great Art of Telling the Truth* (Baltimore: Johns Hopkins Press, 1968), 21–29.

vital chapter in the autobiography of an American artist, this essay is more than remotely analogous to Walt Whitman's "Out of the Cradle," for Melville seems to be saying that his own efforts at short fiction "awaked from that hour" of seminal encounter with Hawthorne's art.

In this instance Melville has given himself "plenty of sea-room to tell the Truth in," another way of saying that highly imaginative fictional content could express the truth of an idea more totally than a literal, logical ordering of fact (133). As John Seelye has pointed out, there is, from the pseudonym on, an intentional transforming of fact into fiction. Melville was in no actual sense "a Virginian Spending July in Vermont." He received his copy of the *Mosses* from his aging Aunt Mary, transformed for purposes of the review into charming, young Cousin Cherry. He concealed the fact that he had previously met Hawthorne and denied that he had wider acquaintance with Hawthorne's work than what was provided by a belated reading of the *Mosses*. All of this is designed to produce an element of freshness, innocence, surprise, and pleasure in the cultural possibilities of America and the personal prospects of a young American.

Cousin Cherry provides more than the natural bounty of strawberries and raspberries that grace the narrator's breakfast board. She serves as the muse who directs the alleged Virginian to discover the rarer bounty—the artistic fruition of Hawthorne's *Mosses*—and to develop the as-yet-unfulfilled potentialities within himself. When she hands him "a volume, verdantly bound, and garnished with a curious frontispiece in green with a fragment of real moss cunningly pressed to a flyleaf," and causes him to spill his raspberries in his excitement, she seems an agent of pastoral fertility affirming various possibilities of creative generation. The moss is a sign of "perennial green," rooting new life in the decaying past, and even Hawthorne's name is a playful part of this pastoral pattern of moss, flowers, and fruit. This "flowering Hawthorne" is also rooted in the wild world of nature; his leaf and blossom are unfolding signs of emergent hope and creative accomplishment. His "ruddy thoughts" fall "into your soul" with "the thump of a great apple . . . falling . . . from the mere necessity of perfect ripeness!" (HHM, 124–26). Later the narrator asserts that "to glean after this man is better than to be in at the harvest of others," but the ultimate consequence is the most meta-phorically daring part of the pattern of creative encounter: "But already I feel that this Hawthorne has dropped germinous seeds into my soul. He expands and deepens down, the more I contemplate him; and further, and further, shoots his strong New England roots into the hot soil of my Southern soul" (HHM, 138–39). The "Virginian" has lost his provinciality and joined in a union that is at first self-consciously American and ultimately international. But even more important, the intellectual stimulation has been such that Melville can convey it primarily in metaphors of erotic excitement—the emotional intimacy such that it turns his own creative potentialities into images of procreative power.

To suggest that his response to Hawthorne's work is more than a fleeting infatuation, Melville finds ways to elevate Hawthorne to superhuman status and then to claim some special status for himself. He draws from every major source of sacred value—religion, literary tradition, the celebration of nature and the scenic sublime, and even popular patriotism—to describe Hawthorne's character and accomplishment. His analogies and allusions produce a combination of literary and dramatic iconography and transform his own enthusiasm into autobiographical art and illuminating cultural comment.

These areas of reference and reverence overlap, but that is in keeping with the spontaneous, enthusiastic feeling of Melville's review. Had he separated the sources of his awe, he might have written a more conventionally discursive piece of literary appreciation. It would have been easier to understand, a good deal less interesting, and much less revealing or prophetic of Melville's own venture into short fiction.

The opening paragraph, as I have suggested, sets the scene of this dramatic encounter in a landscape of mountains, woods, ponds, and an isolated farmhouse. In these circumstances Hawthorne first seems a New England Pan: "His wild, witch voice rings through me; or, in softer cadences, I seem to hear it in the songs of the hillside birds that sing in the larch trees at my window" (HHM, 123). To follow Hawthorne, "an excellent author, of your own flesh and blood," Melville tells his American audience later in the review, is to explore the interior of your own continent or the landscape of your own mind and to discover the sublime wonders of the American condition: "The smell of your beeches and hemlocks is upon him; your own broad prairies are in his soul; and if you travel away inland into his deep and noble nature, you will hear the roar of his Niagara" (HHM, 136–37).

For our alleged visitor from the South, Hawthorne proves a superlative guide to the wonders of nature and human nature, far better than the one the Virginian first chose—Timothy Dwight's *Travels in New England and New York*. In the strategy of Melville's fictive review, Cousin Cherry offers Hawthorne's *Mosses* as better suited for mornings in the haymow than Dwight's *Travels* which she had found there on the previous day. Removing Dwight from the haymow in favor of Hawthorne is a highly symbolic act, far more significant than the mode of playful eroticism might suggest. For Melville it marks the beginning of a new maturity, a new stage of national consciousness. In "The American Scholar" Ralph Waldo Emerson had already prescribed a compound of inspiration and self-assertion as the remedy for an enfeebled condition in American culture, insisting that "we have listened too long to the courtly muses of Europe." Melville's rejection of Dwight is a similar assertion, for he seems to be saying not only that we have listened too long to those European formulations, but also that we have comforted ourselves too long with their bland American imitators, of whom Dwight is a leading example.

Calvinist clergyman and president of Yale, Dwight was one of the more ponderous of the Connecticut Wits. Among his most famous literary productions were an Hebraic epic allegorizing the American Revolution, written in Miltonic style and entitled *The Conquest of Canaan: A Poem in Eleven Books*; an attack on deism, entitled *The Triumph of Infidelity: A Poem*; and *Greenfield Hill: A Poem in Seven Parts*, celebrating the American countryside and its citizenry in the manner of Sir John Denham's *Cooper's Hill* or Oliver Goldsmith's *Deserted Village*. Timothy Dwight was a solid fixture in the American cultural establishment.[3] His *Travels in New England and New York*, published posthumously in 1821 and 1822, is of no more use to Melville's narrative persona than young Redburn's outdated guidebook is to him; neither book corresponds to the world that exists.

In fact such a guidebook becomes an obstacle rather than an aid to understanding. It is as if a tourist were "to travel along a country road," Melville says in his review, "and yet miss the grandest or sweetest of prospects, by reason of an intervening hedge so like all other hedges as in no way to hint of the wide landscape beyond" (HHM, 124). Dwight had become such a barrier or hedge, screening the present and preserving the preconceptions of the past. On this conceptual dead wood the "perennial green" of Hawthorne's *Mosses* generates new life and new opportunities. Melville very likely has Dwight in mind when he denounces servile American imitators of English authors as examples of "literary flunkyism" and adds "we want no American Goldsmiths; nay, we want no American Miltons." And he was just as likely thinking of Washington Irving, when in the same paragraph he relegates to minor status "that graceful writer, who perhaps of all Americans has received the most plaudits from his own country . . . —that very popular and amiable writer, [who] however good and self-reliant in many things, perhaps owes his chief reputation to the self-acknowledged imitation of a foreign model, and to the studied avoidance of all topics but smooth ones" (HHM, 135–36).

Despite, or perhaps because of, his pompous didacticism and his formidable opposition to what he liked to call "infidel philosophy," Dwight had become a false god himself for mid–nineteenth-century Americans. His imitation of seventeenth- and eighteenth-century English models prolonged the authority of the past in matters of lit-

3. The quality of Dwight's mind and the character of his art are conveyed in an early lyric written in obvious imitation of Robert Herrick's advice "To the Virgins, to Make Much of Time." Herrick's poem began:

> Gather ye rosebuds while ye may,
>   Old Time is still a-flying;
> And this same flower that smiles today,
>   Tomorrow will be dying.

Dwight's echo seems to have bounced off *The New England Primer*:

> Look, lovely maid, on yonder flow'r,
>   And see that busy fly,
> Make for the enjoyment of an hour
>   And only born to die.

erary taste and enforced cultural dependence in a broader sense. And Irving was no better for his subservience to Europe and his pandering to an audience that applauded his skillful replay of the same easy pieces. In dramatizing his discovery of Hawthorne and his original use of American material, Melville is something of an iconoclast, trying to turn his fellow Americans from worship of false gods and to communicate the "shock of recognition" that is the central epiphany of his supraliterary experience.

While Dwight has been so widely acknowledged, Hawthorne, Melville says, has been scarcely noticed. This circumstance, he further implies, places Hawthorne in a position analogous to "our Saviour," whose physical appearance gave no hint "of the augustness of the nature within" and enabled him to walk unrecognized among "those Jewish eye-witnesses" who failed to "see heaven in his glance" (HHM, 124). To many of those who know him, Hawthorne seems merely "a pleasant writer, with a pleasant style—a sequestered, harmless man, from whom any deep and weighty things would hardly be anticipated: a man who means no meanings." What Melville discerns, however, is far more profound: "a depth of tenderness . . . a boundless sympathy . . . an omnipresent love." Humor and intellect establish a balance between his "Indian-summer sunlight" and "this great power of blackness in him" (HHM, 127–29). But his values are ignored and his meanings misinterpreted by Americans who bow before another false god or are at least possessed by a false preconception of the literary genius, the cultural messiah whom they await so expectantly: "They fancy he will come in the costume of Queen Elizabeth's day, be a writer of dramas founded upon old English history, or the tales of Boccaccio." These misguided Americans who miss Hawthorne's gifts because he is so totally a part of their own times again relive the experience of those who, "while their Shiloh was meekly walking in their streets, were still praying for his magnificent coming; looking for him in a chariot, who was already among them on an ass" (HHM, 132–33).[4]

---

4. As a proper name, *Shiloh* both "designates the Messiah and refers to the peacefulness of his disposition and his reign." Literally, a "place of tranquillity," it is "the town in central Palestine where the tabernacle was placed immediately after the conquest of Canaan by Joshua." John D. Davis and Henry S. Gehman, *The Westminister Bible Dictionary* (Philadelphia: Westminister Press, 1944), 557.

In several senses, then, Melville's review is an enthusiastic call to fellow Americans to discard the pieties and the preconceptions which blind them to present realities and thereby recognize the genius in their midst. It is, of course, a far-from-selfless act on Melville's part; he would not be content merely to announce that the messiah of American letters had arrived. The splendor of the American Shiloh, Melville seems to believe, would reflect on the emergent literary community in which he counted himself. Proper recognition of Hawthorne would bring joy to his generation of Americans, further encouragement to him, and inestimable cheer to other aspiring writers.

The intensity of his attempt to arouse Americans to what had occurred results from Melville's opinion that both the Epiphany and the Eucharist are communal not individual experiences. As he wrote to Hawthorne in November, 1851, in gratitude for Hawthorne's response to *Moby Dick*, "I feel that the Godhead is broken up like the bread at the supper, and that we are the pieces. Hence this infinite fraternity of feeling."[5] Delighted that his book has communicated matters of significance to Hawthorne, he feels himself not merely participating in a communion ceremony but undergoing transubstantiation himself and subsequently forming a community with others who shared the experience.

A similar conceptual pattern underlies the dramatic exposition of Melville's review. Through his Old and New Testament references, Melville strongly suggests that Hawthorne's book is like those sacred scrolls in the Ark of the Covenant, and the New England barn in which he reads this revealing book is like the tabernacle. The book communicates to him variously and profoundly. In it he has seen the moral landscape of America, heard the roar of Hawthorne's Niagara, perceived a universal guide to human nature, and figuratively at least, fallen in love and found God. Recognizing Hawthorne's accomplishment has further, dynamic effects, or as Melville more significantly puts it: "By confessing him, you thereby confess others; you brace the whole brotherhood." The proper acknowledgment of Hawthorne does not merely enhance his reputation; it assures and

5. Merrell R. Davis and William H. Gilman (eds.), *The Letters of Herman Melville* (New Haven: Yale University Press, 1960), 142.

preserves the opportunity for all other potential shapers of American culture and consciousness. His achievement is their salvation, "for genius, all over the world, stands hand in hand, and one shock of recognition runs the whole circle round" (HHM, 137). It is a joy-filled way of asserting, whether in an aesthetic or a spiritual sense, that it takes one to know one. Having begun with the unprecedented power of one book to communicate, the process leads exuberantly through a stage of communion, to culminate in community.

Quite possibly, Melville's flagrant nationalism, his announced intent "to carry republican progressiveness into Literature, as well as into Life," and his hostility to English dominance over American cultural expression protected him from charges of blasphemy and allied excesses. The seemingly good-natured enthusiasm with which he echoes Emerson's earlier views of America's unique innocence and opportunity shows that his heart is in the right place: "The world is as young today as when it was created and the Vermont morning dew is as wet to my feet as Eden's dew to Adam's." And the blatancy of his assertion "that men not very much inferior to Shakespeare are this day being born on the banks of the Ohio" needs no forgiveness, for when was blatancy ever a sin in America? Most Americans had grown accustomed to hearing and reading that "we are rapidly preparing for that political supremacy among the nations, which prophetically awaits us at the close of the present century," and many would also agree with Melville's corollary that "in a literary point of view we are deplorably unprepared for it" (HHM, 132–36). Melville has repeated enough cultural pieties to cover his possible impieties: there is more means than end in his waving the flag, invoking the Bible, citing the way of nature, or applauding Shakespeare.

He knows that for the genteel upholders of culture Shakespeare is as shocking a counterpart to Hawthorne as Shiloh is for the pillars of piety. But his purpose in comparing Hawthorne to Shakespeare is more complicated than merely to insist that contemporary writers like Hawthorne are already approaching Shakespeare in modern terms. Melville discerned in Shakespeare that same "great power of blackness" so pronounced in Hawthorne and of such concern to Melville himself. It is more than "that Calvinistic sense of Innate Depravity and Original Sin," more than an affirmation of the reality of evil or the presence of some evil principle in human nature; it is more significantly a complaint about and criticism of the way the world is put together and the way that human societies and institutions are permeated by a basic iniquity which they project as inequity. (HHM, 129).

In Melville's view Shakespeare was a strongly antiestablishment writer, an underground critic who used his "dark characters," such as Hamlet, Timon, Lear, or Iago, to challenge conventional assumptions, to insinuate "the things which we feel to be so terrifically true that it were all but madness for any good man, in his own proper character, to utter, or even hint of them." Shakespeare's audiences and even his critics seemed to express greatest admiration for his theatricality and to ignore what Melville finds most enduring and terrifying—his penetration of social sham, his "short, quick probings at the very axis of reality." This Shakespeare, who has been made ultragenteel by the consensus of history, used various forms of symbolic and strategic indirection to master that difficult and "great Art of Telling the Truth." His devious ingenuity was necessary to hint at truths that are unpopular, elusive, or vulnerable to attack from certain segments of society: "For in this world of lies, Truth is forced to fly like a scared white doe in the woodlands; and only by cunning glimpses will she reveal herself, as in Shakespeare and other masters of the great Art of Telling the Truth—even though it be covertly, and by snatches" (HHM, 130–31). The example of Shakespeare seems to impress even more deeply on Melville that a great writer must be a genius at subversion with an awesome responsibility to a concept of truth bound to offend the conventional majority. His art is defined not only by the courage of what he dares to write, but also by the skill with which he conceals his boldest assertions. He must take on faith that there exists an intellectual underground able to appreciate his art.

Melville tries to be such a voice from the underground to Hawthorne and to a potentially larger audience, whom he is trying to educate in the art of covert communication, revealing the "harmless" Hawthorne as another admirably subversive genius who offered glimpses of rarely expressed truth and took "great delight in hoodwinking the world." Such writers, he further suggests, write largely to please themselves and the few like-minded readers they are ever likely to find, the majority of readers being unqualified to judge. And if he should experience wide popularity, such a writer should be suspicious of his accomplishment and "deem the plaudits of the public . . . strong presumptive evidence of his own mediocrity" (HHM, 139–40). It is quite possible that Melville might have been thinking of the considerable stir and favorable comment that followed his earliest published efforts, *Typee* (1846) and *Omoo* (1847), and the less favorable reaction to and frequent misunderstanding of his more ambitious *Mardi* and *Redburn* (both 1849), and *White-Jacket* (1850). Ironically, however, his remarks are most applicable to what he could not yet anticipate—the public reaction to *Moby Dick* (1851), *Pierre* (1852), and the short fiction that followed.

What is even clearer is that Melville was consciously but covertly seeking membership in the very select community of literary genius in which Shakespeare was most prominent and to which Hawthorne had just been nominated. Returning to the idea of the American Shiloh, he asks, "May it not be that this commanding mind has not been, is not, and never will be, individually developed in any one man?" And he immediately extends the question further, in the hope that Herman Melville may also be recognized in the full significance of his role as literary artist–creative communicant–cultural messiah: "And would it, indeed, appear so unreasonable to suppose that this great fullness and overflowing may be, or may be destined to be, shared by a plurality of men of genius?" (HHM, 142).

In one of his opening conceits Melville views a book as an author's progeny, wishing that "all books were foundlings" so that we might ignore the particularities of authorship and recognize the community of genius (HHM, 123). Following this conceit with the extended strategy of intellectual seduction and impregnation, he prepares us to expect some offspring of this encounter. Although he shifts the imagery, he fulfills the expectation, cloaked as it is in metaphor and mythic history: "I somehow cling to the strange fancy that, in all men, hiddenly reside certain wondrous, occult properties . . . which by some happy but very rare accident (as bronze was discovered by the melting of the iron and brass in the burning of Corinth) may chance to be called forth here on earth" (HHM, 143). The off-

spring is here a new alloy, the result, one might say, of the accidental fusion of Hawthorne's iron and Melville's brass and destined to
affect the culture in which it occurred.

Whether or not they affected the culture in any significant way,
Melville's short stories are the offspring of this encounter, and in
theme and technique they reveal their ancestry, the line of descent
stemming not so much from what Hawthorne wrote as from Melville's highly charged, intensely personal reaction. While seeming to
maintain his distance through quasifictional artifice, he creates a narrative–exposition that enables him to participate directly in the
work. He has not so much reviewed Hawthorne's *Mosses* as he has
reviewed his own progress and prospects, revealed his own ambitions, and almost inadvertently shown his true artistry.

It should come as no surprise that his fifteen subsequent short stories reveal an overriding concern with the condition of American
culture, the role of the artist in that culture, and associated themes
of aesthetic, social, and spiritual consequence. In this disarmingly
casual review Melville tips his hand and bares his heart. Foreshadowing later practice in his own short stories, he here employs some
rather astonishing techniques: an extravagant and audacious symbolism, a deceptively indirect narrative style, and a highly innovative
use of allusion. We also find him suggesting the sacramental character of apparently secular circumstances, and in a simultaneous paradox, the secular inroads on sacramental observance. And we are
effectively introduced to the remarkable combination of imagination
and control that enables Melville to mean many unsuspected meanings in his soon-to-appear stories. Of most of them one can say, again
echoing Melville's judgment of Hawthorne's work, that they "are directly calculated to deceive—egregiously deceive—the superficial
skimmer of pages" (HHM, 140). Had these stories been collected in
a single volume in Melville's lifetime, he might have had even
greater reason for inscribing the book to Nathaniel Hawthorne, as
he did with *Moby Dick* in 1851, "in token of my admiration for his
genius."

2

◎◎◎

THE
FALLEN
WORLD

"The Piazza"

Like most of Melville's short stories, "The Piazza" has only recently been rediscovered by critics of American literature, and neither its central concerns nor its relation to the rest of Melville's work has been firmly fixed. In contrast to "Bartleby" or "Benito Cereno," which have drawn so much critical attention and occasioned such amazing critical diversity, "The Piazza" seems to have been generally shrugged off as one of Melville's slighter efforts designed to pad his 1856 collection of stories, so obviously slimmer than earlier collections by Irving, Poe, or Hawthorne.[1]

It has, however, a structurally closer, more artistically organic relationship to the stories which originally followed it (and to the larger body of Melville's short fiction as well) than has Irving's introductory account of himself in *The Sketch Book* or than Hawthorne's essay on "The Old Manse," which introduces his *Mosses from an Old Manse.* "The Piazza" differs most obviously from the introductory strategies

---

1. Brief commentary on "The Piazza" includes the discussion in Richard Harter Fogle, *Melville's Shorter Tales* (Norman: University of Oklahoma Press, 1960), 85–91; and Darwin T. Turner, "A View of Melville's 'Piazza,'" *College Language Association Journal*, VII (September, 1963), 56–62. More extensive interpretation is provided by W. B. Stein, "Melville's Comedy of Faith," *ELH*, XXVII (December, 1960), 315–33; Ilse Sofie Magdelene Newbery, "The Unity of Melville's *Piazza Tales*" (Ph.D. dissertation, University of British Columbia, 1964); Helmbrecht Breinig, "The Destruction of Fairyland: Melville's 'Piazza' in the Tradition of the American Imagination," *ELH*, XXXV (June, 1968), 254–83; and Hyatt H. Waggoner, "Melville and Hawthorne Acquaint the Reader with Their Abodes," *Studies in the Novel*, II (Winter, 1970), 420–24.

of Hawthorne or Irving in that it is a *story* (with some expository and autobiographical elements) written to introduce the themes and techniques of five previously published stories.

Melville, of course, considered Hawthorne an artist far superior to Irving, and it would be a mark of further homage if the strategy of "The Piazza" can be shown to derive from what Hawthorne did in "The Old Manse." The parallels are quite impressive. In each case architectural imagery grounds the account in time and place and then links the more conventional and placid present to the more pronounced contrasts of the past, particularly to the mixed strains of Revolutionary fervor and religious faith. Each house has an adjacent orchard, described in Hawthorne's sketch with markedly Edenic overtones (380–81), and in Melville's story as "white-budded, as for a bridal" but producting "Eve's apples . . . which tasted of the ground" (Piaz., 445). Both accounts contrast the bright, golden sunshine of fairyland with the darker implications of human experience; both contrast genial company and lonely isolation; both quote Emerson without using quotation marks; and both describe botanical and zoological phenomena in curiously opposed, almost parodistic analogues.

In the two most interesting of these parallels, Hawthorne's observations lead to images of bounty, benignity, and blessedness; Melville's to barrenness, blight, and frustration. Hawthorne tells of the "multitudes of bees" which invade "the yellow blossoms of the summer squashes," but he delights to think of the sweetness they will add to the blessings of life, even in "some unknown hive." He recalls having seen twining grapevines along the river bank, serving to "unite two trees of alien race . . . marrying the hemlock and the maple . . . and enriching them with a purple offspring of which neither is the parent" (382, 390).[2] Melville, more perversely, writes "I could not bear to look upon a Chinese creeper . . . which to my delight, climbing a post of the piazza, had burst out in starry bloom, but now, if you removed the leaves a little, showed millions of

2. Page references are to Hyatt H. Waggoner (ed.), *Nathaniel Hawthorne: Selected Tales and Sketches* (New York: Rinehart, 1950) and to Jay Leyda (ed.), *The Complete Stories of Herman Melville* (New York: Random House, 1949). See p. vii for the list of abbreviations used to designate these stories.

strange, cankerous worms, which feeding upon those blossoms, so shared their blessed hive, as to make it unblessed evermore" (Piaz., 443). Later in the story he fashions a crucial symbol of the abortive attempt of two hop-vines to join "in an upward clasp, but the baffled shoots, groping awhile in empty air, trailed back whence they sprung" (Piaz. 452). There are further parallels or reversals in these two deceptively casual but artistically complex pieces, but the ones cited provide a starting point for understanding "The Piazza" and its relation to the rest of Melville's short fiction.

We have in these analogues and inversions another instance of Melville's being stimulated by Hawthorne's work, even as he grew impatient at the occasionally cloying tonal effect or excessive didacticism. It might be that Melville never recognized or admitted to himself the degree to which he imitated or intensified certain elements in Hawthorne's work, for the more significant "shock," as he so effectively phrased it, lay in his recognizing Hawthorne as the artist who showed how the "power of blackness" could dim an unrealistically bright American dream. In stories like "The Piazza" Melville is indebted to his recurring encounters with Hawthorne in person and on the page, using Hawthorne's earlier work to clarify his own meaning and shape his own means, adapting Hawthorne's strategy to his own artistic ends.

The most important aspect of Melville's introductory strategy is that, both as title story and as structural device within the story, the piazza offers prospect and perspective. By *prospect* I mean an extensive view of what lies ahead and a hopeful anticipation of the envisioned results, in both senses a foretaste of what is to follow. And by *perspective* I mean the artistic devices by which a true picture is produced, whether through graduations of color or distinctness for an aerial perspective, through orthographic projection for a sharp, unshaded linear perspective, or in a more literary sense, through symbolic suggestion and artful allusion for an imaginative perspective. By *perspective* I also mean the way something appears from a particular standpoint, as in the phrase *historical perspective*, or in the literary sense the way the point of view and the inherent bias, assumptions, and predisposition of the narrator affect the tale. These subtleties determine the significance and position of "The Piazza," as

well as define the problem and inform the meaning of such stories as
"Bartleby," "Benito Cereno," "The Two Temples," or "Jimmy Rose."
The title story of *The Piazza Tales* effectively introduces not only
that collection but the other nine short stories of Melville as well.

Melville's original intention, when it became possible to publish
in book form the five stories which had appeared in *Putnam's
Monthly* between 1853 and the end of 1855, was to call the collection *"Benito Cereno" and Other Sketches*.[3] The composition of "The
Piazza" was something of an afterthought; of course, it is not as significant a story as "Benito Cereno." "The Piazza" is actually the last
short story Melville is known to have written, and like any good introduction it is more the product of hindsight than foresight, part
summation and part unveiling, as much capstone as cornerstone. It
is evidence that he had recognized his own recurrent concerns in life
and in art and the ends he was trying to attain. A major issue in "The
Piazza" (and as I have suggested, a motif in most of Melville's stories)
is that where one stands determines his view of the world, of truth,
and of reality, and his scale of values, as a matter of course. What he
thinks he sees, however, may well be illusory. This concept of point
of view as theme as well as technique not only connects Melville's
separately published stories, but also joins him and his work with
the twentieth century and constitutes a good part of his modernity.

The formal pattern for this key story is one that recurs throughout
Melville's work—the idea of a quest, but here so reduced in scale as
to seem almost a comic parody of the remote or fantastic adventures
in *Typee* or *Mardi*. W. B. Stein has interpreted it as an ironic put-
down of traditional Christianity—"Melville's Comedy of Faith"—
but I think he overstates the case for Melville's faithlessness. Much
in the story suggests the inadequacy and emptiness of Christianity in
Melville's time, but there is an alternative. Despite a disappointing
and distinctly anticlimactic experience, the narrator remains faithful
in his fashion to the kind of ideal or illusion that sustains art and at
least partially offsets the bleakness of life. Forced to abandon his

---

3. Melville discussed the matter of title and sequence for his volume of short stories in a
series of letters to Dix and Edwards, Publishers, in early 1856. These appear in Merrell R.
Davis and William H. Gilman (eds.), *The Letters of Herman Melville* (New Haven: Yale University Press, 1960), 176–80.

great expectations and settle for lesser satisfactions, the narrator, because he is a man, is somewhat of a loser, but because he gains the insight of an artist, he is not yet wholly lost.

The story undoubtedly hinges on the idea of faith. The prefixed dirge from *Cymbeline* tells us as much: "With fairest flowers / Whilst summer lasts, and I live here, Fidele—" and the circumstances and the following lines of the dirge (which Melville draws upon without citation) tell us more. For Arviragus, lacking self-knowledge, mistakenly mourns the death of the young page (who is really his sister Imogen in disguise and who has been drugged but is not dead) and pledges faithfully to bring flowers to mark the grave. Where, in all this tangle of appearances and high-minded commitment, in this web of double delusion, Melville would seem to be asking, can one have faith in his knowledge of the world?

Like Hawthorne in "The Old Manse," Melville begins by describing his house, its surroundings, and its connections with the past, and like Hawthorne's Old Manse, Melville's "old-fashioned farmhouse" is drawn from the circumstances of the author's own life. Modeled after the house in Pittsfield which Melville bought in 1850 and to which he added a piazza to take better advantage of the view of the valley and Mount Greylock beyond—"to enjoy the calm prospect of things from a fair piazza," as he wrote to Hawthorne in a letter dated June 29, 1851—the house in the story tempts many readers into an autobiographical approach to the story. Even though the narrator reveals his state of arrested innocence, his fanciful turn of mind, his fondness for highly figurative language, and memories of his youth as a sailor in the South Pacific, the autobiographical approach scratches only the surface of the story, its greatest value being to establish a closer relationship between the narrator and the author than exists in most of the other stories and to suggest that we are being introduced to attitudes close to Melville's own, though it would be a mistake to transfer the narrator's naive acceptance of appearance to Melville.

Although the architectural features of the house do not provide a major motif or direct the meaning as in "Jimmy Rose" or "I and My Chimney," they suggest allegorical possibilities. Its age, seventy years in 1856, makes it contemporary with the Constitution of the

United States, but Melville's imagery immediately compounds the possibility of a political or historical analogy with a religious one by suggesting that about 1786 the builders of the house performed a sacred function: "from the heart of the Hearth Stone Hills, they quarried the Kaaba, or Holy Stone, to which, each Thanksgiving, the social pilgrims used to come" (Piaz., 437). As several previous commentators have suggested, "the Hearth Stone Hills" and "the social pilgrims" introduce the note of sociality and friendly communion to counter the dangers of isolation or alienation, a theme common to many of Melville's stories. Melville seems to suggest that a community thus focused on common needs and a common faith no longer exists and that his narrator must find some other source of faith and basis for hope.

Turning from the matter of the age of the house to its location and the view it provides—the "purple prospect" of "Greylock, with all his hills about him, like Charlemagne among his peers"—the narrator begins a series of associations that will connect royalty and divinity, the scenic picturesque and the sources of piety, "the piazza and the pew" (the latter provisions enabling devotees "in these times of failing faith and feeble knees" to sit comfortably while contemplating the power of the religious or the aesthetic sublime). He establishes the picturesque character of the landscape quite literally: "The country round about was such a picture, that in berry time no boy climbs hill or crosses vale without coming upon easels planted in every nook, and sun-burnt painters painting there. A very paradise of painters." Complaining good-naturedly that the house lacks a piazza from which to take advantage of the view, he says the circumstance is as bad "as if a picture-gallery should have no bench; for what but picture-galleries are the marble halls of these same limestone hills? —galleries hung, month after month anew, with pictures ever fading into pictures ever fresh" (Piaz., 437–38). Far less apparent is the device by which he bridges the distance between the superficial pleasures of this picturesque prospect and the sublime possibilities suggested by the lofty and eternally enduring mountain.

The bridge is provided in Emerson's poetic essay on the living sources of religion and art, "The Problem." Still musing on the fortunate situation of the house, Melville's narrator says, "Whoever built

the house, he builded better than he knew; or else Orion in his ze-
nith flashed down his Damocles' sword . . . and said, 'Build there'"
(Piaz., 437–38). The latter part of this statement with its mixed metaphor of heavenly directive and implicit peril overshadows the line
describing Michaelangelo in "The Problem":

> The hand that rounded Peter's dome
> And groined the aisles of Christian Rome
> Wrought in a sad sincerity;
> Himself from God he could not free
> He builded better than he knew;—
> The conscious stone to beauty grew.

I suspect that the reference to Damocles' sword indicates that Melville was interpreting "Himself from God he could not free" in a
highly private way, that he was imparting to God the tyrannical
nature of that dictator who suspended a sword by a single hair to
demonstrate, to Damocles beneath, the perilous fragility of human
happiness. But apart from this, Emerson's lines help identify the
narrator as a man concerned with problems of beauty and help clarify Melville's problem in "The Piazza" as that of the artist in recon-
ciling transcendent illusion with less pleasant empirical fact. In
launching his argument he echoes Emerson's romantic piety in
holding that the divinity in nature inspires the creativity in man.
The narrator thus marks the gravity of this sublime function of nature by insisting that "beauty is like piety" but leavens it immediately in a self-deprecating, comic manner by continuing, "you cannot run and read it; tranquillity and constancy with, now-a-days, an
easy chair, are needed" (Piaz., 438).

The indulgence in the scenic or visual picturesque is essentially a
static affair, the spectator simply recognizing when a natural scene is
in conformity with a specific aesthetic canon and then admiring nature for resembling art or, in more extreme instances, employing
something like a Claude-glass which can simultaneously frame the
scene and impart a golden glow like that of a Claude Lorrain painting. Thus nature by optical alchemy can be turned to art and illusion
can be given color and form. Melville's narrator does not literally
employ such a device, nor does he content himself with such a static
role; but his personal predilections and his literary associations work

for him in a way similar to the Claude-glass to confirm illusion and transmute nature into art. Edmund Spenser's *Faerie Queene* is the lens by which the narrator turns his northern exposure to Greylock into a green and gold fairyland, but he gets some help from *Don Quixote* and *A Midsummer Night's Dream* too.

These literary associations are instrumental in creating what I earlier termed the imaginative perspective in the story. They seem initially to spur Melville into a verbal equivalent of the visual picturesque, and ultimately, because of parallel or conflicting action in the foreground (of nature and reality) and in the imaginative background (of literary allusion and association), cause him to abandon the metaphor of the painted picture and to adopt that of the spectator in a theater. Both his visual picturesque and his verbal picturesque have in common an innocent acceptance of pretense or illusion. In the first instance there is the "charmed ring" in the landscape, formed by "the circle of the mountains"—illusory because when one moves closer to the mountains, "no circle of them can you see" (Piaz., 437). The pretense in his verbal picturesque is the notion that Greylock's imposing character is like that of Charlemagne and that every sunrise and sunset is a coronation ritual which the narrator, still lacking a piazza, watches from "the hillside bank near by, a royal lounge of turf—a green velvet lounge, with long, moss-padded back." Infatuated by the fanciful analogy that so extends the sublime majesty of the landscape, he describes how, at the head of his grassy lounge, "there grew (but, I suppose, for heraldry) three tufts of blue violets in a field-argent of wild strawberries; and a trellis, with honeysuckle, I set for canopy. Very majestical lounge, indeed." But even kings are not totally secure, and alluding to Hamlet's father, the narrator foreshadows the sad lesson of the major action of the story when he says that "here, as with the reclining majesty of Denmark in his orchard, a sly earache invaded me" (438). The earache, which culminates in the king's death, seems thematically related to Damocles' sword and to the dark shadows which dim the narrator's view and jar his equanimity by the end of the story. The theatrical reference here anticipates the concluding metaphor, which effects strategic compromise between the static detachment of the visual picturesque and the painful helplessness of immersion in empirical reality.[4]

Explaining that he can afford a piazza on only one side of the house, the narrator quarters the surrounding horizon to determine his best vantage point. East, south, and west all offer promising vistas, some with Christian overtones, some with reminders of annual renewal in nature. He chooses the most challenging and least hospitable exposure to the north, as if drawn to the Olympian authority of Greylock almost by command: "So Charlemagne, he carried it. It was not long after 1848; and somehow, about that time, all round the world, these kings they had the casting vote, and voted for themselves" (Piaz., 439). Melville's allusion to the abortive revolutions of 1848 casts the narrator as something of a monarchist, though living in a republic. In his customary imagery, he casually identifies with King Hamlet, Canute, and Oberon. But it is more likely that he means in a self-mocking way to draw attention both to the perilous quest that he will soon undertake in pursuit of a chivalric ideal and to his own somewhat misguided sense of sovereignty. By the end of the story, that noble ideal seems no more substantial than the illusion that from high on the mountain his own house looks like a marble palace inhabited by some King Charming.

Despite the ridicule of neighbors who scorn a piazza to the north, the narrator carries out his choice, enjoying it in summer when it seems "the cool elysium of my northern bower" and in winter when "once more, with frosted beard," he can "pace the sleety deck, weathering Cape Horn." His eye is constantly drawn to "the purple of the mountains" where he detects some uncertain gleam "snugged away . . . in a sort of purpled breast-pocket, high up in a hopper-like hollow." He cannot even be sure whether this spot is on a slope or on a summit, for though these mountains seem enduring and eternal in their enpurpled majesty, their outlines are indistinct and visually deceptive. Under the proper conditions—"witching conditions of

---

4. The tactic of a detached spectator with an addiction to the picturesque might have been suggested by Washington Irving's use of an inscription on the title page of *The Sketch Book* establishing Geoffrey Crayon as a "mere spectator of other men's fortunes and adventures"—a narrator interested in, but fearful of, further involvement in human affairs.

light and shadow" on "a wizard afternoon in autumn," with the sky as
"ominous as Hecate's cauldron"—he can find the "spot of radiance,
where all else was shade." And there he imagines is "some haunted
ring where fairies dance" (Piaz., 440–42).

This is the realm of naive literary fancy and illusion which he
hopes to reach by an "inland voyage to fairy-land." When, after a
spring shower, he sees the far end of a rainbow touching the distant spot, he is determined to pursue the promised treasure. Even
though a practical neighbor thought it some abandoned old barn,
the narrator, who "had never been there," nevertheless "knew better" (Piaz., 440–42). But an illness that is too real to ignore forces
him unromantically to bed in a chamber which offers no view of the
mountains, and not until September can he again think of pursuing
the golden gleam.

So strong is this attraction that it draws the now-convalescent narrator away from his moody contemplation of another thematic icon,
the beautiful blossoms which conceal the sordid and destructive life
beneath, their beauty like a surface illusion masking the underlying
unpleasantness: "I could not bear to look upon a Chinese creeper of
my adoption, and which, to my delight, climbing a post of the piazza
had burst out in starry bloom, but now, if you remove the leaves a
little, showed millions of strange, cankerous worms, which, feeding
upon these blossoms, so shared their blessed hue, as to make it unblessed evermore—worms, whose germs had doubtless lurked in
the very bulb which, so hopefully, I had planted". Dismissing the
lesson of innate evil in the blighted flowers, the narrator sets out like
a knight on horseback to reach the enchanted and unchanging Fairyland, knowing only, from his reading of Spenser, that "it must be
voyaged to, and with faith" (Piaz., 443–44).

"Road-side golden-rods, as guide-posts, pointed, I doubted not,
the way to the golden window . . . through grass-grown ways . . .
traveled but by drowsy cattle . . . and a pasture . . . so moistly
green . . . with golden flights of yellow-birds—pilots, surely, to the
golden window": thus the narrator reads into the New England landscape the route to Spenser's green and gold world. As he climbs
higher, the road is still fringed "with winter-green," the "swaying fir-
boughs . . . still green in all." But there are challenges to faith be-

neath the apparent affirmation of the green: " On I journeyed . . .
by an old saw-mill, bound down and hushed with vines . . . on, by a
deep flume clove through snowy marble, vernal-tinted, where
freshet eddies had, on each side, spun out empty chapels in the
living rock; on where Jacks-in-the-pulpit, like their Baptist name-
sake, preach but to the wilderness; on where a huge, cross-grain
block, fern-bedded, showed where, in forgotten times, man after
man had tried to split it, but lost his wedges for his pains—which
wedges yet rusted in their holes; on, where, ages past, in step-like
ledges of a cascade, skull-hollow pots had been churned out by
ceaseless whirling of a flintstone—ever wearing, but itself unworn. "
These are signs of failure not of faith, hints of disillusionment and
man's physical and spiritual impotence, mockeries of Christian affirmation. The red apples in a nearby orchard, he calls "Eve's apples;
seek no furthers," but tasting one proved no delight: "It tasted of the
ground" (Piaz., 444–45). The experience is reminiscent of the disenchanted comment in the first sketch of "The Encantadas": "In no
world but a fallen one could such lands exist" (Enc., 51). Despite
these signs, the narrator will not yet admit, as he continues to as-
cend, that his is a fallen world or that he is a fallible being.

What had seemed such a golden beacon from below turns out to
be "a little, low-storied, grayish cottage," its previously beckoning
gaiety now "nun-like," its glowing roof "deeply weather-stained," the
golden window now "fly-specked . . . with wasps about the mended
upper panes," and the hoped-for fairy queen simply "a pale-cheeked
girl," abysmally lonely. There is no gold in this world, and the green
no longer connotes fertility but neglect and decay. The eavestrough
is overgrown with moss, the clapboards "green as the north side of
lichened pines, or copperless hulls of Japanese junks, becalmed."
The house is rotting, but the narrator, now having rationalized his
fondness for the picturesque into what Melville in *Pierre* called the
povertiresque, supposes the "shaded streaks of richest sod" along the
base of the house and before the settling entrance to be evidence of
"its fertilizing charm" (Piaz., 446–47). At this point his illusion which
had added imaginative depth and occasional wit to his experience
becomes a dangerous delusion, not simply coloring but distorting
and misinterpreting natural fact. Had he gone on to deny the un-

pleasantness of Marianna's isolation and continued to conceive of her as Spenser's Una and an embodiment of Platonic perfection and immutability, he would have fallen victim to his own destructive innocence. The narrator is an unseemly middle-aged caricature of the Red Cross Knight, fancifully expecting such fulfillment of truth, beauty, and love as in Spenser's allegorical union of Red Cross and Una or Arthur and Gloriana. But such, in Melville's opinion, is not the human condition: to demand it of life is to invite dangerous delusion; to expect it, however, might be sustaining and purposeful illusion.

The encounter with Marianna produces a change in the style of the story. The narrator drops his fanciful references and reports only the dialogue that passes between them. The story takes on the form of drama—the narrator no longer a spectator but a protagonist, painfully immersed in unexpected realities. From his first devotion to the picturesque, to his imaginative attempt to convert his surroundings into a theatrical performance, to his present involvement in life that is too real, he has changed his perspective and undermined his faith. As his prospect is altered, it yields a totally different truth.

From Marianna's crumbling cottage, his own house seems in "a far-off, azure world." To the girl, orphaned and isolated but for an overworked brother, the only house visible in the distance seems made of marble, and, glittering in the sunset, it must be the home of "some happy one." When the narrator points out that the sunrise gilds her house equally well, she answers in disbelief: "This house? The sun is a good sun, but it never gilds this house. Why should it? The old house is rotting. That makes it so mossy. In the morning, the sun comes in at this old window, to be sure—boarded up, when first we came; a window I can't keep clean, do what I may—and half burns, and nearly blinds me at my sewing, besides setting the flies and wasps astir—such flies and wasps as only lone mountain houses know. See, here is the curtain—this apron—I try to shut it out with them. It fades it, you see. Sun gild this house? Not that ever Marianna saw." Her experience admits no pastoral myth or fictional fairyland. As if to show the disenchanted side of another treasured dream, Marianna adds, "They went West, and are long dead . . . who built it" (Piaz., 448–49).

Still unwilling to grant the truth of Marianna's perspective, the narrator is not deluded enough to insist on the exclusive accuracy of his own:

> "Yours are strange fancies, Marianna."
> "They but reflect the things."
> "Then I should have said, 'These are strange things,' rather than, 'yours are strange fancies'" (Piaz., 449).

He thereby acknowledges that only in a world fallen far short of his expectations can such things exist. He is aware suddenly not only of the power but of the extent of blackness in his once-bright world, as he notes "a broad shadow stealing on, as cast by some gigantic condor . . . which by its deeper and inclusive dust . . . wiped away into itself all lesser shades of rock or fern." When the cloud passes, Marianna speaks of a lesser shadow as a friendly dog whose company she looks forward to at the same time each day. The narrator, commenting on this illusion which offers her slight comfort, asks whether "shadows are as things . . . lifeless shadows are as living things?" He has been looking for Una, the ideal unity in Plato's highest realm, and found instead the lonely girl, who, like those confined in Plato's cave, must believe in the reality of the shadows they see. Some of her shadows, such as that of a once-familiar birch, appear no more in her world where nature offers no solace, for "the tree was struck by lightning, and brother cut it up." Like much of her life, it has become a shadow of a shadow. There are no sounds of merriment; neither birds nor boys venture so far. Her isolation is total, but she makes some limited accommodation to her alienation from humanity: "Sometimes 'tis true, of afternoons, I go a little way, but soon come back again. Better feel lone by hearth, than rock. The shadows hereabouts I know—those in the woods are strangers" (Piaz., 450–52).

She cannot sleep for thinking about her isolation. When the narrator suggests that prayer and "a fresh hop pillow" might help, she admits to having tried both without result, or even the least narcotic relief, and points out the window, "where side by side, some feet apart, nipped and puny, two hop-vines climbed two poles, and, gaining their tip-ends, would have then joined over in an upward clasp, but the baffled shoots, groping awhile in empty air, trailed back whence they sprung" (Piaz., 452). This image, so expressive of the frustrated union and difficulty of communion even for people of good faith, stands as the best iconographic clue to the meaning of the story. However, anticlimactically, it does not conclude the story.

The only hope left to Marianna, she confesses, would be for her just once to "get to yonder house, and but look upon whoever the happy being is that lives there." The narrator obviously has two choices: to reveal himself as that person, not very grand and no longer very happy, or to leave Marianna with the faint hope supplied by her illusion. He takes the latter choice. According to W. B. Stein, the story thus ends in the narrator's cowardly betrayal of himself as well as of the potential heroine. I am not so certain that the narrator is actually lying when he tells Marianna that for her sake he wished that he "were that happy one of the happy house you dream you see; for then you would behold him now, and, as you say, this weariness might leave you" (Piaz., 452–53). If this imagined trip to Fairyland had been a fairy tale, he might reveal himself and break the curse of Marianna's lovelessness. But this story is the introduction to such unsentimental and unsettling stories as "Bartleby," "Benito Cereno," and "The Bell-Tower," and though he has been guilty of sentimentally deluding himself, the narrator has temporarily dispensed with sentiment and appraised the situation realistically.

In short he knows that he is not "that happy one" in Marianna's dream because such a person does not exist any more than Una or Fairyland. To deprive Marianna of her illusion and add to her stock of painful truths might darken her world completely and constitute a worse betrayal of faith. When feeble men are relieved of their sustaining illusions by some force like O'Neill's iceman, they crumble pathetically. Mark Twain expressed the same idea in an item from *Pudd'nhead Wilson's New Calendar*, found in Chapter 23 of *Following the Equator*: "Don't part with your illusions. When they are gone you may still exist but you have ceased to live."

And what of the narrator? Deprived of his illusions, does he cease to live? Not at all. No doubt sadder and wiser, he returns to his piazza and effects a compromise with the conditions of life. He has learned that the world has more dimension to it than the picturesque scene he once admired. Having left his piazza to venture into that world, he tested his facile romantic faith and found it empty fancy. His quest carried him through a fallen world peopled by burdened men and women, their freedom circumscribed, their ambitions thwarted, their self-realization blocked. Marianna is the first of these, and "The Piazza" is the curtain raiser. The narrator's compromise is to make the piazza "my box-royal; and this amphitheatre, my theatre of San Carlo. Yes, the scenery is magical—the illusion so complete." His capacity for illusion has been shaken but not destroyed. It can no longer dominate his life or enable him blandly to ignore the darker truths, and "every night, when the curtain falls, truth comes in with darkness. No light shows from the mountain. To and fro I walk the piazza deck, haunted by Marianna's face, and many as real a story" (Piaz., 453).

In sticking to his piazza by day, he makes clear his commitment to a theater of hope, artifice, and illusion, keeping his distance but not disengaging himself from the world of less pleasant realities. As his illusions were threatened, so was his faith in the power of the imagination, and it continues to be as "truth comes in with darkness" and "no light shows from the mountain." Or more accurately, his experience has given a darker cast to his imagination—in contrast to the Claude-glass which characterized him earlier. It has altered his perspective and prospect significantly, but faith in the shaping imagination is the only faith that can sustain him. In this sense his piazza has become his pew, and the elements of artifice and illusion are essential to his art. He has recognized the darker truths of existence "in this world of lies" but not integrated them into his art. Keeping them separate, he is not yet the artist who knows fully and expresses forcefully "this great power of blackness."

Although the story has an ascertainable American locale, it has less specifically American subject matter than the stories which follow. While it details an essentially romantic quest for the realization of a dream, the goal has not been specifically the American Dream, as in "The Bell-Tower" or "The Two Temples." It is the more general version of the dream perpetuated in legend, literature, and religion. It is the illusion which encourages at least a temporary suspension of disbelief; which informs so much of Shakespeare or Spenser or Cervantes; and which, even if it is shown to be a delusion in a particular instance, remains essential in giving form to art and direction to life. With special reference to the recurrent concerns of Melville's art, it is the imaginative masquerade that, properly understood, serves to unmask the hidden character of nature, of man, and of human institutions.

Like the grandest of Melville's characters, this narrator has discerned the mask of appearance and the role of illusion but remains content to lift the curtain rather than "strike through the mask." If he thinks, or rather if the reader thinks, he can conveniently and comfortably separate the bright day-world from the dark night-world, the interpenetration of the two in the stories which follow should disabuse him of that delusion and undermine the security or complacency of his own innocence.

"The Encantadas"

Because "The Encantadas or Enchanted Isles" consists of a series of mixed descriptive, narrative, and expository forms, the work has been a rather special challenge to twentieth-century readers.[5] In all likelihood "The Encantadas" would not have seemed so unconventional to nineteenth-century readers who were familiar with the kind of literary miscellanies published by Irving, Poe, and Hawthorne. Melville's designating the ten sections of "The Encantadas" as "Sketch First," "Sketch Second," and so on, and publishing them in three installments in *Putnam's Monthly* under the pseudonym "Salvator R.

5. The first significant comment on "The Encantadas" sought to identify Melville's many quotations and the most important sources in the literature of travel and personal record, *e.g.*, Leon Howard, "Melville and Spenser—A Note on Criticism," *Modern Language Notes*, XLVI (May, 1931), 291–92; and Russell Thomas, "Melville's Use of Some Sources in 'The Encantadas,'" *American Literature*, III (January, 1932), 432–56.

More recent criticism has been concerned with ascertaining the unifying theme or themes of the ten sketches and demonstrating the contextual appropriateness of Melville's epigraphs and allusions, *e.g.*, Fogle, *Melville's Shorter Tales*, 92–115; Newbery, "'The Encantadas': Melville's Inferno," *American Literature*, XXXVIII (March, 1966), 49–68; and Robert C. Albrecht, "The Thematic Unity of Melville's 'The Encantadas,'" *Texas Studies in Literature and Language*, XIV (Fall, 1972), 463–77.

Tarnmoor" recalls Irving's quaint and playfully metaphorical ascription of *The Sketch Book* to Geoffrey Crayon. But Melville uses the resemblance to emphasize several important literary and pictorial contrasts between his portfolio of sketches and that of such a genteel predecessor as Irving: (1) between the conventionally bland travel accounts of Americans abroad and his own perception of an exotic land, (2) between the superficially attractive idealizations of conventional landscape painting and surrealistically repellent aspects of his sketches, and (3) between the contrived terror of gothic artifice and the ingrained misery and horror of real life on these equatorial islands. Above all, he emphasizes the contrast between an innocent, inexperienced trust in the validity of appearances and the multitude of inevitable deceptions and betrayals that permeate human experience. Like the two sides of the tortoise, penance is the ever-present obverse of promise.

Melville may have used a pseudonym because he had accepted an advance from Harper Brothers for a proposed work on the Galapagos tortoise after having submitted "The Encantadas" to Putman's.[6] But the pseudonym he chose seems as much a calculated clue as a clever jest or a somewhat dishonest dodge. He invented "Salvator R. Tarnmoor" as a shorthand means of expressing his awareness of and dissatisfaction with the false idealizations of the conventional picturesque, an attitude he spelled out more carefully in "The Piazza." No doubt Melville hoped that he had not taken the name of Salvator Rosa, the seventeenth-century Italian painter, in vain.

Like Claude Lorrain, Salvator Rosa was precursor of the picturesque landscape treatments of eighteenth-century English painters whose work became a benchmark for nineteenth-century American canons of art. Whereas Claude's renditions, which are more in keeping with the mood of "The Piazza," sought to express the sublimity of nature through art, there is more romantic turbulence in Salvator Rosa's work; and his rocky landscapes and evocative ruins, his brigands and battle scenes are in keeping with the surface and subject matter of "The Encantadas." But the underlying subject and implicit meanings of the sketches in Melville's portfolio double back after

6. Jay Leyda, *The Melville Log*, (2 vols.; New York: Harcourt, Brace and Co., 1951), I, 485.

seeming to start in the direction of the picturesque or the sublime. His use of "Tarnmoor" to complete the contrapuntal pseudonym nods toward Poe and the vocabulary of gothic theatricality, but while announcing his concern with terror, he also indicates his disdain for conventional literary or pictorial means of evoking it. Figuratively, "The Encantadas" recalls the terrors of Hell; literally, it details the horrors of life. Alluding to the curse that began with the islands' creation, Melville seems intent on proving that any promise of salvation is only as true or as false as the picturesque art and artificial sublime of his pseudonymous "Salvator."

I claim no novel interpretation in associating "The Encantadas" with inquiry into horror and evil. R. H. Fogle saw Melville's sketches of the islands as constituting "a microcosm of complex reality" like the *Pequod* or the *Neversink*, and he believed that they bore inescapably on "the Fall of Man and of the world." Ilse S. M. Newbery states the central theme as "the effect of evil on life" and describes Melville's grouping of the sketches as "ringed like Dante's into various circles of damnation." Robert C. Albrecht restates the theme as Melville's absorption "in the predator behavior of man and in the hell man thereby creates for himself."[7] Even though Newbery disagrees with Fogle's formulation, I think there is a good measure of accuracy in each view.[8] But I think none of them has stated Melville's hypothesis fully nor distinguished thesis and

7. Fogle, *Melville's Shorter Tales*, 92–93; Newbery, "Inferno," 50; Albrecht, "Thematic Unity," 463.

8. Despite Melville's own statement that "In no world but a fallen one could such lands exist" (Enc., 51), Newbery rejects Fogle's terminology of the Fall because, as she explains, "Melville stresses his view that the world was created evil, and . . . has remained basically unchanged from the moment it 'exploded into sight.'" Her argument is that the presence of evil from the beginning precludes any concept of a Fall. My suggestion in this apparent dilemma is that "fallen world" does not necessarily mean that it was once better in reality than it is now, but that the real world always falls short of the ideal.

In disagreeing with Fogle's "microcosm" view, Newbery stresses Melville's effort to distinguish the islands from what pertains in the rest of the world, a world of change, growth, and human associations in contrast to the static, sterile Encantadas. Here I think she has read Melville more literally than she should. Although he meant to show the Encantadas as different, perhaps even unique, I think the difference lies in the stark inhospitality of the islands, with almost nothing to temper their unadorned barrenness. They are the world with all its comforting amenities stripped away, perhaps more an abstraction of underlying reality than "a microcosm of complex reality," but undeniably representative, it seems to me, of the way he felt about some important aspects of man and nature.

method sufficiently in this quasiclinical examination of ecological relationships and theological implications.

There is virtual unanimity that the first four sketches form a structural unit, fulfilling an introductory, scene-setting function, and highlighting the moral as well as the physical character of the Encantadas. Because most comment has emphasized the first two sketches, "The Isles at Large" and "Two Sides to a Tortoise," I would like to remedy the inbalance and call more attention to the fourth sketch, "A Pisgah View from the Rock," which is as important to the underlying method and ultimate meaning of "The Encantadas" as are the quotations from Spenser or the ideas from Dante. But we must begin with the first sketch and the two passages from the *Faerie Queene* that head it.

In the first passage the ferryman warns the Red Cross Knight against stopping at the Wandering Islands, "For those same Islands, seeming now and than, / Are not firme land." This instability of the islands, their seeming to be what they are not, raises the theme of illusion, and the distressed traveler who sets foot on one of them "may never it secure, / But wandreth evermore uncertein and unsure" (Enc. 49).[9] In a physical sense he is condemned never to leave the islands; in a more figurative sense he is condemned to share the inconstancy and instability of the islands; and bereft of his previous faith and certainty, he is forever disillusioned and harshly disenchanted. The second passage from the *Faerie Queene* describes the cave of Despair, "Darke, dolefull, dreary, like a greedy grave," where "wandering ghostes did wayle and howle." Both passages have direct application to the subject and tone of Melville's first sketch, which actually intensifies the penal and penitential aspects of Spenser's lines.

The sketch opens with a challenge to the reader to imagine a Pacific island, but the images created have far more in common with an urban wasteland than a Polynesian paradise:

> Take five-and-twenty heaps of cinder dumped here and there in an outside city lot; imagine some of them magnified into mountains, and the

9. The lines from Spenser, as well as the quotations from "The Encantadas" are taken from Leyda (ed.), *The Complete Stories*. Howard's "Melville and Spenser" not only identifies the Spenserian sources but also cites Melville's alterations.

vacant lot the sea; and you will have a fit idea of the general aspect of the Encantadas, or Enchanted Isles. A group rather of extinct volcanoes than of isles, looking much as the world at large might, after a penal conflagration (Enc., 49).

There is no benign "Let there be light" connotation to this perverse parody of the Creation, the act by which these lands were "exploded into sight" (Enc., 103). The "clinker-bound" coast rims lands of unparalleled desolation, unchanging seasons, and unrelieved sorrows, where "rain never falls." The environmental conditions set the evolutionary limits to what can survive:

> Little but reptile life is here found: tortoises, lizards, immense spiders, snakes, and that strangest anomaly of outlandish nature, the *iguana*. No voice, no low, no howl is heard; the chief sound of life here is a hiss (Enc., 50–51).

One underlying implication in this ecological description is markedly ethological as well—that the Creator of such an infernally harsh and physically limited world set similar limits on the moral behavior of the resident creatures. The inherent meanings culminate in the narrator's observation, "In no world but a fallen one could such lands exist," a statement paradoxically implying that every observer begins with the innocence of high expectations but faces the destined disillusionment of discovering his own fallen condition (Enc., 51).

There are two further, though subordinate, topics in this first sketch. One is the reason-defying action of wind and sea in this island world; the other is the appearance and character of the creature which gives the islands their second Spanish name, *Galapagos*, the tortoise. The "capricious" tides, the "light, baffling, and . . . unreliable" wind, the "perplexing calms," and the unpredictable currents amplify the "most deadly daunger and distressed plight" of Spenser's warning lines and lead to numerous delusions—confusing navigators, causing mapmakers to err, and precipitating the islands' primary designation in Spanish, the *Encantadas*, or Enchanted Ones. The discussion of the tortoises, which continues into the next sketch, also extends Spenser's description of Despair's cave, for this first sketch ends with the narrator's remarking how, long after his visit to the islands, he was haunted by "the ghost of a gigantic tortoise" bearing a cryptic legend on its back (Enc., 52–54).

Rock Rodondo, the focus of the third and fourth sketches, offers prospect, perspective, and instruction in point of view much like the piazza of Melville's especially written introductory story, and what Melville called "A Pisgah View from the Rock" helps us gloss "the two sides" of the tortoise. The lines from Book II of the *Faerie Queene* which preface the third sketch cite the ravening birds which sit and wait on "the Rock of vile Reproch." The stratified bird societies which Melville describes range from the ungainly and zoologically ambiguous penguins at the base through the layer of pelicans ("a penitential bird . . . haunting the shores of clinkered Encantadas"), through the stratum of the gony or gray albatross, to orders of gannets, haglets, jays, sea-hens, sperm-whale birds, various gulls, and stormy petrels. Melville's observations rival Charles Darwin's in their ethological and evolutionary implications, but Melville's suggestions are more extensive. The strata follow some principle of order in nature but it seems less a principle of divine order than of diabolical decree, and its connotations are as penal, penitential, and tormented as the stratified circles of Dante's *Hell*. Having done this, Melville suddenly shifts the allegorical suggestion from a netherworld concept to the more familiar power structures or hierarchical stratification of the world we know best; thus, the bird societies seem "thrones, princedoms, powers, dominating one above the other in senatorial array" (Enc., 60–63). The effect is much like that of a Byzantine icon symbolically depicting a traditional moral and religious scene from the past but conveying in less obvious but no less symbolic terms additional meanings derived from the painter's contemporary culture.

In "Sketch Fourth" the narrator makes his way to the top to gain his "Pisgah View from the Rock." The reference, of course, is to that passage from Deuteronomy (34: 1–5) describing how Moses ascended from the plains of Moab to a ridge in the mountains called Pisgah, from which the Lord showed him the promised land of Gilead (and where he also died). The two-line epigraph, from Book I of the *Faerie Queene*, challenges the reader to complete the passage in order to grasp Melville's use of it: "That done, he leads him to the highest Mount, / From whence, far off he unto him did shew." The subsequent, though unquoted, lines describe the Red Cross

Knight's version of the New Jerusalem from atop the Mount of Contemplation, again a vision of a promised place of peace and joy for those chosen people purged of sin and guilt. The view from Rock Rodondo, however, is strikingly different from the promises of Old and New Testament texts. It resembles "the universe from Milton's celestial battlements" (a fallen world) and "a boundless watery Kentucky" (not only wilderness but also dark and bloody ground). Melville refers to it as "yonder Burnt District," using the same metaphor that referred to areas swept by the fervor of evangelical revival, such as the Great Awakening, the metaphor simultaneously implying holiness and hellfire (Enc., 66). The "Pisgah View" is the conceptual key to such opposed or contradictory meanings.

From the specific instance of Moses on Pisgah, the term probably became more secularized in referring to a pleasant prospect from some high vantage point. But I suspect Melville knew something more of the word's meaning in Hebrew: "a cleft or split," implying in a phrase like "a Pisgah view" not only the broad prospect from the heights but also the inevitable discrepancy when one looks out from a lower point of view. Thus the phrase, while referring to a land of promise and boundless possibility glimpsed from on high, also suggests a cleft view of experience, so that when we descend from the heights, the fallen world always belies our expectations or presumed promises. Melville's use of the phrase as a principle of existence in "The Encantadas" means more than *imperfection*, applying also to discrepancy, contradiction, illusion, delusion, and error. These result inevitably, it would seem, from the observer's position, distance, perspective, predisposition, or frame of reference. In Melville's hands the Pisgah principle summarizes the appearance–reality debate and characterizes the world of natural facts and human relationships as a series of concealments, deceits, implicit contrasts, surprising connections, and inherent contradictions. Whereas Emerson was invigorated by his *correspondences*, Whitman intoxicated by his *eidólons*, Melville took little comfort in the symbolic irony that permeated his world, making the Encantadas the stage for a drama of disenchantment. When he insisted on at least two sides to a tortoise—or a buccaneer or a narrator—he was more intent on teaching and testing his reader than on merely telling a story.

The duality inherent in Melville's Pisgah principle not only helps explain "The Encantadas," but is also at the heart of several other stories he completed later in 1854, the same year he published "The Encantadas." In those stories—"The Two Temples," "Poor Man's Pudding and Rich Man's Crumbs," and "The Paradise of Bachelors and the Tartarus of Maids"—the Pisgah principle becomes the structural plan. Each story offers a split view of a single issue— religious communion, attitudes toward poverty, and the consequences of moral innocence and impotence—and they are all familiarly discussed as diptychs, an appropriate metaphor borrowed from the hinged painted icons that depict two related scenes of spiritually symbolic significance. What has not been adequately realized, however, is the degree to which "The Encantadas" foreshadows the diptychs and constitutes Melville's first fully conscious attempt to link Paradise and Tartarus in a transcendent iconological dichotomy.

Description of the bleak, devastated beaches in "Sketch First" calls attention to the "decayed bits of sugar-cane, bamboos, and cocoanuts" washed up "from the charming palm isles to the westward and southward; all the way from Paradise to Tartarus" by "the conflicting currents which eddy throughout." These stranded hints of vital life on other isles contrast with the "dead shells" and Plutonian rocks of this fallen world and lead the narrator to characterize the Enchanted Isles as "Apples of Sodom," possessing "the aspect of once living things malignly crumbled from ruddiness into ashes." There are, it seems, two sides to the Creation: Apples and Sodom, ruddiness and ashes, life and death. The next sentence further emphasizes the islands—which seem to waver when viewed from shipboard—as the permanent locus of death when viewed by one on shore, their position now "fixed, cast, glued into the very body of cadaverous death" (Enc., 51–53). There are two distinguishable but related modes of perception going on here: (1) that of the stationary observer gaining a Pisgah view of the contradictory elements in what he sees, and (2) that of the mobile observer whose shifting point of view reveals the contradictory elements. The latter is the dominant mode in "The Piazza," but when the narrator turns to scrutiny of the tortoise, it becomes clearer that the former is the dominant mode of perception in "The Encantadas." In each case discovery leads to dichotomy and disillusionment; understanding leads to ambiguity.

Melville draws upon two mythic roles for the tortoise before the narrator sits down to a demythologizing supper of tortoise steaks and tortoise stews. He first mentions the "long cherished" sailors' superstition that "all wicked sea-officers, more especially commodores and captains, are at death . . . transformed into tortoises; henceforth dwelling upon these hot aridities, sole solitary lords of Asphaltum." He further describes these fallen figures of former authority as "self-condemned" and expressing "lasting sorrow and penal hopelessness" (Enc., 53). Whether Melville knew the etymology of *tortoise* or not (though it is likely that he did, since he had contracted with the Harpers to issue that detailed work on tortoises), he employs the etymological and mythological conceit imbedded in an Ancient Greek word for tortoise—*tartaruchos*, one confined to Tartarus, that underworld to which the spirits of the wicked are perpetually condemned.

As implied in the first Spenserian epigraph, the narrator carries a measure of the curse with him from the islands. In a remote Adirondack hideaway, in all the picturesque Salvatorean surroundings of "deep-wooded gorge, surrounded by prostrate trunks of blasted pines," he imagines "sudden glimpses of dusky shells, and long languid necks," and "vitreous inland rocks worn down . . . into deep ruts by ages and ages of slow draggings of tortoises in quest of pools of scanty water." At the other end of the social spectrum, "in scenes of social merriment," the curse still persists and the "optical delusion" of wandering ghosts comes out of the darkness. Especially in a setting of gothic theatricality "at revels held by candlelight in old-fashioned mansions, so that shadows are thrown into the further recesses of an angular and spacious room, making them put on a look of haunted undergrowth of lonely woods. . . . I have seemed to see slowly emerging from those imagined solitudes, and heavily crawling along the floor, the ghost of a gigantic tortoise, with 'Memento*****' burning in live letters upon his back" (Enc.,54). The first sketch thus ends striking the tone that Melville emphasized in his conclusion to "The Piazza": there, in his imaginary "theatre of San Carlo," "when the curtain falls, truth comes in with darkness";

and the narrator is "haunted by Marianna's face, and many as real a story" (Piaz., 453). The legend "burning in live letters" is no *memento mori* but rather a *memento vitae*, and the penitential tortoises emblematically extend their Tartarean existence from the fallen world of the Encantadas into the somewhat less anguished world of mid–nineteenth-century America, a promised land that Melville was not alone in apprehending in penitential terms of quiet desperation.

The second sketch explicitly calls for a Pisgah view in its title, "Two Sides to a Tortoise," and calls our attention to the second important mythological role of the tortoise—the Hindu conception of the tortoise as avatar of Vishnu and foundation or support for the world.

The Spenserian epigraph to this sketch cites creatures more ugly and horrifying than nature could bear but then suggests that "these fearfull shapes" are only illusory. Melville offers no such calming assurance, though he recognizes that the tortoise has its bright side as well as its dark. The bright underside, however, is visible only if one turns the tortoise on its back. This feature is hardly a basis for optimism since the tortoise in so unnatural a position cannot right itself and is vulnerable to human predators seeking meat, oil, or shell. Yet most critics, with the exception of W. B. Stein, use the narrator's words to insist on Melville's Manichean balance of good and evil. After describing the helpless, upturned tortoise, the narrator somewhat patly urges, "Enjoy the bright, keep it turned up perpetually if you can, but be honest, and don't deny the black" (Enc., 56). The Pisgah view posits "two sides to a tortoise," but the bright side is exposed through the concerted force and will of the aggressor and maintained through the painful and unnatural inversion of the tortoise. Its effectiveness as a bright beacon of hope seems very insubstantial and illusory, controverting the assurance of Spenser's lines which so easily dispatch the appalling and dreadful aspects of existence. From Melville's position on Pisgah, the promise is more precarious than the penance.

As the reference to Hindu myth suggests, the tortoise merits reverence rather than the rude treatment it gets. It is a living link to the antediluvian world, an example of fossil life incarnate. The three tortoises captured and ultimately consumed by the narrator and his shipmates "seemed newly crawled forth from beneath the foundations of the world" (where the other myth locates Tartarus). Their scars are the hieroglyphics of terrestrial experience; their configuration suggests "three Roman Coliseums in magnificent decay." In this regard, the narrator further suggests that the tortoises ought to interest the scientist as well as the theologian, for they carry evidence not merely of antiquity but of the evolutionary beginnings of life, evidence of the Creation (Enc., 57).

Yet observation of tortoise behavior counters the suggestions of reverence or worshipful antiquity. Ponderous and stubborn, stupid and blindly resolute, they seem "the victims of a penal, or malignant, or perhaps a downright diabolical enchanter"—as if the Creator had diabolically condemned them to their Tartarean existence. If Melville can suggest two sides to the Creator, we ought to recognize two sides to the narrator too, for he feels no compunctions about making "a merry repast from tortoise steaks and tortoise stews," and afterward converting the dark concave shells into souptureens and the bright "yellowish calipees into three gorgeous salvers." As if to say that here are two sides to a symbol also, the narrator has made a utilitarian burlesque of his earlier moral maxims, drastically devalued the symbolic bases of his scientific and religious ruminations, and demythologized the imaginative appeal of the natural world. Those "three gorgeous salvers" will equip no salvator nor serve to protect or save anyone any more than they saved the unfortunate tortoises. Against his better nature, he uses his Pisgah perspective to turn a quick profit and committed an act of grievous transgression against his own transcendental perceptions.

The variance inherent in the Pisgah view and in the corollary principle of shifted perspective extends to Rock Rodondo itself. Those at sea invariably mistake it for a sail atop "a glad populous ship," while those making their way to its summit "know it to be a dead desert rock" (Enc., 61, 65). In truth, however, neither can wholly deny the opposing view. The multitudes of fish inhabiting the rocky grottoes below the waterline and the swarms of noisy birds above—one white, whistling bird aptly called the "Boatswain's Mate" at the top—make it "a glad populous ship" at the same time as we learn that it is "a dead desert rock." Error and illusion are endemic in this "enchanted" environment, but the "enchantment" does not signify, as Newbery has argued, "the ominpotence of evil."[10] Rather it refers to that state of variant perceptions where appearance and reality are continually shifting, and contradictories must include, not exclude, each other. As the narrator says, ostensibly referring to ascending the rock for "a comprehensive view of the region round about": "Yet soft, this is not so easy" (60, 65).

From the fourth sketch through the tenth the Pisgah principle continues to shape the narrative: all the sketches are concerned with duplicity, most of them relating to the simultaneous conception of the islands as land of promise or refuge and place of penance and despair. The geographic and demographic survey of Narborough and Albemarle islands in the fourth sketch describes one nearly surrounded by the other "like a wolf's red tongue in his open mouth," and the census suggests a vision that might have made Moses backtrack from Pisgah and its unknown promises to the known dangers of Egypt:

Men	none
Ant-eaters	unknown
Man-haters	unknown
Lizards	500,000
Snakes	500,000
Spiders	10,000,000
Salamanders	unknown
Devils	do.

So unpromising are most of the other islands glimpsed from the summit of the rock, that the narrator dismisses them as an "archipelago of aridities, without inhabitant, history or hope of either," citing his greater interest in those four islands to which human beings were lured by the promise of refuge or profit (Enc., 70, 73).

The fifth sketch is a sort of historical aside, a brief note concerning the U.S. frigate *Essex* and its pursuit of a strange vessel in 1813. The mysterious ship, showing American colors in the morning and English later in the day, escaped before a strong breeze as the Ameri-

10. Newbery, "Inferno," 51.

can frigate lay becalmed, its crew unable to explain the engimatic double identity of the other ship (Enc., 74–75).

Barrington Isle, the first of the four which were sites of significant human settlement, opens the question of the two-sidedness of a buccaneer. The lines from Spenser's *Prosopopia: or Mother Hubberds Tale* preceding "Sketch Sixth" state the intention of the fox and the ape to outwit the authorities and gain their due share of the land's wealth. Like the buccaneers, who "waylaid the royal treasure-ships plying between Manila and Acapulco," the fox and the ape recognize no law but that of their own making. The irony of Melville's continuing view from Pisgah is that for these buccaneers (undeniably pirates, murderers, robbers, and revelers) Barrington Isle was a promised land, "a secure retreat," "a harbor of safety," and a "bower of ease." They were hardly the chosen people of the Old Testament or the virtuous remnant of the New Testament, but for them the promise of Pisgah was more certain than for any others. Not only a safe haven, Barrington Isle has good water, shelter, and anchorage as well as food, fuel, and pleasing landscapes. Here the buccaneers carved stone sofas, softened them with turf, and seemed to enjoy pure "peacefulness and kindly fellowship with nature." Here they turned from "the toils of piratic war" and "came to say their prayers." "Could it be possible," the narrator asks, "that they robbed and murdered one day, reveled the next, and rested themselves by turning meditative philosphers, rural poets, and seat-builders on the third?" It is possible, he goes on, if one "consider the vacillations of a man." And he concludes that "among these adventurers were some gentlemanly, companionable souls, capable of genuine tranquillity and virtue." In a world where truth is so relative and judgment so uncertain, where there are always two sides to a tortoise, men are even more complex and many-sided—murderer and meditative philosopher, robber and rural poet (Enc., 76–79).

The circumstances of the next sketch, "Charles's Isle and the Dog-King," are drawn from actuality and designed to show still another side of an adventurer. The subject of the sketch, modeled after one José Villamil, a general in Ecuador's war of liberation whom Melville mistakenly connects with Peru, was rewarded for his patriotic bravery and service with the deed to Charles's Isle. Unlike the fraternal community of the buccaneers, the resultant society had no suggestions of virtue and ease. That Melville intends some connection and contrast with the previous sketch seems likely because he again quotes from the lines of the unprincipled fox and ape of *Mother Hubberds Tale* who use their freedom and fortune to subjugate others:

> We will not be of anie occupation,
> Let such vile vassalls born to base vocation
> Drudge in the world, and for their living droyle,
> Which have no wit to live withouten toyle.

And he also describes the leader and his subjects in this colonial enterprise taking "ship for the promised land," again reminding us of one dimension of the view from Pisgah (Enc., 80–81).

The character of this enterprise was revealed when the leader boarded the ship with his "disciplined cavalry company of large grim dogs," who snarlingly kept "the inferior rabble" in line. The "Dog-King" quickly became a bloody tyrant, further surrounded himself with "an infantry body-guard" supplementing the dogs, and established a law-and-order society that decimated the population. His paranoid policy persuaded him that the list of his enemies was truly prodigious, "that all who were not of the body-guard were downright plotters and malignant traitors." Trying to bolster the dwindling population, he resorted to kidnaping sailors from visiting ships and inevitably created the proper climate for a rebellion as bloody as was his tyranny. The rebels proclaimed a republic but perverted their alleged democracy into "a permanent *Riotocracy*, which gloried in having no law but lawlessness." Their "asylum of the oppressed" was actually "the unassailed lurking-place of all sorts of desperadoes, who in the name of liberty did just what they pleased" (Enc., 81–85). Another "promised land" had become an anarchic hell, and the Pisgah principle has exposed two sides of an heroic leader, linked tyranny and anarchy, and revealed the duplicity of political slogans and political entities.

"Norfolk Isle and the Chola Widow" is probably the best known of the sketches but not the best understood. The three epigraphs all concern pity and grief resulting from deception. The first, again from Book II of the *Faerie Queene*, describes the siren whose apparent sorrow, agony, and calls for help drew seamen to their deaths. The second, from Thomas Chatterton's *Mynstrelles Songe from Aella*, laments the death of a lover who is actually alive. The third, from the same ultimate source as the epigraph to "The Piazza," is William Collins' version of the dirge from *Cymbeline* and involves a compounding of deceptions, one of which is again a lament for an apparently dead youth who is neither dead nor the young man the speaker assumes him to be. Hunilla, the Chola widow, however, is a genuinely pitiable and long-suffering woman who has been deceived and degraded and whose acquaintance with death has some of the appearance but none of the consolation of art.

Young and recently married, she had come to Norfolk with her husband and brother, lured by the promise of high profits from tortoise oil. The abundance of tortoises seemed at first to confirm their hopes, but an accident in which the two men were drowned and her misplaced faith in the French captain who had brought them to the isle, turned her honeymoon into a private hell. The captain, who had insisted on being paid in silver when he deposited his passengers, swore to return, but was never seen again. In the Encantadas every promise bodes deceit, and by the end of her ordeal, Hunilla is a stoic veteran of the Encantadas.

Even perception deceives. The scene of her husband's and brother's deaths, so terrifying in all its implications, is recounted as a more artful illusion than were the dramatic deceptions in the epigraphs:

> The real woe of this event passed before her sight as some sham tragedy on the stage. She was seated in a rude bower among the withered thickets. . . . The thickets were so disposed that in looking upon the sea at large she peered from among the branches as from the lattice of a high balcony. But upon the day we speak of here . . . Hunilla had withdrawn the branches to one side, and held them so. They formed an oval frame, through which the bluely boundless sea rolled like a painted one. And there, the invisible painter painted to her view the wave-tossed and disjointed raft, its once level logs slantingly upheaved, as raking masts, and the four struggling arms undistinguishable among them, and then all subsided into the smooth-flowing creamy waters, slowly drifting the splintered wreck; while first and last, no sound of any sort was heard.

Death in a silent picture; a dream of the eye; such vanishing shapes as the mirage shows (Enc., 90–91).

The enchantment is such that she seemed a spectator at a "sham tragedy," helplessly viewing "a silent picture." "With half a mile of sea between," the narrator asks, "how could her two enchanted arms aid those four fated ones?" He seems to mean that life itself is an enchantment (recalling the long-lived tortoise "with 'Memento*****' burning in live letters upon his back") and death the ultimate disenchantment. Surely this is not too sinister a reading for a passage that concludes with a more pointed question and answer: "Ah, Heaven, when man thus keeps his faith, wilt Thou be faithless who created the faithful one? But they cannot break faith who never plighted it" (Enc., 91). The ultimate self-deceit would be to count on being saved by the crafty captain or the not-so-benevolent Creator or the "downright diabolical enchanter" or "the invisible painter" or that nonexistent Salvator who allegedly authored "The Encantadas."

Having buried her husband, Hunilla, like some primitive Pacific Antigone, piously sought to recover her brother's body—but never gained that elusive satisfaction. The narrator strongly hints but stops short of specifying "those two unnamed events which befell Hunilla" from ships that did stop briefly, but left without her. Such treatment was in utmost contrast to the "silent reverence of respect" paid Hunilla by the narrator's shipmates, who not only rescue her, two of her dogs, and her stock of tortoise oil, but also contribute secretly to the sum realized from the sale of that oil (Enc., 95, 97, 101). Yet no kindness can wipe out the memory of her having for so long shared Tartarus with the tortoises.

The last paragraph of Hunilla's story has been most often interpreted as an affirmation of that Christianity from which Hunilla never swerved: "The last seen of lone Hunilla she was passing into Payta town, riding upon a small grey ass; and before her on the ass's shoulders, she eyed the jointed workings of the beast's armorial cross" (Enc., 101). But the underlying principle and the total context of "The Encantadas" posits a denial for every apparent promise, a disappointment for every apparent affirmation. If some readers re-

spond, like James Russell Lowell, to the upbeat note of Christian affirmation in the last Madonna-like image of Hunilla, it is at the cost
of ignoring her long season of torment, which may not yet have
ended.[11] Having known love and loss, crushing indignities, prolonged pain and loneliness, Hunilla makes the forlorn Marianna of
"The Piazza" seem fortunate by contrast.

Ironically enough, her rescue seems due less to her patient prayer
and her "little brass crucifix . . . worn featureless, like an ancient
graven knocker long plied in vain," than to the circumstance of a
sailor's good-natured intemperance (Enc., 99). None of the narrator's shipmates except one, "unwontedly exhilarated" by a morning
tipple, which spurred him to leap atop the windlass, saw the tiny figures on shore. The narrator even puns about the man's high spirits,
the spirituous liquor which caused them, and the sort of spiritual
high associated with salvation: "Being high lifted above all others
was the reason he perceived the object . . . and this elevation of his
eye was owing to the elevation of his spirits; and this again—for
truth must out—to a dram of Peruvian pisco . . . secretly adminis-
tered . . . by our mulatto steward" (Enc., 87). There might be more
than a tweaking of temperance advocates in this Pisgah view of
pisco, which here challenges the specifics of special providence.

Jay Leyda has suggested that the criticism of Christianity in this
sketch may well have been muted by the Scribner's editor who also
rejected "The Two Temples," which he felt offensive to the religious
sensibilities of some readers. In the letter explaining his rejection,
Charles Briggs also apologized for excising several words from the
last sentence of Hunilla's story—an omission in all likelihood
prompted by his wish to protect Melville and the magazine as well
to shield tender sensibilities from the troubling themes of a literary
heretic.[12]

"Hood's Isle and the Hermit Oberlus" probes more deeply into
the degradation and degeneracy of a man who has no apparent re-
deeming virtue and who fully merits his sentence to Tartarus. For

11. Newbery has stated the minority view quite forcefully: "The content of Christian comfort in this passage . . . is practically nil. What is left of Christ is his Passion but not his victory,
and what the cross symbolizes is not redemption but a community of suffering in which even
the animal world is included" ("Inferno," 65).

12. Leyda (ed.), *The Complete Stories*, 460.

the epigraph, Melville again draws from the description of Despair
in Book I of the *Faerie Queene*:

> That cursed man, low sitting on the ground
> Musing full sadly in his sullein mind;
> His griesie locks, long growen and unbound,
> Disordred hong about his shoulders round,
> And his face; through which his hollow eyne
> Lookt deadly dull, and stared as astound.

With sunken cheeks and ragged clothes, Spenser's figure of Despair
becomes Melville's model of irretrievably fallen man. Oberlus is a
vicious, misanthropic parody of Adamic man, and the sketch in its
entirey a perversion of the pastoral dream.

The sketch could even be viewed as an anti-idyllic portrait of a
Robinson Crusoe existence. It is a Pisgah view of Defoe's celebrated
hero, who fashioned for himself such a tolerably comfortable life on
the isle of Juan Fernandez, which Melville, curiously enough, had
mentioned as one of the nearby cluster in "A Pisgah View from the
Rock" (Enc., 67).

Oberlus is introduced as a white European "bringing into this
savage region qualities more diabolical than are to be found among
any of the surrounding cannibals," and like Conrad's Kurtz in *Heart
of Darkness*, he attempts to subjugate and enslave any whose misfortune brings them his way. His "den of lava and clinkers" contrasts
with the ingenious, civilized amenities of Crusoe's dwelling, and his
guileful attempt to capture a Negro sailor is a perversion of Crusoe's
relationship to Friday. His efforts at agriculture produce "a sort of
degenerate potatoes and pumpkins." His hoe seems "elbowed more
like a savage's war-sickle than a civilized hoe-handle"; his appearance when planting was "so malevolently and uselessly sinister and
secret, that he seemed rather in act of dropping poison into wells
than potatoes into soil." Propagation and pollution seem inseparable
aspects of his agricultural efforts (Enc., 102–104).

He is a figure of monstrous degeneracy, laboring under some
curse that makes him appear the "beast-like" "victim of some malignant sorceress," his "rags insufficient to hide his nakedness, his
freckled skin blistered by continual exposure to the sun; nose flat;
countenance contorted, heavy, earthy; hair and beard unshorn, pro-

fuse, and of fiery red." The curse that brought him to Hood's Isle links him to his companion tortoises in Tartarus, "and he seemed more than degraded to their level," his "sole superiority . . . was his possession of a larger capacity of degradation; and . . . something like an intelligent will to it." More redolent of evil than his Tartarean environment is the hell he has created within himself by undisciplined egotism, vanity, hatefulness, and lust for power over others. It seems as if the "vitreous cove," the "wide strand of dark pounded black lava," his "den of lava and clinkers," and his bestial, misanthropic behavior are outward signs of his inner hell (Enc., 102–104).

Melville also suggests a moral kinship with Caliban, the "salvage and deformed slave" who inhabits the island on which Shakespeare's *The Tempest* is set. "This island's mine by Sycorax my mother," Oberlus says at one point, claiming the same descent and dominion as Caliban, though he never follows Caliban's redemptive determination to seek forgiveness and grace. (These references by allusion or incident to the *Faerie Queene, The Tempest,* or *Robinson Crusoe* are attempts not only to deepen the implications of the sketch by similarity or contrast but also to show how life follows art.) Another striking difference between Caliban and Oberlus, of course, is that Caliban was a primitive, meeting civilized Europeans for the first time; Oberlus, a supposed representative of superior European culture in his first contact with primitive conditions. That Oberlus should be more cruel and deceitful than "the surrounding cannibals" asserts Melville's belief, present in his writing from *Typee* through *Billy Budd,* concerning the consequences of contact between representatives of civilization and primitive cultures, from the American West to remote Pacific isles: the savagery of noble Christian intentions could be far more reprehensible than the ignoble savagery of the primitives.

Although Oberlus' "ursine suavity" enables him to capture but not to keep the Negro he intends to enslave, he does succeed in enslaving several sailors who do his dirty work and even murder for him as they prey upon unsuspecting vessels that put in for fresh vegetables and water. In a small boat stolen from a visiting vessel, Oberlus and his cutthroat army set out for Peru, but Oberlus arrives alone at Guayaquil, after leaving a self-serving, witty, and apparently deceitful explanation of his actions. He sets out to woo a potential Eve to aid in colonizing his island kingdom, "which doubtless he painted as a Paradise of flowers, not a Tartarus of clinkers," but his amours are interrupted (Enc., 109–11).

His appearance raises suspicions, and when he is caught in an act of apparent arson, he is thrust into another hellish environment—a windowless prison "built of huge cakes of sunburnt brick," housing "villainous and hopeless inmates . . . in all sorts of tragic squalor." And in this not unfamiliar environment, Oberlus again rules, becoming "the central figure of a mongrel and assassin band; a creature whom it is religion to detest, since it is philanthropy to hate a misanthrope" (Enc., 112). His inner hell had again forced him to fashion his own Tarturus, and that is the curse he carried with him to and from the Encantadas—or so the narrator would have us believe.

There is no doubt that the narrator comes down harder on Oberlus than on Villamil, the tyrannical Dog-King whose acts and attitudes are hardly more justifiable. He seems more manipulative of reader sentiment in the story of Oberlus, telling us what we should think rather than presenting the basis for our conclusions. The Pisgah pattern leads us to expect two sides to a hermit; instead we are exposed to a heretofore unseen side of the narrator. And this raises a further question: what if Oberlus's letter is not only self-serving but closer to the truth than the secondary sources from which most of the information stems? In the letter he claims to have been "exiled from my country by the cruel hand of tyranny," to have tried to leave the island by honest means, to have been driven in desperation to stealing, and to "have been robbed and beaten by men professing to be Christians" (Enc., 110–11).

The possibility that Melville may be up to some trick involving narrative perspective is strengthened by the changes he made in the original letter which he found in Captain David Porter's *Journal of a Cruise Made to the Pacific Ocean*. He changed the name of the ship which Porter's hermit stole for his escape from *The Black Prince* to the *Charity*, very likely to suggest that the only charity he received he had to steal.[13] And then he expanded the hermit's mention of his

---

13. *Ibid.*, 461.

"old hen" to a lengthier joke on charity, for the "old fowl" allegedly
nesting on eggs "proved to be a starveling rooster, reduced to a sit-
ting posture by sheer debility"—perhaps to suggest that Oberlus
was repaying his fellow men in kind for the sort of charity he had received (Enc., 111). Either the letter is deceitful and we trust the
narrative, or the narrative is deceitful and we should trust the letter
—a conundrum appropriate to the world of the Encantadas where
the reader has learned that one cannot believe what he sees, what
he hears, what he feels, or perhaps, what he reads.

The epigraph prefixed to the last sketch also stems from Spenser's
description of the cave of Despair in the *Faerie Queene* and constitutes the epitaph of many nameless dead, citing the "old stockes and
stubs of trees. . . . / On which had many wretches hanged beene."
Among the wretches whose misery-filled existence on one or another island is marked by some half-obliterated relic are various ref-
ugees: sailors seeking to escape some tyrannical captain and rarely
finding asylum, stranded tortoise hunters abandoned by their com-
rades, or seamen summarily sentenced to solitary confinement by
wrathful captains. Their remains populate a necropolis, which, like
some European monasteries, entombs the dead in the walls that
house the living. Others fortunate enough to die within range of the
Encantadas thereby avoid burial at sea and lie interred in this remote but convenient Potter's Field, the graves of the most fortunate
graced by the effort of "some good-natured forecastle poet," aspirant
to membership in the Graveyard School by writing such an example
as Melville provides:

> Oh, Brother Jack, as you pass by,
> As you are now, so once was I.
> Just so game, and just so gay,
> But now, alack, they've stopped my pay.
> No more I peep out of my blinkers,
> Here I be—tucked in with clinkers!   (Enc., 113–16)

Aside from having written what could have become his own epitaph, Melville has again borrowed from and made some interesting
changes in a few lines from Porter's *Journal*:

Gentle reader, as you pass by,
As you are now, so wonce was I;
And now my body is in the dust
I hope in heaven my soul to rest.[14]

Both epitaphs present the ultimate disparity in point of view—that
the living and the dead, but Melville's version reduces the formality,
accents the geniality and vernacular tone, and, most important of all,
eliminates any sentimental hint of rosy salvation. Unlike the verse
he found in Porter's *Journal*, Melville's provides no Pisgah view of
the soul in heaven, choosing to conclude the work with an equivalency rather than the patterned disparities that characterize most of
it: the damned soul in Hell or the live being in the fallen world share
the same cinder-heaped view in a clinker-strewn Tartarus. He will
not posit the promised land in heaven after dispelling the illusion
that it exists on earth.

In Melville's view, this "fallen world" is the discovery of every
moral explorer who gains insight into its inherent contrasts, deceptions, and contradictions, and who grows disenchanted in the process. His discovery uncovers nothing new but reinforces the unpleasant truth of an old despair. The world has not changed since it
first came into being, and the old diabolism may be denied but not
mitigated. In the fallen world penitential suffering, callous exploitation, injustice, and deceit lay the basis for lasting despair, and the
Pisgah principle, which promises something much better, also pre-
dicates something much worse.

In an indirect way "The Encantadas" is also concerned with Melville's recurrent interest in the problem of art and illusion. As he
makes clearer in "The Piazza," the process of disenchantment (intensified by the concentrated lessons of life on the Encantadas) is a
necessarily preliminary stage for the artist who must expose and
abandon some illusions to produce the more potent illusions of art,
his imaginative reconstruction of reality becoming an act of homage,
of defiance, and quite possibly of redemption. Working consciously
with illusion, he must avoid the destroying delusion that results

14. *Ibid.*, 461.

from narrow insistence on the truth of one's perceptions or preconceptions in a world where the Pisgah principle prevails.

Although "The Encantadas" is not, strictly speaking, the kind of short fiction we are accustomed to in the story, tale, or novella, it is a form of highly imaginative nonfiction with strong links to much of Melville's subsequent fiction and poetry. Most obvious in the diptych stories completed or published in the same year as "The Encantadas," the inherent principle of dualistic complement and contrast becomes overt structural strategy. And even when it is not obvious in the structural form, the Pisgah principle remains a thematic constant in the duplicities of *The Confidence-Man* and the moral ambiguities of *Billy Budd*.

3

⊚⊚⊚

A PISGAH VIEW
OF OLD WORLD
AND NEW

"The Two Temples"

None of the stories Melville wrote between 1853 and 1856 did much
to bolster his waning reputation or depleted royalty accounts, but
"The Two Temples" did least for Melville in any tangible way. Both
the editor and publisher of *Putnam's*, while admiring the story,
found it too potentially offensive to the religious sensibilities of many
readers, and so it was never published in Melville's lifetime.

It is of interest now not only as a story in its own terms but also for
the way it fits with Melville's other stories and strengthens certain
thematic and formal relationships. "The Two Temples" is one of several stories, including "The Lighting-Rod Man" or "Jimmy Rose,"
which should have offended American religious sensibilities, had
they been understood. It is also like "Poor Man's Pudding and Rich
Man's Crumbs" and "The Paradise of Bachelors and the Tartarus of
Maids" in that it is constructed of facing panels contrasting New
World and Old, offering a Pisgah view of human societies but not
one in which the New World is automatically the land of promise
and fulfillment. And it is like Hawthorne's "Celestial Railroad" or
"Minister's Black Veil" or Emerson's "Divinity School Address" in
exposing painful perversions of religious purpose and meaning. Melville, however, was less the preacher and more the pathologist than
his literary contemporaries. His intent in "The Two Temples," as in
much of his short fiction, was to show by oblique and symbolic
means that beneath the apparently living tissue and virtuous pro-

51

nouncements of mid–nineteenth-century American society was a
spiritual deadness, a startling insensitivity to the communal needs of
the individual. By going deeper than conventional American self-
appraisal, he asserted that the basic rights and values that defined
America were in fact going under.

We do not learn until the second half of the story (the half that is
set in London) that the narrator is a physician, but this fact is important since each half of the two-part story constitutes an examination
and description of a series of social symptoms culminating in a rather
ironic and unexpected diagnosis. In the first part of the story, set in
New York, the narrator as physician is subordinate to the narrator as
pilgrim who comes, prayerbook in hand, to worship humbly at the
"marble-buttressed, stained-glass, spic-and-span new temple." Modeled after the recently completed, elegant, and exclusive Grace
Church, Melville's first temple is guarded by a "great, fat-pauched,
beadle-faced man" who denies entrance to the modestly dressed
narrator (TT, 149). Here irony is heaped on irony and Melville begins his allegory without departing from the very tangible reality of
New York's streets.

The temple is first of all a symbol of what American piety has become, and second, like the Wall Street law office in "Bartleby," a
symbol of what American society has become. The dream of Christianity has been its promise of salvation for the meek and humble,
and one segment of the American Dream has been liberty and
equality within a system where special privileges based on class had
no place. But Grace Church, as here represented, graces its ample
pews with wealthy and well-dressed parishioners; it has no grace for
the common man. And classless America is identified with segrega-
tion and exclusion based on superficial signs of status, the sort of inequity and iniquity associated in the American Dream with the misery, privilege, and decadence of the Old World.

"Temple First" is thus a double-edged critique of hypocrisy in
American piety and American society. Its meaning hinges on our
recognizing the narrator as an essentially honest, if somewhat naive,
believer in the American Dream. He acts as if freedom of worship in
the church of his choice extended to each individual, as if class distinctions had been canceled by the affirmations of democracy, as if

church and state were duly separate, and as if the courts served to protect and extend the principle of liberty and justice for all. His brief experience at the Sunday service at Grace Church and his appearance before the judge on Monday morning dispel every comforting feature of this American Dream. In his wakeful nightmare the New World acquires most of the worst features of the Old and loses its uniqueness, which is probably the essential quality of the dream.

In "Temple First" the sequence of experiences continues to build until they culminate in an "appalling din" that releases the wrath and justice of ordered society upon the innocent narrator. The first warning on "this blessed Sunday morning" occurs when "the fat-paunched, beadle-faced man" rebuffs the narrator, who, as he is forced out of the nave, feels himself "excommunicated" or at least "excluded," his fault being a coat a bit too shabby to permit him to mingle with the congregation in one of "these splendid, new-fashioned Gothic Temples." The gothic style, of course, is distinctly European; the "new-fashioned Gothic" in America hints at where the story is heading (TT, 149–50).

The second premonition is provided by the narrator's notice of "glossy groups of low-voiced gossipers nearby," dressed in the gorgeous finery "of royal dukes, right honorable barons." Of course they are not what they seem, for democratic America stands against such artificial prerogative. They are not even members of this exclusive congregation, only lackeys in glittering garb whose function is to ornament the "noble string of flashing carriages drawn up along the curb." Had Melville gone on in this way, he would have sounded like Thorstein Veblen on the conspicuous consumption among America's wealthy, but Melville's mode, especially in his short fiction, is to present imaginative glimpses of elusive and frequently unpopular truth rather than sober and considered reflection on troublesome matters. Still his depiction of the conspicuous display outside the church, inside it, and in the architecture itself lays the basis for his implicit charges of un-Christian and antidemocratic values in the church and un-American attitudes in American society at large (TT, 149–50).

Noticing a small door outside the church and assuming that it leads to a place in the tower from which he might "in spirit, if not in place, participate in those devout exultations," the narrator decides to try this other mode of entry. His aim is still to "take part in the proceedings," to seek even at some distance the grace and communion to which the church is pledged and to participate in the political community to which the society is pledged. In a crucial moment he steals through the side door and makes his way up the stairs, asserting "I will not be defrauded of my natural rights." He reaches a small platform, the first of several stops on his way up into the bell tower, and finds himself enclosed on three sides by richly colored stained glass windows which cast fantastic sunrises, sunsets, rainbows, falling stars, and other pyrotechnical effects into the air and onto the wall. But despite all this psychedelic splendor, he may as well have been, he says, in "a basement cell in 'the tombs'," for he can see nothing outside his cell until he scratches a peephole in the center of one of the stained glass windows. What he then sees is the beadle-faced man chasing three ragged little boys into the street. He does not dwell on the scene, but it does have iconographic significance that further heightens the inverted epiphany at the center of the story. Here, within the church, the poor inherit the wrath of the official guardian, and Christ's injunction to "suffer the little children to come unto me" becomes something like "the little children shall suffer if they dare" (TT, 150–51).

Proceeding further up the tower, the narrator finds a small circular window which affords a view of the congregation about a hundred feet below. But the window, designed for purposes of ventilation, is covered with a fine screen and transmits a hellish blast of hot air, scorching his face, as he looks down upon the assembled worshipers. He can hear the priest and make the proper responses, he can hear the organ and the uplifting hymns, but the screen darkens his view of all the proceedings below. Like Parson Hooper's black veil in Hawthorne's story, this screen "had the effect of casting crape upon all." In Hawthorne's story the piece of crape that darkens the minister's vision and hides his face signifies the minister's belief in the innate sinfulness of all men. His unyielding insistence on this belief removes him from any joyful participation in human community, or as Hawthorne elsewhere phrases it, he has broken "the magnetic chain of humanity." The darkening screen in Melville's story, however, signifies a different truth—not that of the individual who has through pride and isolation broken that "magnetic chain of humanity" but of organized society and institutionalized religion that have blasted the hopes of democratic community and distorted the meaning and intent of Christian communion. However, the narrator, believing still in the benignity of things as they are (or as he thinks they are), tries to discount the dark view of circumstances through the screen. He will not admit—though the reader is supposed to recognize—the power of blackness to delineate some of the less pleasant aspects of life in mid–nineteenth-century America (TT, 152–53).

Despite his efforts to compensate for his blackened vision of the assembly below, some disturbing alterations of reality result from his new perspective. Cynicism is not normally part of his nature; yet as he stands "in the very posture of devotion," responding with prayerbook in hand, the scene below begins to seem a sumptuous theatrical spectacle. The chants proceed according to script; the priest appears a practical actor, entering and exiting dramatically. His reappearance is marked by quick change of costume and his presence reinforced by "melodious tone and persuasive gesture." As Emerson had diagnosed in his personal journal and at his unexpectedly controversial address to Harvard divinity students, the priest was playing a role, fulfilling a form. The spirit languished as the literalist went through his paces. Communion, Emerson insisted, ought to be a living experience, not a dead letter. (It is of interest to recall the personal crisis that led to his resigning his pulpit when he began to feel that he was furthering a form and serving a cold institutional purpose.) Lack of integrity is the unspoken charge against the priest in Melville's story, the priest who ironically tells his affluent congregation through his chosen text: "Ye are the salt of the earth" (TT, 53–54). The irony in this choice of the minister's text is simultaneously an indictment of Christian ethics and democratic practice, and the narrator, from his unaccustomed vantage point, gazes down not at the Promised Land of the American Dream but at an image of reality permeated by hypocrisy and social pretensions.

The narrator's experience has been unsettling, but it will reach nightmare proportions before he is free again to walk the streets.

Trying to exit by the same route as he had entered, he finds the door securely locked. He had come to the church, a source of Salvation, to be part of a worshiping community, but finds himself isolated and imprisoned. Climbing again to his high perch and looking down into the vast hall, he imagines himself "gazing from Pisgah into the forest of Old Canaan" and the unusual perspective alters expectation and illuminates hidden truth. His eye falls on "a Puseyitish painting of a Madonna and child" on one of the lower windows but its iconographical impact on him makes it seem "the true Hagar and her Ishmael." As I have suggested, Melville has used a series of symbolic revelations to heighten the sense of terror and alarm, and I think this Pisgah view of hallowed Madonna and Child as social outcasts—outsiders in this magnificent temple of Christian worship—is the culmination of Melville's epiphanic method, developed long before James Joyce articulated its possibilities for short fiction (TT, 154–55).

Melville's narrator awakens to the full terror of his experience when he pulls a bell rope to call attention to his predicament. Instead of some gentle peal or gong, he sets off a thunderous reverberation, as if he had tripped some earthshaking burglar alarm and roused the world to his irreverent intrusions. Hauled off by the beadle-faced man, he is handed off to three policemen, who recognize him "as a lawless violator, and a remorseless disturber of the Sunday peace." Like Bartleby, who also despaired of the possibility of significant communication, genuine community, or spiritual communion, the narrator of "The Two Temples" is led off to the Tombs. His fate is more comic than tragic, but it is black comedy, black as the vision that transforms the infant Christ into the outcast Ishmael. He comes before a judge the next morning, is quickly found guilty, fined, reprimanded, and released. There is as much justice in the Halls of Justice as grace in Grace Church.

"Temple First" has provided an overview of the American Dream and the hope of Christianity, but through a screen, darkly (TT, 156–57). Melville has impressed upon us that the atmosphere of our institutions is, as Emerson earlier insisted in his "Divinity School Address," one where what were once expressions "of admiration and love . . . are now petrified into official titles, kill[ing] all generous sympathy and liking."

If the cumulative revelations of the first half of Melville's diptych darken the dream of spiritual communion and democratic community, the iconography of the second half somewhat sentimentally restores his faith in man and the possibilities of spiritual regeneration. "Temple Second" is set in London. The narrator has been unexpectedly dismissed from his position as private physician to an ailing wealthy young American lady, and he is for the moment impoverished and in debt. Like Ishmael, he is "forlorn, outcast, without a friend," "a penniless stranger in Babylonian London" with its "fiendish gas-lights, shooting their Tartarean rays." He feels caught up and swept along in "unscrupulous human whirlpools," and expecting every man's hand to be turned against him, he has a series of encounters that reverse the sobering experiences of "Temple First" (TT, 157–59).

The "blessed oasis of tranquility" in the midst of this urban pandemonium is not a church but a theater, a temple of entertainment, where a noted actor is on this Saturday night appearing as Cardinal Richelieu. Even if he had the shilling for admission, the narrator does not feel a theater could satisfy his psychological needs. Tired, depressed, abandoned, he is an alien in search of human fellowship. His need, as he explains it, is the same as what drew him to Grace Church: the "cheer" that results from "making one of many pleasing human faces," from "getting into a genial humane assembly of my kind," the satisfaction that "at its best and highest, is to be found in the unified multitude of a devout congregation." Still, he is pulled by the desire to see this performance. He is saved from the folly of pawning his overcoat "by a sudden cheery summons in a voice unmistakably benevolent." The caller, who seems a workingman by his dress, extends a ticket which he is unable to use and urges the embarrassed narrator to take it and enjoy the show. In a single instant he has had cheer and charity thrust upon him, qualities he may have needed before but had never been offered "ere this blessed night." A minor miracle has taken place and an even greater one awaits him in the theater (TT, 159–61).

His entry into this second temple through a small side entrance
and his ascent up many twisting stairs repeats his experience in
"Temple First," with the important exception that he is *welcomed* to
the theater, which strangely embodies many of the characteristics of
a church. The tickettaker at the top of the stairs looks out of a little
booth "like some saint in a shrine, [his] countenance . . . illumi-
nated by two smoky candles." The orchestral music recalls the organ
melodies of Grace Church, and as he looks from his seat high in the
shilling gallery down through the hot, smoky air at the massed audience below, he feels the resemblance even more. But now he is not
alone; he has "most acceptable, right welcome, cheery company
. . . quiet, well-pleased working-men, and their glad wives and sisters, with here and there an aproned urchin, with all-absorbed,
bright face, hovering like a painted cherub over the vast human
firmament below." After a brief moment when he involuntarily
seeks in his pocket for the prayerbook which is not there, one of the
aproned urchins approaches him with a pot and pewter mug. Forced
by his poverty to refuse what he assumes is coffee, he is recognized
by the boy as an American. But the boy answers hospitably, "Well,
dad's gone to Yankee-land, a-seekin' of his fortin; so take a penny
mug of ale, do, Yankee, for poor dad's sake." With the mug of dark
ale in his hand, the narrator confesses that he has no penny, to
which the boy replies, "Never do you mind, Yankee; drink to honest
dad." Moved by this gracious gesture, the narrator offers a toast:
"With all my heart, you generous boy; here's immortal life to him!"
The boy moves away smiling and finds there are many more takers
of his ale. Deeply affected by this second act of unexpected charity
given so cheerfully, the narrator feels new life and new hope through
this secular sacrament: "That unpurchased penny-worth of ale re-
vived my drooping spirits strangely. Stuff was in that barley malt; a
most sweet bitterness in those blessed hops. God bless the glorious
boy!" Whether by accident or intent, Melville has linked in human
action three words which are strongly linked etymologically—*cheer,
charity, Eu-charist*, the latter unmentioned but playfully suggested
in the revival of spirit (TT, 162–64). (*Eucharist* is still the word for
"thank you" in modern Greek, meaning literally "by your favor" or
"by your grace.")

Although the most important action seems to be in this topmost balcony, there are noteworthy things down below too. Mr. Macready's performance as Richelieu, the statesman–priest, is apparently a superb achievement, more moving and genuine than the priest's performance in "Temple First." The audience in the first instance seemed "one of buried, not living men"; in the second case "the enraptured thousands sound their responses, deafeningly, unmistakably sincere. Right from the undoubted heart." The first priest was a dissembler who deceived himself, the second a consummate actor who, as actor, was "the real thing." What he had accomplished, Melville suggests, was far more than "mere mimicry." He had elevated his art and his audience and converted a vast number of disparate individuals, the narrator among them, into a harmonious and "gladdened crowd" (TT, 165).

The question this raises is "what is it then to act a part?" Such a question concerning the interpenetration of life and art is one which we are more accustomed to find in Henry James than in Melville. But Melville's implied conclusion in this parable of the priest–actor and the actor–priest is very close to James's suggestion that "the real thing could be so much less precious than the unreal," that an artful approach to life and an awareness of its symbolic moments can be more penetrating, revealing, and "real" than a thoroughly realistic approach. If this seems a side issue in Melville's story, it is, nevertheless, a relevant one, for it is an acknowledgment that while art is built on illusion, it is the kind of illusion that can sustain life and unmask other deceits.

Melville developed his second sketch, like the first, through a series of cumulative revelations, reaching a climactic, if somewhat sentimentally ironic, epiphany in the cup of ale so freely given. This may seem a fictional device considerably in advance of his time, and indeed it is, but Melville did have a model, or at least a precedent, in the work of the two contemporaries I mentioned earlier. There is a ready connection with the symbolic tales and tableaus of Hawthorne; there is a less obvious but no less important connection with the technical and the thematic elements of Emerson's "Divinity School Address," a deeper relationship than any I have yet mentioned.

Without ever instructing his listeners or readers in what he was doing, Emerson began his address by describing sacramental mysteries, such as baptism and the Eucharist, in terms of what takes place freely in nature and in human experience. Whether he was right or not, he undoubtedly felt that an audience schooled in religious symbolism would grasp his meaning and agree with the deritualizing of the sacraments in order to make them live. He also implored, "All who hear me, feel that the language that describes Christ to Europe and America is not the style of friendship and enthusiasm to a good and noble heart, but is appropriated and formal." Melville did not hear him, but he certainly did read him. And what the narrator, when he blessed "the glorious boy" and drank "to honest dad," felt in the depths of his heart was the lesson the Emerson read in Jesus, who "saw that God incarnates himself in man, and evermore goes forth anew to take possession of his World."

My point in all this, however, is not to propose the "Divinity School Address" as a source for "The Two Temples" but to suggest a cultural connection that brings us back again to the American Dream and its implication for religion. We have perhaps no more articulate statement of the American Dream, its individual and national implications, than "The American Scholar." (It is a prescription for curing the pathological alienation and sterility of "Temple First.") I do not have to insist either that the "Divinity School Address" focuses the main ideas of "The American Scholar" on the narrower field of religion and the ministry and actually incorporates the Kingdom of God in the American Dream. And if, as I have tried to show, there are strong thematic as well as technical parallels between the "Divinity School Address" and Melville's "The Two Temples"—especially "Temple Second"—then I may be justified in suggesting that even the London half of Melville's diptych has more than a peripheral relevance to the matter of the American Dream.

Let me put it differently before being accused of the tactic of guilt by association. "Temple First" clearly describes the American Dream rendered nightmare by increasingly rigid social organization and materialistically rather than humanely ordered social forces. In the America of "Temple First" the Puritan ethic, with its inevitable emphasis on the Kingdom of Goods, has taken precedence over the

Christian ethic and its injunction to "love thy neighbor as thy self."
The result has been an isolating and divisive kind of individualism
that subverts the communal hope of both democracy and Christianity. "Temple Second" clearly abandons the American scene in finding relief from the nightmare of alienation, but it seems to me that
the therapy by which our physician heals himself is more than the
accidental experience of an American down and almost out in London: it is still the stuff of the American Dream. What Melville has
implicitly questioned, however, is not the meaning of the dream or
even its connection with the promised kingdom of Christian thought.
In his own way he seems to have affirmed these. Rather, he challenges, though somewhat obliquely, the self-styled role of America
as the redeemer nation (wherein there are seemingly insurmount-
able obstacles to redemption) and the idea of America as the necessary locus for realization of the American Dream. The symbolic
strength of the dream survives, despite what has happened to its
substance. Its power in London after being dispelled by the circumstances in New York seems to make Melville more American than
ever in demonstrating that the dream is not dead, even though the
nightmare has revealed in indisputably real terms the threat of
America's going under.

"Poor Man's Pudding and Rich Man's Crumbs"

"Poor Man's Pudding and Rich Man's Crumbs" is the second of the
three two-part stories Melville published or attempted to have published during 1854, each contrasting a highly graphic situation of
New World origin with Old World circumstances. This juxtaposition
sometimes produced an unexpected analogue, at other times an
ironic inversion. Whether the two scenes turned out to be con-
gruent or incongruent, the method was one of thematic reinforcement and sudden, if not always obvious, illumination. When most
successful, Melville's diptychs (a remarkably apt term for these
stories since a diptych consists of two related sacred scenes) convey
an epiphanic experience, but not necessarily a revelation of unexpected divinity. Melville's epiphanies more often illuminate a lack of
divinity in human relationships and a corresponding lack of humanity in supposedly divine institutions. And the crosscultural contrast

which marks "The Two Temples," "Poor Man's Pudding and Rich
Man's Crumbs," and "The Paradise of Bachelors and The Tartarus of
Maids" frequently counters the myth of uniqueness, exceptionalism,
or benignity so often underlying the American self-image.

On first reading "Poor Man's Pudding and Rich Man's Crumbs,"
one is strongly impelled to agree with R. H. Fogle that its two parts
contrast American and British poverty in order to assert that "whatever the differences of time and place, the misery of poverty is, has
always been, and will continue to be, the same everywhere."[1] More
studied reading convinces me, however, that while the story focuses
on poverty, its purpose is to illuminate the diminishing role and the
meaning of *charity* in Christian society, and the consequent lack of
communal feeling or concern in the New World or the Old.

In this purpose "Poor Man's Pudding and Rich Man's Crumbs" is
closely linked with "The Two Temples," which contrasts the lack of
grace, charity, and justice in American spiritual and secular affairs
with the narrator's unexpected experience of joyful human community sparked by two acts of selfless, faith-restoring charity. The word
charity appears ten times in one paragraph in "The Two Temples."
In "Poor Man's Pudding and Rich Man's Crumbs" the word appears
about twenty times, often in combination with *alms, beneficence,*
and *philanthropy*; and in the second part of the story *charity* becomes as subtly insistent and multimeaninged a word as *prefer* in
"Bartleby." In "The Two Temples" Melville set up an etymological
pattern linking *cheer, charity,* and the unmentioned but unmistakable *Eucharist,* which climaxes the story. This pattern continues in
"Poor Man's Pudding and Rich Man's Crumbs" but with less emphasis on the possibility of cheering communion of souls and more
on the hollowness and hypocrisy of what passes for charity and effectively sunders community in the superficially Christian societies of
Old World and New.

The title of the story calls attention to the two meals which shape
each half of the diptych, those two meals which so inadequately sustain the poor diners. Each meal, in fact, serves to emphasize the social and psychological divisions, the unbridgeable gaps in society,

1. Richard Harter Fogle, *Melville's Shorter Tales* (Norman: University of Oklahoma Press,
1960), 40.

parodying the egalitarian promises of community and the possibilities of communion. Most pointedly in the second sketch the Lord Mayor's Charity (which makes available to London's poor the remains of the Lord Mayor's feast of the previous night) is a frightening rendering of the Lord's Supper wherein the host's charity goes far beyond condescension and becomes ill-concealed contempt. In this crosscultural exploration of values, Melville is first social critic exposing the comforting rationalizations of the blandly complacent, well-to-do class in America and the grossly self-indulgent, supremely conspicuous consumption of the European aristocracy. But the social criticism is really the first half of a conceit by which Melville, like a metaphysical poet, tries to dramatize the spiritual delights of God's grace and to bemoan its inaccessibility in the world we know—the world which Edward Taylor in "Meditation Eight" says "no food for Souls e're gave," where all but the firmest Christian are impoverished, for "the World's White Loafe is done, / And cannot yield thee here the smallest Crumb."[2]

In the opening sketch, labeled "Picture First," the narrator is introduced to a set of bland rationalizations and cruel self-deceptions by his guide, a vacuous but enthusiastic poet named Blandmour—whose name itself suggests the inability to mourn deeply or to recognize tragedy. Blandmour's view "that the blessed almoner, Nature, is in all things beneficent; and . . . considerate in her charities" launches a parody of the belief that in America a redemptive nature nurtures the body and renews the spirit. For Blandmour the new fallen March snow is "Poor Man's Manure"; melted and bottled it becomes "Poor Man's Eye-Water." A cup of rainwater becomes "Poor Man's Egg," and a compound of readily available natural substances becomes ."Poor Man's Plaster," so effective in alleviating bodily injuries. Before he finishes his catalog of how Nature favors

2. Of course Melville could not have known Taylor's poetry and never shared the fervor or the firmness of his faith, but Melville's fascination with the way men's practice ran counter to their professed faith prompted him to use such theological bench marks in his literary technique.

The passage from John 6:51, from which Taylor drew for "Meditation Eight" was probably known to Melville: "I am the living bread which came down out of Heaven; if any man eat of this bread he shall live forever." And in an ironic way it constitutes the iconographical focus for each half of Melville's diptych.

the poor, Blandmour tries to tempt the narrator, who is his guest, into sampling the ultimate treat—"Poor Man's Pudding." Behind all this enthusiastic hyperbole may stand the benign figure of Emerson, whose explication of nature's role had progressed from "Commodity" to "Spirit," and whose comments on poverty at times seem to resemble Blandmour's. For example, in the section on "Discipline" in *Nature*, Emerson suggests, to use Melville's formulation, that poverty is "Poor Man's Preceptor," or that snow is "Poor Man's Property": "Debt . . . is a preceptor whose lessons cannot be foregone, and is needed most by those who suffer from it most. Moreover, property . . . has been well compared to snow,—if it fall level today, it will be blown into drifts tomorrow." This latter observation, which announces a principle of compensation in nature, seems to be disproved by the experience of Melville's narrator, who asks his guide and host, "How is it that wind drives yonder drifts of 'Poor Man's Manure' off poor Coulter's two-acre patch here, and piles it up yonder on rich Squire Teamster's twenty-acre field?" (PMP, 167–69).

Poor Coulter's bare, damp, ill-ventilated dwelling is the setting for the main action of "Poor Man's Pudding." Like Blandmour, so oblivious to the suffering of the poor, Coulter bears a tag-name which signifies that he has been reduced to the condition of an implement for tilling the soil, rather than, as Emerson would have it, a fully developed "Man on the farm." The Coulters' hospitality is genuine but not without embarrassment. The condition of their bleak lives is a corrective to the sentimentalities of pastoral myth. Illhoused, overworked, underpaid, undeniable victims of callous exploitation, the Coulters are nevertheless far from being likely prospects for a revolutionary cause. Because American values do not recognize poverty, except as the consequence of a lack of virtue and industry, the Coulters are woefully ignorant, for they do not in a sense know how poor and debilitated they are. Along with Blandmour and, no doubt, Squire Teamster, who extracts maximum value from Coulter's labors, they believe that charity demeans, that nature provides, that God is good, especially to the self-reliant man, and that, as William Ellery Channing wrote, "Moral and religious culture is the great blessing to be bestowed upon the poor."[3] The only book that the narrator notices in their home, so conspicuously bare of conventional amenities or attempts at aesthetic leavening, is "an old volume of Doddridge" (PMP, 171). (Melville probably had in mind the Rev. Philip Doddridge, an advocate of the power of piety and positive thinking, "Suited to Persons of Every Character and Circumstance," as he phrased it in one of his titles. The main character in one of Melville's later stories, "Jimmy Rose," expresses his contempt for such pious panaceas as Doddridge's by terming them "Poor Man's Plaster.") At any rate, this amalgam of secular and religious placebos keeps the Coulters proud and apparently whole in spirit, even as their bodies shrivel and their children die in infancy. Mrs. Coulter, in particular, pallid in her current pregnancy and buffeted by misfortune and loss, seems as poignant as Marianna in "The Piazza" as she struggles vainly against harsh environmental odds for some fleeting consolation: "Strive how I may to cheer me with thinking of little William and Martha in heaven, and with reading Dr. Doddridge there—still, still does dark grief leak in, just like the rain through our roof" (PMP, 175).

Staunch as the Coulters remain in their devotion to prominent American virtues and verities, the true quality of their lives is conveyed in the terms which describe their appearance and that of their surroundings: "an infirm-looking old shed," "a half-rotten, soaked board," an "enfeebled chair," "the ineffectual low fire" with its "sad hissing and vain spluttering," the "rankish" salt pork, the "bitter and mouldy" pudding, and the "cheerless," "blue, resigned eye" of Mrs. Coulter. The source of both the narrator's pity and the Coulters' pride lies in their failure to recognize the extent of their subjugation and helplessness before brutifying circumstances. Coulter unwittingly mentions the horse he hopes to buy from Squire Teamster in order to carry his wife to the distant church. He has already "christened it 'Martha.'" But his essential kindness and blindness to irony

3. William Ellery Channing, "Ministry for the Poor," *Works* (17th ed.; 6 vols.; Boston: Walker, Wise, and Co., 1862), IV, 279. Channing argues that the Christian spirit is the greatest gift to the poor, that hunger is a lesser hazard than overeating, and that the happiness of the poor has its own peculiar dignity and honor. This address was delivered in 1835 and appeared in the first edition of Channing's *Works* in 1841.

and sexual innuendo prevent him from seeing how completely a horse named for his wife (and dead daughter) expresses their subservience to Squire Teamster, who profits from their all-too-limited strength. Only through the cruel ironies of ordinary life can the "poor man's pudding,"—which the narrator found so unpalatable, but which Blandmour found so worthy of praise—have any connection with "the living bread which came down out of heaven" to assure men of life everlasting" (PMP, 170–77).

Just as there was nothing of the conventionally picturesque in the debunking of pastoral myth and the exposure of the hopelessly dependent yeoman in "Picture First," there is nothing of the tourist's picturesque in the London setting of "Picture Second" and the meditation on "Rich Man's Crumbs." Both sketches serve to reject the kind of social insensitivity and moral blindness that stems from too strong a predilection for the picturesque. There is a shared snobbishness in Mrs. Glendinning's blandly benignant admiration of what Melville termed the *povertiresque* in *Pierre* and Washington Irving's embarrassingly extravagant admiration for the history-laden and regally redolent shrines of British antiquity in *The Sketch Book*. Of course, it would not be the first time that Melville used Irving as a target for social and literary barbs, having described him disdainfully in "Hawthorne and His Mosses" as "that graceful writer, who . . . has received the most plaudits from his country . . . that very popular and amiable writer . . . who perhaps owes his chief reputation to the self-acknowledged imitation of a foreign model, and to the studied avoidance of all topics but smooth ones." Melville's topic in "Rich Man's Crumbs" is certainly not a "smooth one," for he is determined to show the gracelessness of an aristocratic and ostensibly graceful society and the maddening heartlessness of an ostensibly humane act of charity.

Melville's sketch is set in 1814, after Napoleon's defeat at Waterloo, to provide historical justification for such an assembly of "grateful and gorgeous aristocracy" as the emperors, regents, kings, and other beautiful people who dined off "solid silver and gold plate" at the Guildhall Banquet. On the day after the sumptuous feast, the narrator is taken by his uniformed guide, a minor civic official, to admire one "of the noble charities of London"—the remains of the feast generously made available to an eager, struggling mass of London's poor (PMP, 178–79).

So "lean, famished, [and] ferocious" is this "squalid mass," that they seem "a mob of cannibals," or a "murderous pack," the narrator himself "seething in the Pit with the Lost." The guide draws a glittering weapon from his belt to protect himself and the narrator from the danger presented by these recipients of the Lord Mayor's civic grace. But by his words this guide would imply that blessed are these poor souls who have the blue tickets of admission enabling them to sup where "less than twelve hours before" there supped such lords and nobles as "His Imperial Majesty, Alexander of Russia; His Royal Majesty, Frederic William, King of Prussia; His Royal Highness, George, Prince Regent of England; His world-renowned Grace, the Duke of Wellington . . . and innumerable other nobles of mark." To drive home his point that such "a generous, noble, magnanimous charity" blandly conceals a calloused contempt for the lesser ranks of society, Melville has another civic official address the narrator as "Graceless ragamuffin," while thrusting at him a broken pastry with the admonition to "be thankful that you taste of the same dish with Her Grace the Duchess of Devonshire." The painful discrepancy between what the world dignifies as "Grace" and what is generally worthy of "Grace" is so absurb that only such puns enable Melville to express and yet to contain his outrage, to suggest a critical view of the reigning establishment but to stop short of supporting a revolutionary threat even as he sees it developing (PMP, 179–82).

At this point in Melville's story a further complication emerges as the narrator struggles to establish his identity and disengage himself from the mob. His coat has been "fouled and torn," he has been mistaken for one of London's poor, and when his guide corrects this mistake, a colleague urges him to remove the narrator quickly before "the grand crash"—the certainty of which he is experienced enough to expect. And when it comes, it is as much a paradigm of revolution as Hawthorne's surrealistic spectacle in "My Kinsman, Major Molineaux":

The yet unglutted mob raised a fierce yell. . . . They surged against the tables, broke through all barriers, and billowed over the hall—their bare tossed arms like the dashed ribs of a wreck. It seemed to me as if a sudden impotent fury of fell envy possessed them. That one half-hour's peep at the mere remnants of the glories of the Banquets of Kings, the unsatisfying mouthfuls of disembowelled pasties, plundered pheasants, and half-sacked jellies, served to remind them of the intrinsic contempt of the alms. In this sudden mood, or whatever mysterious thing it was that now seized them, these Lazaruses seemed ready to spew up in repentant scorn the contumelious crumbs of Dives (PMP, 182–83).

Escaping from the tumult of "the greatest of England's noble charities," the narrator is forced to follow the protective measures of his guide: "Wedge—wedge in—quick . . . hit that man—strike him down! hold! jam! now! now! wrench along for your life!" The reader, however, is forced to contrast these mutually escalating hostilities with the ties of community that charity is supposed to reinforce between men. The contrast suggests that this social perversion of communion and community accomplishes not God's work but the devil's, and there is an ironic iconographic appropriateness in the laughing representations at one end of the Guildhall of Gog and Magog, Satan's cohorts in his war against the Kingdom of God. Melville thus suggests, quite unmistakably, that these forces have good reason to rejoice at the covert inhumanity that passes in the world for grace and charity (PMP, 183, 181).

But this recognition does not solve the problem of the narrator and his role in the story. He is a man of sensitivity and insight, but while he sympathizes with the Coulters, he is loath to criticize Blandmour and never considers the possibility of an appeal to Squire Teamster in the Coulters' behalf. He comments in "Picture First" that "the best one can do is to do nothing," and eases himself out of the pain that his insight provokes by romanticizing the American poor who "never lose their delicacy or pride." In "Picture Second" he remarks with similar blandness that misery in urban London maddens, wheras in rural New England it softens. He reveals something of his own values when he mentions that he "had declined all letters but one to my banker," and he suggests something of his own lack of moral engagement when he characterizes himself as a curious but

neutral spectator who "came but to roam and see" (PMP, 175–79).[4]
He is offended when his torn clothing causes him to be mistaken for
one of the miserable poor and envies the unruffled uniform of his
unflappable guide, which so effectively protects that gentleman from
"all tumblings and tearings" (PMP, 183). It seems to me that what
he envies in this is more than his guide's badge of distinction and respectability; it is the perpetuation of authority and tradition, which
treat poverty as inevitable and have established conventions, including the use of force, for dealing with it. The uniformed guide is himself an embodiment of secure, substantial, royally subsidized, beef-
eating Britain; the tattered American an indication of the insecurity
or uncertainty of those basic beliefs which deny or ignore poverty and discourage charity. Or to put it differently, his tatters
are the consequence of the inevitable "tumblings and tearings"
bound to take place in all human societies, but especially in an
avowedly egalitarian society with ill-concealed class distinctions.
Like the narrator in "The Two Temples," whose shabby coat ex-
cludes him from communion in New York's Grace Church, this
narrator's clothes serve to reveal a serious flaw in the fabric of
American society.

The narrator, who feels fortunate in reaching his lodgings merely
bruised and battered, seems a much lesser man than the one who
penetrated Blandmour's rationalizations. Grateful for his escape, he
implores that "Heaven in its kind mercy save me from the noble
charities of London . . . and Heaven save me equally from the 'Poor
Man's Pudding' and the 'Rich Man's Crumbs'" (PMP, 184). While
thus asking selfishly for the grace that would spare him from ever
needing the pretensions that pass for grace in New World and Old,
he also asks that he be spared the responsibility of having to act on
the basis of his insights—action that would run counter to tradition,
convention, and respectability. Whether Melville intended it or not,
his narrator would strike a good many alert students of literature as

---

4. This characteristic of the narrator as an uninvolved spectator with a predilection for the
picturesque reinforces my earlier suggestion that Melville's strategy of "Picture First" and
"Picture Second" might have been motivated by Irving's *The Sketch Book*. Like Irving's Geoffrey Crayon, Melville's narrator is a "mere spectator of other men's fortunes and adventures."

something of a cop-out. He has recognized the inadequacy of charity in each instance and really done nothing about it.

The two-part story suggests then that despite its central place in church doctrine, charity in Christian countries does not originate in heartfelt sympathy, nor does it join men and obliterate class lines through a recognition of their common need for social and spiritual community. In situations which parody the sacrament which embodies God's grace, charity serves rather to isolate and dehumanize the unfortunate "have-nots" and to insulate the prosperous "haves." Conditions may differ widely in Old World and in New, but Melville's meditation on grace considers the human condition a matter of sad congruence in these worlds of social difference.

"The Paradise of Bachelors and the Tartarus of Maids"

Unexpected similarities underlying ostensible differences also emerge from Melville's last and longest two-part story, "The Paradise of Bachelors and the Tartarus of Maids," in many senses his most daring and subversive story. Only his most careful readers could begin to appraise his apparent envy for the life style of London's bachelor lawyers or his announced "homage to the pale virginity" of the girls employed in a New England paper mill (PBTM, 210). His purpose was ironic in both cases. His modern Templars parody crusaders for justice and Christian community; they are impotent, effete caricatures of their medieval counterparts. Subjected to an obsessive puritanism, his New England maids remain physically chaste while exposed to a system of technological exploitation that violates their wills, perverts their nature, and transforms the New World garden into a metaphorical hell. Within an atmosphere of moralistic paternalism, they have lost their freedom and innocence, and their experience illuminates the nightmare side of the American Dream. Both halves of his diptych draw from Melville's personal experience, but they are not autobiography in the ordinary sense. Although some literary historians approach Melville's stories as if to prove that Melville really lived at a particular time and in a particular place, the real value of stories like "The Paradise of Bachelors and the Tartarus of Maids" lies in their revealing what Melville thought about what he lived through—how his imagination transformed and connected disparate circumstances in a highly symbolic process that infused meaning into experience.

Melville had gained many of the impressions recorded in "The Paradise of Bachelors and the Tartarus of Maids" during a four-day period in December, 1849, when he visited, dined, and breakfasted at Elm Court, Lincoln's Inn, and the Erectheum Club. His experiences, as recorded in his *Journal*, seem to have been uniformly pleasant; the dinners were "glorious," the company "fine fellows," and even in midweek these gatherings lasted "till noon of night." It was the first of these occasions that he termed in his *Journal* "The Paradise of Bachelors," but his entries also make clear that he was not fully of this carefree company. On the day before his first visit to the Temple, he mentioned buying a silver fork for his infant son Malcolm and then working on the manuscript of *White-Jacket* before sending it to his publisher, who "though he has paid his money, has not received his wares." And just before his first dinner at the Temple, Melville recorded that "a letter was left for me—from home! All well and Barney [Malcolm] more bouncing than ever, thank heaven."[5] These associations are enough to make clear that he had more in common with the "Benedick tradesmen," who are more worried about the "rise of bread and fall of babies," than with the "banded bachelors" of "The Paradise" and that while the *Journal* and later story seem so approving, Melville as guest and then as narrator might not have so totally envied his hosts' euphoria (PBTM, 185). He was more concerned with reporting the unusual ambiance of their lives and investing it with meaning for the reader than he was in joining their band, sharing their pleasures, and adopting their values.

The autobiographical basis of "The Tartarus of Maids" lay in a visit by Melville to a paper mill about five miles from Pittsfield in late January of 1851. His only recorded remark on this visit seems to be in a letter to Evert A. Duyckinck about two weeks later on a sheet which was one of a "sleigh-load of this paper" from Carson's Old Red Mill. Jay Leyda suggests that Elizabeth Melville's second pregnancy, occurring at the same general time, probably sparked the fantastic

5. Herman Melville, *Journal of a Visit to London and the Continent, 1849–1850*, ed. Eleanor Melville Metcalf (Cambridge: Harvard University Press, 1948), 75–81.

conceit linking aggressive technology and submissive femininity.[6]
Uncertain as this suggestion must remain, it is clear that "The Tartarus of Maids" and "The Paradise of Bachelors" to which it is
coupled are characterized by suppressed eroticism and sexual guilt
when the narrator of "The Tartarus" is confronted by the suppression of Eros.

Interest in "The Tartarus of Maids" continues for two easily recognizable reasons. First, it is one of the strongest explicit (and even
stronger implicit) denunciations of industrialism—and the kind of
servitude and loss of will it entails—by an articulate American during the period which comprises our literary as well as our technological coming-of-age. Second, it is the first full-blown example of
Melville's strategy of artistic concealment, his technique of expressing controversial, at times scandalous, and usually unpopular views
symbolically, but then embedding his symbols so deeply in situation, description, or oblique allusion that few of his contemporaries
could fully grasp the multileveled meaning. These techniques of
concealment were what William Charvat meant when he wrote that
Melville in the 1850s "was discovering ways of speaking to, without
withdrawing from, a public he was dependent upon."[7] Indeed, he
may have been the first major American writer to have written for an
underground audience, never quite certain that any such audience
even existed.

In fashioning his experiences into a diptych Melville no doubt
wanted his audience to view the two panels as both contrasting
and complementary—"Paradise" and "Tartarus," "Bachelors" and
"Maids"—the quality of each sketch apparently opposite, one essential trait of the characters apparently similar. Lacking any strong
links in plot, the two vignettes are nonetheless related in ultimate
meaning. Both graft real details onto an underlying fantasy, but
neither depicts a fully satisfactory mode of life. Melville never
seemed concerned with constructing a central mediating panel.

6. Herman Melville to Evert A. Duyckinck, February 12, 1851, in Merrell R. Davis and
William H. Gilman (eds.), *The Letters of Herman Melville* (New Haven: Yale University Press,
1960), 119. Leyda's suggestion is in *The Melville Log* (2 vols.; New York: Harcourt, Brace and
Co.), I, 403–404.

7. William Charvat, *The Profession of Authorship in America, 1800–1870*, ed. Matthew J.
Bruccoli (Columbus: Ohio State University Press, 1968), 240.

The obvious contrasts in the titles are further reinforced by contrasts between the Old World and New, or at least Old England and New, between free indulgence and rigid discipline, and before the end of the second sketch, between submissive and suffering femininity and aggressive impersonal force. It is the second that has been more provocative, and I mean to look at the first only long enough to establish some links and suggest the unity of the whole design. It is really the imagery that couples the insulated satisfaction of the "bachelors" and the exposed misery of the "maids," and though the direction of the imagery has been obvious to modern readers, its full implications have been seldom realized. Perhaps for reasons of politeness, discussion has always stopped short of completely elucidating the playful audacity and the desperate horror that mark Melville's attitude toward his audience and his response to a crisis of his time.[8]

There is an initial parallel in the way the narrator (in the first tale simply an American ostensibly admiring the ease, tradition, and gentility of England; in the second more significantly a "seedsman" seeking to purchase envelopes for his business) describes the entrance to the site of major action. To get to the Paradise of Bachelors "by the usual way is like stealing from a heated plain into some cool, deep glen, shady among harboring hills." Melville recalls that "it lies not far from Temple Bar." In the mid-nineteenth century, the *Oxford English Dictionary* informs us, Temple Bar was "the name of the barrier of gateway closing the entrance into the City of London from the Strand," the connotation in Melville's sketch being the bar between city and sanctuary. Having penetrated this gateway–barrier, he finds the site is like "Eden's primal garden" sweeter than "the oasis in Sahara." There are parks and flowerbeds with "the Thames flowing by" as once "flowed the mild Euphrates." This island of tranquillity is one of the Inns of Court in London, a perfect retreat for one "sick with the din and soiled with the mud of Fleet

8. Of course "The Tartarus of Maids" is no longer virgin territory for the critic either, three major analyses being E. H. Eby, "Herman Melville's 'Tartarus of Maids,'" *Modern Language Quarterly*, I (March, 1940), 95–100; W. R. Thompson, "'The Paradise of Bachelors and The Tartarus of Maids,': A Reinterpretation," *American Quarterly*, IX (Spring, 1957), 34–45; and Beryl Rowland, "Melville's Bachelors and Maids: Interpretation through Symbol and Metaphor," *American Literature*, XLI (November, 1969), 389–405.

Street—where the Benedick tradesmen are hurrying by, with ledger-lines ruled along their brows, thinking upon rise of bread and fall of babies." It exists then as a protective cocoon, an envelope of tradition and gentility in the midst of the arid impersonality and disorder of the city. But it is not an available retreat for the married men who are pressed by rising prices and falling babies (calling attention to the germination conceit of the second tale); it is for the bachelor barristers who have not a care in the world. The terms which describe this "Paradise"—sweet, charming, august, delectable, dreamy—invite the reader to enter the "soft seclusion" of "this serene encampment" and "in mild meditation pace the cloisters; take your pleasure, sip your leisure . . . go linger in the ancient library; go worship in the sculptured chapel . . . dine among the banded Bachelors. . . . Not dine in bustling commons . . . but tranquilly, by private hint, at a private table" (PBTM, 185).

The protection of this Old World retreat is without parallel in the New, yet the second story begins with a boldly ironic, bitterly contrasting variation of the same pattern. Here, too, the narrator must penetrate a gateway to reach his destination. But the path is less defined semantically, and the landscape lies dense with symbolism, like the neogothic images in an Ingmar Bergman film. To emphasize both the similarity and the difference in these two imaginative journeys, Melville uses the identical sentence pattern, but reveals immediately the unattractiveness of the route and the undesirability of the goal: "It lies not far from Woedolor Mountain in New England. Turning to the East, right out from among bright farms and sunny meadows, . . . you enter ascendingly among bleak hills" (PBTM, 195). From this point on, the approach to the mill (which the narrator discovers in a frigid hollow) is described in terms so frankly physiological and so nearly scatological that their appearance in a mid-nineteenth-century issue of the highly respectable *Harper's Magazine* documents not only Melville's audacity but also the unsuspecting innocence and complacency of editor and audience.

On first reading, it is easy to miss these connotations in the description of the landscape; they become more obvious after Melville develops his theme of machine production and the perversion of human reproduction inside the paper mill. Only then is it also clear that shocking the genteel reader was not one of Melville's major intentions. He may have delighted in deceiving the reader, but his main aim was to express imaginatively the emotional impact of what he felt to be a general crisis for humanity: the widespread existence of a mechanistic, life-deadening, freedom-denying set of values emphasized in America by increasing industrialization.

His initial experience in the actual paper mill led to a mixed reaction. In his letter to Duyckinck, dated February 12, 1851, he could jest about the convenient source of cheap paper, the proximity of his new friend Hawthorne, or possibly, the raw material in his visit to the Old Red Mill: "A great neighborhood for authors, you see, is Pittsfield." The more he thought about it, the more the circumstances of the mill must have seemed unnatural—a sisterhood of erotically deprived and economically exploited girls. In the symbolically subversive mode of his art, he went a step beyond and tried to suggest how the moralistic justification for increased material production not only bent the mind or blighted the body but most profoundly perverted the promise and character of American life.

Several analyses of the American literary imagination have shown how the contradiction between agrarian and industrial social orders was expressed not simply as a conflict of forms or even values but as a conflict between two psychic states. One recurrent pattern in our literature from the 1840s on presents the unmistakably aggressive machine "invading the peace of an enclosed space, a world set apart or an area somehow made to evoke a feeling of encircled felicity,"[9] a pastoral world expressive of serenity, femininity, submissiveness. In this light, the passage described in each half of Melville's diptych assumes additional significance.

In the first, the "Paradise" is a haven of oral nurture where no pain, trouble, or responsibility can jar the tranquillity or mar the infantile comfort of these celibate brethren. They are served by a "Socrates," who asks no irritating questions, leads men to no unseen truths—who, in fact, helps them to lose themselves, rather than

9. Leo Marx, *The Machine in the Garden* (New York: Oxford University Press, 1964), 29. Melville attaches the same connotations to pastoral landscape when he describes Redburn's exit through the Narrows and into the sea. Redburn is launched upon life by passage through and abandonment of the verdant pastoral images of this last cleft of land.

know themselves, by supplying an endless array of bottles and a huge Jericho horn of choice snuff. In all this self-indulgence there is "nothing loud, nothing unmannerly, nothing turbulent" (even the snuff did not stimulate a sneeze). Their bachelor passions are spent on the study of old Flemish architecture or Oriental manuscripts in the British Museum, the praise of wine, and for the more active brethren, the private perusal of the *Decameron*.

As the story develops, it suggests that their pain-free existence is more a pupal state than a paradise. Insulated by layers of tradition, these modern Templars protect no Holy Sepulchre and serve no Christian purpose. Their cloistered retreat from painful reality also marks their degeneration from monkish austerity and militant sense of purpose into decadent luxury. In his *Journal*, Melville described a visit to one of the courts where he had seen "the Lord High Chancellor Cottenham—an old fellow nearly asleep on the bench." This inattention to justice might have suggested to him that the bachelor lawyers labor not to secure justice but "to check, to clog, to hinder, and embarrass all the courts and avenues of Law." Just as their "helmet is a wig," their holy war has become idle wit (PBTM, 187). This particular area of the Old World has become barren and unproductive; its comforts amount to an abdication of justice and responsibility. The serene retreat is a state of moral impotence and psychological regression, and in its own way represents as complete, though less apparent, a sense of life-deadening values as the mechanized hell of the New England maids.

Some readers may still insist on taking Melville's narrator at face value when he praises the pleasures of these fortunate bachelors. If so, they must explain an inane lapse of taste in the story—or admit that lapse to be a calculated pun on person, place, and thing. Recalling the generation of bachelors who have sampled the pleasures of the Temple, the narrator can express himself only through poetry and chooses "Carry me back to old Virginny!" (PBTM, 189). This is a peculiar selection for Melville, unless he means to undercut his narrator's celebration of celibacy by having *Virginny* refer to a particular girl or to the more vital and virgin New World. (And of course the virgin state is in a sense his preoccupation in the second sketch, or more properly, an extended metaphor which informs each sketch, for his bachelor barristers remain untouched by any conception of or commitment to the concerns of suffering humanity—unlike the pseudonymous "Virginian" who was so deeply affected by his encounter with Hawthorne's *Mosses*).

The virgin state, we generally assume, is one of innocence and potential productivity, and Melville plays upon this assumption in a shockingly paradoxical way, using a pattern which he has previously employed, most dramatically perhaps in *Moby Dick*. In Chapter 102, where Ishmael has entered a primitive temple of nature formed by the massive skelton of a sperm whale and is driven to consider the analogy between human and natural productivity, there is an extravagant allegory of American experience: "Ishmael deliberately making his way to the center of primal nature only to find, when he arrives, a premonitory sign of industrial power." [10] In "The Tartarus of Maids" Melville renders the allegory even more boldly and employs one of the chief motifs of *Moby Dick*—the ambiguity of whiteness (not only associated with innocence and evil but also with virginity and sterility)—to express a horrifying contradiction of American experience.

We recognize that Melville's narrator, whose "seeds were distributed through all the Eastern and Northern States, and even fell into the far soil of Missouri and the Carolinas," is metaphorically entering the womb of nature, the center of creation as he proceeds from "sunny meadows" up "bleak hills" then into the hollow where the factory lies hidden (PBTM, 195–96). The physiological dimension of the allegory suggests very quickly that there is also a psychosociological analogy here. This analogue-making process is the attempt of the literary imagination to form its response to certain repressive and perhaps destructive forces in life, and the sexuality by which the analogy moves links what Melville finds most intimately human and most insufferably mechanical. In the case of the industrialization of the New World, Melville confronted a phenomenon so recent and so dramatic that no adequate conventions existed for communicating it to an audience. This is what propelled him onto the terrain later mapped by Freud, and in Melville's own time, but in somewhat different terms, by Karl Marx.

10. *Ibid.*, 312.

We also know that Melville himself visited the mill to buy writing paper, so it is not too farfetched to see the "seedsman" as a projection of the writer–artist. (Remember Melville's account of how Hawthorne "dropped germinous seeds into my soul.") So his seeds "distributed" throughout the states are the most valued and potent aspects of his writing. Yet the process by which they are distributed —put up in "yellowish paper, folded square," "stamped, and superscribed with the nature of the seeds contained"—is an ironic parody of the publishing business and the writer's need to conform to it. The seed-filled envelopes "assume not a little the appearance of business-letters," and the seedsman-writer is, not involuntarily, part of the business system he detests (PBTM, 197). He can never be certain whether they will take root or in what soil they may fall. In "Bartleby" we are more pessimistically informed of how many such attempts at human communication end at the Dead Letter Office, no readers to be found. But this matter is only a tangential concern in "The Tartarus."

It is the feminine contours of Nature that Melville, virtually anticipating the concern of modern psychoanalytical critics with anal and urethral characteristics, describes in the opening paragraphs of his "Tartarus."[11] The denuded hills "gradually close in upon a dusky pass, which, from the violent Gulf Stream of air unceasingly driving between its cloven walls of haggard rock, as well as from the tradition of a crazy spinster's hut having long ago stood somewhere hereabouts, is called the Mad Maid's Bellow-pipe." This is no sentimentalized Mother Nature but an outraged force rendered demonic by turbulent counterforces which extract and exploit the resources of nature for artificial production. "Tartarus" indicates the nether region of dehumanizing factory labor; the opening paragraphs focus on the nether regions of a femininely formed Nature immobilized by aggressive technological exploitation. Consider the second paragraph:

> Winding along at the bottom of the gorge is a dangerously narrow wheelroad, occupying the bed of a former torrent. Following this road to its highest point, you stand as within a Dantean gateway. From the

11. I am thinking particularly of the discussion of these terms in Norman Holland, *The Dynamics of Literary Response* (New York: Oxford University Press, 1968), 31–62.

steepness of the walls here, their strangely ebon hue, and the sudden contraction of the gorge, this particular point is called the Black Notch. The ravine now expandingly descends into a great, purple, hopper-shaped hollow, far sunk among many Plutonian, shaggy-wooded mountains. By the country people this hollow is called the Devil's Dungeon. Sounds of torrents fall on all sides upon the ear. These rapid waters unite at last in one turbid brick-colored stream, boiling through a flume among enormous boulders. They call this strange-colored torrent Blood River. Gaining a dark precipice it wheels suddenly to the West, and makes one maniac spring of sixty feet into the arms of a stunted wood of gray-haired pines, between which it thence eddies on its further way down to the invisible lowlands (PBTM, 195–96).

Both the traditional literary reference and the gynecological imagery are integral to the story: the narrator, neglecting the implied warning to all those who enter here, will find among other things that this Blood River has been harnessed to move the productive machinery.

Of course there is a discrepancy between the kind of "return to the womb" which Melville pictures here and the more familiar layman's notion of this concept. Melville was, I strongly suspect, aware of this, and in view of his two-part structure, I think that he intended this reversal of expected meaning to heighten the inherent irony of his experience. It is also possible that Melville could not even maintain the security of an idyllic, enclosed place in the woods, such as Hawthorne or Thoreau described, because he was horrified that industrialism had penetrated far deeper than his contemporaries had imagined. The "Tartarus" is, after all, a tale more horrifying than any of Poe's. Its theme has attracted successive generations of science-fiction writers: the instinctive horror of going back to the source of life only to discover that "life" is obsolete, that the "artificial" and "mechanical" has triumphed completely over the "natural" and "organic." Combined with the first half of the diptych, the "Tartarus" ironically spells out a cruel paradox; for while the womb of the New World is far more productive than the tradition-laden refuge of the Old World, it is in human terms far more destructive and deadly.

Melville's was essentially a tragic view of material accomplishment, a view which he characteristically expressed by presenting muted contradictions in a world where familiar things suddenly become more important than their recognizable reality entitles them

to be. There are few of the pseudosupernatural allegations of Hawthorne, whose fancy also led him to associate the signs of technology
with access to infernal regions in a more self-conscious, Bunyan-like
allegory. For Melville human nature could be bad enough without
reference to an abstract embodiment of evil. But he had no less an
attraction to allegory as a vehicle for his sinister views. If Hawthorne
was prone to italicize his symbols, Melville seemed to guard his
from discovery, for he saw allegory as the actual way of the world—a
world in which true meanings are obscured by dense layers of ambiguous and contradictory reality which most people do not want to
peel away.

The paragraphs already quoted from the "Tartarus" certainly exemplify these layers of ambiguity and contradiction in the image of
Nature vulnerable and violated. Melville continues his description,
employing the same technique to emphasize the exploitation and
devastation which resulted with the shift from an agrarian to a
machine technology, from accommodation to the ways of nature to
the new freedom to master and exploit nature. The once-picturesque
landscape has become a scene of blight and collapse: the nearby pin-
nacles suggest a romantic Rhineland but the only ruins are those of
"an old sawmill, built in those primitive times when vast pines and
hemlocks super-abounded throughout the neighbouring region."
Blackened logs and spikey stumps, "here and there all tumbled together in long abandonment and decay," extend the atmosphere of
ruin and mark the gloomy depletion of virgin forest. And in striking
contrast to the blackness of the shorn landscape, there stands, near
the bottom of the hollow, "a large whitewashed building, relieved,
like some great whited sepulchre against the sullen background of
mountain-side firs." In his covert and allusive way, Melville is beginning his denunciation of the scribes and Pharisees, the confidence men of the modern economy who praise the benefits of industrial progress but conceal its cost. Thus the "whited sepulchre" of
the "whitewashed" paper mill, the symbol of productive enterprise
irrevocably established in the womb of nature, will emerge, paradoxically, as the mill of death whose production masks the con-
current destruction (PBTM, 196).

Melville, as we well know, frequently employed color symbolism for thematic purposes—particularly the apparent polarities of black and white, the common association of *black* with dark, sinister, malignant forces; *white* with purity, goodness, truth, joy. Peeling away these familiar connotations, Melville delights in cynically suggesting the areas of identity between black and white, exploring the gradations of conflicting connotation which language can offer, and, in the "Tartarus," challenging his reader to be clinician as well as critic.

The whiteness becomes more prominent as the narrator passes through the area described in the opening paragraphs, draws near the whitewashed factory, and actually begins his tour of the machinery. The time of the visit is January and the snow and cold are, of course, appropriate. But the images of cold and whiteness culminate in a larger metaphor. We read of the summit "smoked with frost," "white vapors" rising from "its white-wooded top"; of "the intense congelation" which "made the whole country look like one petrifaction"; of "vitreous, chippy snow" like "broken glass"; of "forests . . . feeling the same all-stiffening influence, their inmost fibres penetrated with the cold . . . as the fitful gusts remorselessly swept through them"; of maples "brittle with excessive frost," "snapped in twain like pipestems." Superficially, this is a description of a seasonal extreme, of an impersonal nature destroying as well as creating; but in view of what came before and what comes after, this cluster of images of cold and white and brittle vulnerability, ending with "the unfeeling earth," strongly suggests nature physically paralyzed, organically barren, and morally inert in almost complete surrender to man-directed forces (PBTM, 197).

There is only token resistance as the least of these forces, the narrator's horse (named Black), labors to penetrate the Black Notch. "Flaked all over with frozen sweat, white as a milky ram, his nostrils at each breath sending forth two horn-shaped shoots of heated respiration," he is the animal representation of the kind of masculine force which is most mechanical in nature. Melville stresses this identity not only by using the phallic simile of the "milky ram" (primarily a male sheep, also a device for battering or forcing a gate) but by reminding us slyly of the physiological metaphor and the Dantean reference in the opening paragraphs of the "Tartarus." As horse and passenger reach the Bellows-pipe, "the violent blast, dead from behind, all but shoved my high-backed pung up-hill." Benefiting from this tail wind, which "shrieked through the shivered pass, as if laden with lost spirits, bound to the unhappy world," the horse "slung out with his strong hind legs," swept "grazingly through the narrow notch, [and] sped downward madly past the ruined sawmill. Into the Devil's Dungeon horse and cataract rushed together" (PBTM, 197– 98). Confronted with this submerged level of physiological turbulence, we ought to remember that in "The Paradise of Bachelors," "though they took snuff very freely, yet not a man so far violated the proprieties, or so far molested the invalid bachelor in the adjoining room as to indulge himself in a sneeze" (PBTM, 194). Melville, like Hawthorne in *The Scarlet Letter*, views both man and nature in the New World as exhibiting a distinct lack of restraint; and with fewer established social restraints, moral and metaphysical problems are thrown into stark relief.

Further similarity—and a significant difference—between the charging horse and the intruding machine are borne out in successive passages. The headlong rush of the horse, we are told, could be checked by a driver who "with one foot braced against the dashboard . . . rasped and churned the bit, and stopped him just in time to avoid collision." Later passages will show the force of the machine to be irresistible and unstoppable; in the atmosphere of the factory the horse, so vital and powerful as he broke through the Notch, will be found "cringing and doubled up with the cold." But at this point Melville is more anxious to stress the similarity: by the device of the narrator's free association, tinged "not less with the vividness than the disorder of a dream," he links not only horse and machine but "Tartarus" and "Paradise" as well (PBTM, 198–99).

He tells how the sight of "the grim Black Notch" recalls the "first sight of dark and grimy Temple Bar," how the horse "darting through the Notch, perilously grazing its rocky wall" recalls "being in a runaway London omnibus, which in much the same sort of style . . . dashed through the ancient Arch of Wren." The whitewashed factory buildings themselves, nearly invisible in the snowy hollow and against "the mountains . . . pinned in shrouds," strangely appear "the very counterpart of the Paradise of Bachelors, but snowed upon, and frost-painted to a sepulchre." Once the sounds of the

whirring machinery break through the snowy camouflage, and the
narrator discerns the austere, comfortless buildings, looks back on
the "deep-cloven passages" through which he has come, and realizes
the isolation of the location, his unconscious mind helps establish
the unlikely connection—"what memory lacked, all tributary imagination furnished." The high-gabled factory, "with a rude tower—for
hoisting heavy boxes," stands "among its crowded outbuildings and
boarding houses, as the Temple Church amidst the surrounding offices and dormitories." He never really explains the womblike similarity of the stark, practical, no-nonsense New World and the mel-
lowed and static Old World, but his imagery continues to suggest
covert parallels and revealing contrasts (PMTB, 199–200).

There is obvious irony in the unlikely comparison of the mad,
roily Blood River, the shrill and piercing wind, and the ice-crusted
town square with "the sweet, tranquil Temple garden bordered by
the Thames," but a far more subtle sort in the growing realization
that the moral impotence of the well-fed lawyers who are blind to
pain and ignorant of social responsibility has been magnified into an
immoral power striking at the heart of humanity. Looking around for
contented bachelors, the narrator meets only cold, white-faced, un-
derdressed, obviously miserable girls. Their pallor and cold are in
contrast to the "dark-complexioned, well-wrapped personage" who
points out a shelter for the horse (PBTM, 200–201). Later identified
as a bachelor, as well as overseer and principal proprietor of the
works, he is referred to as "Old Bach" (but it might as well be "Old
Scratch" for his position in this Tartarus and his complacent oblivi-
ousness to the suffering he inflicts).

The interior of the mill is part of the frigid whiteness, for it is "in-
tolerably lighted by long rows of windows, focusing inward the
snowy scene without." And what stands revealed immediately is the
utter hopelessness of the employees: "At rows of blank-looking
counters sat rows of blank-looking girls, with blank, white folders in
their blank hands, all blankly folding blank paper." Melville had not
run out of words. *Blank*, like *white*, with which it has meaning in
common, here has a range of meaning from "bare"; to "disconcerted
and emotionless"; to "unmarked"; to "futile," "unproductive," and
"fruitless"; to "unrelieved," "helpless," and "resourceless." Their

work, as well as the kind of life it shapes for them, is nugatory. Like the bachelor Templars, who in their brotherhood of celibacy still maintain a secular facsimile of their monkish origins, the girls form a sisterhood of sterility, whose white habit marks their new order (PBTM, 201–202).

Unhappily, these ascetics perform rites that are not only self-abasing, but also self-sacrificing:

> In one corner stood some huge frame of ponderous iron, with a vertical thing like a piston periodically rising and falling upon a heavy wooden block. Before it—its tame minister—stood a tall girl, feeding the iron animal with half-quires of rose-hued note-paper which, at every downward dab of the piston-like machine, received in the corner the impress of a wreath of roses.

The narrator "looked from the rosy paper to the pallid cheek, but said nothing" (PBMT, 201). Here is the first of the images which suggest the extent of their exploitation by the machine, their strength being drained in the manufacture of the rose-hued paper which bears an emblem of sentimental femininity.

Another nearby machine cruelly parodies the genteel pursuits in which these girls should engage. It has "long, slender strings, like any harp," but these are not for music. They are the means of impressing lines on the blank foolscap sheets which one girl passes to another. The narrator noted that the first girl's brow " was young and fair," the other girl's "ruled and wrinkled," and as he watched, the girls changed places—the only variation in the monotonous rhythm of their work (PBMT, 201–202). This incident, so like one of Dante's glimpses of damned souls, reminds us of those "Benedick tradesmen . . . with ledger-lines ruled along their brows, thinking upon rise of bread and fall of babies." It leads to the narrator's wonder that so much of the paper produced should be blank foolscap rather than finer quality. This in turn suggests John Locke's metaphorical tabula rasa. Melville's extended conceit now becomes clearer: we are viewing a process that goes from education (impressing sentimental symbols and unvarying lines on blank paper, by blank-looking girls, at blank-looking counters) back to gestation. The excessive amount of foolscap, in contrast to the more aristocratic "cream-laid and royal sheets," conveys Melville's pessimistic view of that divine, democratic average that so inspired Whitman at the same moment in our history.

The more limited connotations and implications of the passage are easier to fathom. The peculiar kinship between the girls and the material they work with troubles the narrator most deeply throughout his visit. But he was not unique in his reaction. Fredrika Bremer, the Swedish novelist who very hopefully visited the Lowell mills to see "the young ladies" at their work, was also troubled "by the relationship of the human being and the machinery" and by the fact "that some of 'the young ladies' were about fifty." She, too, sensed a perversion of motherhood: "Thus, for example, I saw the young girls standing—each one between four busily-working spinning jennies . . . and guarding them much as a mother would watch over and tend her children. The machinery was like an obedient child under the eye of an intelligent mother."[12] Melville's image is even more extreme and guilt-laden. He follows the direction of Miss Bremer's comment but sees the machine as a stronger force, usurping procreative functions, and the final product as some cruel parody of natural offspring, "taking" a rosy hue from one girl, a fair appearance from another, lines like a wrinkled brow from a third. Even the simple descriptive adjectives are deceptively ambiguous and serve to link the girls and the paper: *blank* paper is that which is left *white* or *fair* or *unsmudged*; *ruled* and *wrinkled* easily apply to both. And the girls are *ruled* in several senses: the anxiously lined brow, of course, but they are also *ruled* by the regulations governing their conduct and work procedures (which Melville has covertly likened to the code of a religious order), and finally by the tyrannical machine which they serve.

Religious *service* (which was satirized in "The Paradise") is, in fact, parodied in the very next passage:

> Perched high upon a narrow platform, and still higher upon a high stool crowning it, sat another figure serving some other iron animal; while below the platform sat her mate in reciprocal attendance.

12. Fredrika Bremer, *The Homes of the World*, trans. Mary Howitt (2 vols.; New York: Harper Brothers, 1854), I, 210.

Not a syllable was breathed. Nothing was heard but the low, steady overruling hum of the iron animals. The human voice was banished from the spot. Machinery—that vaunted slave of humanity—here stood menially served by human beings, who served mutely and cringingly as the slave serves the Sultan. The girls did not so much seem accessory wheels to the general machinery as mere cogs to the wheels (PBTM, 202).

The sense of abject subordination is as strong here as in a firsthand complaint Melville might have read in that overpraised literary phenomenon, *The Lowell Offering*. In a story entitled "The Spirit of Discontent," a factory girl complains of the pace of life which does not allow "time to eat, drink, or sleep": "Up before day, at the clang of the bell—into the mill, and at work, in obedience to that ding-dong of a bell—just as though we were so many living machines. I will give my notice tomorrow: go, I will—I won't stay here and be a white slave."[13] She was, we can be sure, comparing her condition to that of a black slave in the South. We cannot be certain about the "white slaves" of Melville's tale, for, as the *OED* reveals, "white slavery" could by midcentury refer to prostitution, an irony Melville may or may not have intended.

Some of the same meaning informs the record of an enthusiastic English visitor to the Lowell mills—but his ingenuous imagery often seemed to undermine his approval. In a large upstairs workroom at one of the Middlesex Corporation mills, where "our senses are half dizzied by the noise":

Shuttles fly in all directions; and we listen with pleased wonder to the descriptions of our friend who is obliged to bawl his information into ears unused to the sounds of SPINDLEDOM. Then there were carding machines of strange and mysterious structure which often performed their duties in so astonishingly easy a manner, that the girls who stood looking at them seemed almost to be works of supererogation. And they would have been useless too, only for a careless and sly way these ma-

13. Charles Knight (ed.), *Mind Amongst the Spindles* (Boston: Jordan, Swift & Wiley, 1845), 37. An observant French visitor had the same impression of the girls at Lowell, "whose movements are regulated like clockwork," for he termed them "the nuns of Lowell," who "instead of working sacred hearts, spin and weave cotton." Michel Chevalier, *Society, Manners and Politics in the United States* (Boston: Weeks, Jordan, 1839), 129, 143.

chines had of snapping a thread or so now and then, just as if they wanted an excuse for stopping to peer into the pretty faces around, and dally with the fair fingers which just touched them, as if chidingly, and set them going on again as though nothing had happened.

He has trouble keeping his "coat tails from being nipped by cogged wheels which showed their teeth as if longing for a meal of 'devil's dust.'" He promises to tell more about the girls by saying, "After we have gone through the garden, we will discourse of the flowers."[14] The narrator in Melville's tale also asks about flowers (he ostensibly asks whether there are any bachelors' buttons—from old shirts), but is told directly, "None grow in this part of the country" (PBTM, 204). The English visitor did go on to "discourse of the flowers" because he found these working girls were so much better off materially than their English counterparts, and this stilled his fears. Melville, however, was far more interested in the psychological, ecological, and spiritual implications of industrial technology, and in this sense his virginal maids have been drastically deflowered—and unsexed as well. In his view the American ethos held the seeds of ecological disaster. That the iconography of the two divergent accounts should be so similar suggests the intensity of this cultural crisis, Melville's response integrating theme and form in a fantastic fable of dehumanization, the other creating an awkward imbalance as economic good sense quells the implications inherent in the imagery.

One of Melville's most ironic devices is the character of Cupid, who guides the narrator through the rest of the mill. More than the Socrates who brought comforts to cloud the mind in the first tale, Cupid belies his name. He looks right, but by word and deed shows himself a heartless little devil. He knows what makes this particular world go 'round and it certainly is not love.

His duties are vague but he seems a conscientious guide as he shows the narrator first the powerful heart of the mill, the "incessantly showering," constantly circulating "dark colossal water-wheel, grim with its one immutable purpose." The narrator sees that it is the Blood River, emblematic of the violent exploitation of nature

---

14. John R. Dix, *Local Loiterings and Visits in the Vicinity of Boston* (Boston: Redding, 1845), 76–78.

and humanity, that turns the wheel which transmits the power and sets "our whole machinery a-going" (PBTM, 203).

With a single, apparently stupid question the narrator suddenly extends the allegory to make it a national indictment. "You make only blank paper; no printing of any sort . . . ? All blank paper, don't you?" he asks, and Cupid answers, "Certainly; what else should a paper-factory make?" (PBTM, 203). Here at the heart of the New World, its inmost nature under examination, he again employs the Lockean metaphor—the unmarked, virgin paper—and uses it to suggest cultural and intellectual barrenness—the absence of any innate ideas.[15] The paper factory has become the microcosm of progressive America, the workshop of the world, but Melville can take no pride in its products or its procedures.

In the next room, where the girls stand "like so many mares haltered to the rack," they shred white rags and fill the air with "fine, poisonous particles, which . . . darted, subtiley, as motes in sunbeams, into the lungs." The "erected sword" which each girl uses in her work seems to signify that sentence has been passed: prisoners of sex and of society, "through consumptive pallors of this blank, raggy life, go these white girls to death." In contracting this white death, they seem "their own executioners." The rags on which they work may have some incidental meaning too. They are gathered locally and "some from far over sea—Leghorn and London" (PBTM, 203–204). If we remember that allegorically the production of paper represents the manufacture of a population by industrial procedures, the rags which go into the paper suggest a further level of misanthropy. They are what the Old World sends to the New to swell the population—to be assimilated and refashioned in endless conformity.

When the narrator asks his guide why the girls look "so sheet-white," the boy answers with an ambiguous twinkle, "I suppose the handling of such white bits of sheet all the time makes them so

15. This is very close to what Henry James meant when he suggested that the image of America in Hawthorne's *American Note-Books* "is characterised by an extraordinary blankness—a curious paleness of colour," which "indicates a simple, democratic, thinly-composed society." And for this reason, of course, James was strongly sympathetic. James, *Hawthorne* (Ithaca: Cornell University Press, 1956), 33, 36.

sheety" (PBTM, 205). Again Melville depends on ambiguity to either elude or inform his reader; for *sheet* refers not only to bed covering or to paper, but also the performing of penance (originally, the *OED* reveals, for fornication), and these penitential connotations further enshroud the tension between religious and sexual elements in the story.

My reading is strengthened by the narrator's judgment on Cupid's remark: "More tragical and more inscrutably mysterious than any mystic sight, human or machine, throughout the factory, was the strange innocence of cruel-heartedness in this usage-hardened boy" (PBTM, 205). Ostensibly the boy lacks any social consciousness; allegorically, the comment cuts much deeper. For this "usage-hardened boy" has, like the girls, served as his own executioner by allowing himself to be severed from his traditional function.

To Melville, the encounter with the machine seemed to foreshadow the end of humanity. Many of the circumstances which inspired Whitman's first version of "Song of Myself" in 1855, his expansive vision of the possibilities for the individual in America, led also to Melville's dirge for America in 1855. If Whitman's view of technology could secure his miraculous "Passage to India," Melville's provided only a ticket to Tartarus. At about the same time as the publication of Melville's story, Thoreau concluded that "we do not ride on the railroad; it rides upon us," but it was Henry Adams who later responded most keenly to these implications of industrialism. Melville, Thoreau, and Adams seem to have written less for their own times than for ours. This illusion, due in part of course to our own perspective, is most directly conveyed by that section of *The Education of Henry Adams* which most closely parallels "Tartarus" in meaning—"The Dynamo and the Virgin." The sense of crawling along a knife-edge that "divided two kingdoms of force" is common to both works, and Adams' assertion that "in America neither Venus nor Virgin ever had any value as force—at most as sentiment" suddenly illuminates some of the dark in the "Tartarus." Recognizing that "the Woman had once been supreme," that "in France she still seemed potent, not merely as a sentiment but as a force," Adams asked, "Why was she unknown in America?" The

Puritan sense of sin and the repression of sex provided most of the answer; the eager acceptance and rapid multiplication of the means of material progress supplied the rest. The energy, the mystery, the fecundity of woman paled before the new sources of power symbolized by the dynamo. Her spiritual force and her reproductive power could not compete: "An American Virgin would never dare command; an American Venus would never dare exist." Sex in Adams' America was supplanted by the machine, and the historian, like the scientist, pursued the track of new forces.

Thus, in Melville's tale, Cupid, the offspring of a Venus who dares no longer exist, illustrates the same meaning. He should exalt the power of love, but instead cynically ignores sexuality and serves as guide to and exponent of the power in the machine. The system of the New World paper factory first regulates, then uses, and finally replaces utterly the creative power of Eros. This is Melville's central irony, the core of his meaning: that the force of the machine is in the New World the most nearly equivalent, in shaping human society, to the creative force of sexual vitality, but that in value the two forces are poles apart. As the new ethos is to the ancient Eros, so the new economy is to traditional ecology.

The climax of Melville's tale occurs as Cupid unveils the mechanical process that in a grotesque parody mocks conception, rationalizes gestation, and industrializes birth. "That's the machine that makes the paper" and "cost us twelve thousand dollars only last autumn," Cupid announces as they reach the center of Melville's brave new world. "Carelessly," he taps the vats of "white pulp" which are "the first beginnings of the paper," and points out the "one common channel" that sends the "white, wet, woolly-looking stuff" "to the great machine." In a room "stifling with a strange blood-like, abdominal heat, as if here, true enough, were finally developed the germinous particles lately seen," they follow every intricacy of the productive process, which takes "only nine minutes." To test the precision of the machine the narrator writes "Cupid" on a bit of paper and places it where the process begins. Exactly nine minutes later the marked sheet emerges barely distinguishable from countless others, and the narrator remembers that "a scissory sound smote my ear, as of some cord being snapped," and that "for a moment a curious emotion filled me" (PBTM, 205–207).[16]

Melville's narrator convinces himself that what he has watched was "a mere machine," but Melville tries to suggest that it is a good deal more. As the narrator considers this technological marvel, "still humming with its play," he is "struck as well by the inevitability as the evolvement-power in all its motions." Further questions produce more testimony to the absolute perfection of the machine, and the narrator now records, "Something of awe now stole over me." Gazing upon "this inflexible iron animal," he is terrified not by the ponderous grotesqueness of the thing but by its "metallic necessity" and "autocratic cunning." Before this symbol of supreme power, he stands "spell-bound and wandering in my soul." But the mystical vision which he experiences is no ecstatic knowledge of supreme goodness; it is again cruel, chilling parody:

> Before my eyes—there, passing in slow procession along the wheeling cylinders, I seemed to see, glued to the pallid incipience of the pulp, the yet more pallid faces of all the pallid girls I had eyed that heavy day. Slowly, mournfully, beseechingly, yet unresistingly, they gleamed along, their agony dimly outlined on the imperfect paper, like the print of the tormented face on the hankerchief of Saint Veronica.

If we look again to his allusion for a clue, we find no Christian concept of God's suffering for mankind but a Melvillean inversion—mankind marched to its collective Golgotha by the will of the implacable, godlike machine which has efficiently combined the *locus* and *modus* of creation and damnation (PBTM, 208–209).

16. Although the image of the cord being snapped at the moment the paper emerges fits neatly into Melville's allegory, I suspect that it, like the image of the invaded hollow, is part of a larger pattern of association that suggests a simultaneous beginning and end, a sudden but irrevocable separation. Thoreau, for example, contemplating the electrifying changes wrought by the railroad in "Sounds," writes, "We have constructed a fate, an *Atropos*, that never turns aside." And Melville, in *Israel Potter*, yokes an image of technology with the fate that cuts off the thread of life. Describing the "mechanical magic of discipline" with which the men of the *Serapis* worked their "death-dealing batteries," Melville says, "They tended these rows of guns as Lowell girls the rows of looms in a cotton factory. The Parcae were not more methodical; Atropos not more fatal; the automaton chess player not more irresponsible" (Boston: L. C. Page, 1925), 226. But the best example is undoubtedly *The Education of Henry Adams* which is permeated by the sense that technology has irrevocably severed the continuity of culture and obviated the function of religion, love, and feminity.

The tour is over, the vision completed, only a few amenities remain before the narrator can return to a more conventional world. After praising the "great machine" as "a miracle of inscrutable intricacy" (the kind of phrase Melville likes to apply to figures of supreme authority), he finds opportunity to ask why in such factories "female operatives, of whatever age, are indiscriminately called girls, never women." The answer of the old bachelor proprietor, who never thought of this before, is that they are "generally unmarried": "For our factory here, we will not have married women; they are apt to be off-and-on too much." Thus we are again reminded by verbal play that the world of the paper factory is the antithesis of sex, that machine production is not reconcilable with human reproduction.

He also implies that the Puritan ethic is as thoroughly an expression of masculine dominance as any *machismo* might be, but that the debased puritanism of mid–nineteenth-century America can simultaneously exploit women yet preserve their innocence and purity by viewing them as work objects rather than sex objects. Melville's Old Bach is the straitlaced progenitor of Hugh Hefner. At the realization that "these are all maids," the narrator feels again the strange emotion he felt while watching the great machine, and the chill blanches his cheeks. He hastens to leave this place of fantastic frigidity, pauses for an instant at the Black Notch to think of Temple Bar, then shoots through the pass, eager to leave this shocking view of the future already implied in the present. Like the narrator of "Bartleby," in his final exclamation, he reveals not only his guilt but also his growth in understanding and sympathy: "All alone with inscrutable nature, I exclaimed—Oh! Paradise of Bachelors! and oh! Tartarus of Maids!" (210–11).

The "Paradise" he described could sustain no manly existence and his paradoxically frigid "Inferno" synchronized creation and damnation. He saw the repression of Eros in the decadent Old World of morally ignorant, tradition-shielded bachelors, and even more starkly the suppression of Eros in the aggressive New World of regulated maids. To convey his vision he allegorized the clash of two principal images of value: (1) evoked by the normal associations of nature—the landscape and feminine fertility—and (2) evoked by industrial technology—machines, efficiency, lack of warmth and feeling. The collision of these images produces a sense of danger and dislocation, as we have seen not only in the conscious artistry of Melville but also in the less conscious response of other witnesses. Only Melville, however, among his mid–nineteenth-century contemporaries responded so dramatically, casting the system of the machine in opposition to warmth and·comfort, to health and beauty, to love and sympathy, to individualism and pride in craftmanship, to free will, or to any sense of harmony with nature. It threatened every physical, psychological, organic, and spiritual attribute of humanity.

By setting the factory and its machines in opposition to the warmth and fertility of both nature and women, Melville made it the symbol of the mechanistic, the utilitarian, and ultimately the inhumane character of industrial technology. He contrasted factory production (quantitatively superior to older methods) with human reproduction in a fantastic conceit to demonstrate its efficiency and its destructiveness. Indirectly he also revealed his contempt for a democracy of quantity, of foolscap mediocrity. The greatest crime, however, is that by rendering love meaningless, technology translates the feminine workers into an anonymous, enslaved work force, comsumes their vitality, and debases all human creativity.

Beginning with actual experiences in Old and in New England, Melville constructed a kind of confessional story in which he hinted at sensual indulgence and sexual fulfillment as hoped-for ideals, but this wish pales before the frightening revelation of cultural impotence, deprivation, and sterility. In each part of Melville's story an autobiographical vignette becomes a national indictment and the cumulative revelations form a series of inverse and ironic epiphanies disclosing the nature of man and of the dark force that fashions the future.

Melville was working both within and outside an American cultural mythology. Since Henry Nash Smith detailed the notion of America as an agrarian paradise, particularly in the nineteenth century, many have shown how that idea seemed to define the purpose and promise of the nation's existence.[17] Melville neither rejected nor ignored this cultural myth; instead he reacted with heightened sensitivity to the force which most emphatically contradicted this view and undermined all its assumptions—the force of the machine, which turned virgin land and potential paradise into potent hell and, for Melville, served to polarize all human experience.

In its sense of horror, its Manichean polarities, its sense of the severance of past and present, this vision of Herman Melville forcefully dramatizes a distinctive and recurrent aspect of American experience. And the meaning of this vision—compounded of shock and sympathy—is crucial to our understanding of contemporary American culture as well as the forces which shaped it.

17. Henry Nash Smith, *Virgin Land: The American West as Symbol and Myth* (Cambridge: Harvard University Press, 1950).

4

◎◎◎

TRUTH
COMES IN WITH
DARKNESS

"The Bell Tower"

"The Bell-Tower"—published in 1855, the same year as "The Paradise of Bachelors and the Tartarus of Maids" and "Benito Cereno"—is an important link between them. Although it seems a much slighter effort, "The Bell-Tower" actually brings together the two very grave and distinctly American cultural dilemmas explored in the other two stories—the dehumanizing quality of industrial labor and the denial of humanity inherent in chattel slavery.

The fact that "Benito Cereno" appeared a few years before the Civil War and dealt in such gruesome detail with the consequences of a Negro slave revolt aboard a Spanish ship has deterred many readers from appreciating the story and prevented a few from understanding it on its own terms or recognizing its relation to Melville's other fiction of the 1850s. F. O. Matthiessen, for example, in his seminal study, *American Renaissance*, too readily linked the oppressive sense of blackness which enshrouds the last days of the Spanish captain's life with the explicit villainy of the Negroes. Matthiessen contended that such symbolism was socially unfortunate and left troublesome moral questions unanswered.[1] The events of our own

---

1. F. O. Matthiessen, *American Renaissance: Art and Expression in the Age of Emerson and Whitman* (New York: Oxford University Press, 1941), 508.

time, however, help us to perceive the network of cultural stereotypes which prevents Amasa Delano, the American captain, from
getting beneath the surface of puzzling appearances to a horrifying
reality; in addition, our times help us to see in the clever leader of
the Negro mutiny a forerunner of Malcolm X. Only by the values of
a society and a religion that denied him manhood could Babo be
termed a criminal of Satanic proportion; to his own people who survived him, he could only be an unusually resourceful leader of nearly
mythic stature, a prophet of greater violence to come if no enlightened changes occur in the decadent, morally impotent Old World of
Benito Cereno and the blissfully innocent and morally impervious
New World of Amasa Delano.

The main thrust of "The Bell-Tower," as Charles A. Fenton con-
vincingly explained, reveals Melville's imaginative distrust of mid–
nineteenth-century technology.[2] But a secondary thrust is announced
in the first of Melville's three epigraphs to the story, which not only
reminds us of "Benito Cereno" but also initiates at least a partial reply to Matthiessen's objection: "Like negroes, these powers own
man sullenly; mindful of their higher master; while serving, plot revenge." By this epigraph Melville asserts that elements which we
view as servile serve paradoxically to enslave their masters, that
masters and slave shape each other's destiny, and moreover, that a
slave's awareness of a higher law than social codes and man-made
legislation holds the promise of freedom and keeps rebellion brew-
ing. He claims simply that natural rights apply to all men and that
despite the involuntary conditioning or the conscious effort which
subordinate some men, natural law will subvert local law and custom. Perhaps the Italian Renaissance setting of the story (which reminds some readers of Poe and others of Hawthorne) kept many of
Melville's readers in 1855 from discovering in "The Bell-Tower" not
only a rejection of technological progress but also a fearful response

---

2. Charles A. Fenton, "'The Bell-Tower': Melville and Technology," *American Literature*,
XXIII (May, 1951), 219–32.

to that other contemporary phenomenon—the institution of Negro slavery.[3]

To suggest that this story is in part Melville's response to slavery is not to insist that the story is explicitly about the slavery issue in mid–nineteenth-century America. The story is about a Renaissance "mechanician" (an artist–inventor whose human origins are unknown) who seeks to outdo nature in creating a complex mechanical system that will serve simultaneously as a practical, utilitarian device, as an example of the inventor's own unrivaled ingenuity, and as a monument to national greatness. His striving for perfection and power is a hubristic echo of Hawthorne's Brand and Aylmer; he is the artist of the powerful, as Owen Warland was "the artist of the beautiful." When the machine smashes its creator, it seems simply to confirm the pat poetic justice of Melville's second epigraph ("The world is apoplectic with high-living of ambition; and apoplexy has its fall") and the more general philosophical irony of his third epigraph ("Seeking to conquer a larger liberty, man but extends the empire of necessity"). But throughout the fabric of the story Melville has woven a pattern out of biblical and mythological allusion, specific incident and echoes of mid–nineteenth-century racial controversy—a pattern which by its recurrent motifs outlines the natural law dooming masters to fall victim to their slaves.

The targets of both the main thrust of the story (the unquestioning faith in technological progress) and the subordinate thrust (man's

---

3. Some of Melville's attention to the issue of slavery is discussed by Charles H. Foster, "Something in Emblems: A Reinterpretation of Moby-Dick," *New England Quarterly*, XXXIV (March, 1961), 3–35; and Howard R. Floan, *The South in Northern Eyes, 1831 to 1861* (Austin: University of Texas Press, 1958), 131–47. A very thorough general treatment of racial issues is Laurie Jean Lorant, "Herman Melville and Race" (Ph.D. dissertation, New York University, 1972). More recent and also relevant are Joyce Sparer Adler, "Melville's 'Benito Cereno': Slavery and Violence in the Americas," *Science & Society*, XXXVIII (Spring, 1974), 19–48; Edward S. Grejda, *The Common Continent of Men: Racial Equality in the Writings of Herman Melville* (Port Washington, N.Y.: Kennikat Press, 1974); Charles E. Nnolim, *Melville's "Benito Cereno": A Study in the Meaning of Name Symbolism* (New York: New Voices Publishing Co., 1974); two essays by Carolyn L. Karcher, "Melville's 'The Gees': A Forgotten Satire on Scientific Racism," *American Quarterly*, XXVII (October, 1975), 421–42, and "Melville and Racial Prejudice: A Re-evaluation," *Southern Review*, n.s., XII (Spring, 1976), 287–310; and Kermit Vanderbilt, "Benito Cereno': Melville's Fable of Black Complicity," *Southern Review*, n.s., XII (Spring, 1976), 311–22.

domination of the processes of life and enslavement of "lesser" beings) constitute an extension of human exploitation and control beyond the limits of individual or social safety. Together, these two
forces are flaws in the design of this hopeful and commercially successful society, the seeds of its own self-destruction. It seems clear
from the materials of Melville's story that his fictional Renaissance
state, his new world born of an old, allegorizes mid–nineteenth-
century America.

In terms that recall the description of Vivenza, another allegorized
version of the United States, in Chapter 161 of *Mardi*, we are told of
a proud and rich commercial state which has its origin "in a high
hour of renovated earth, following the second deluge, when the
waters of the Dark Ages had dried up, and once more the green appeared." This brave and enlightened new world, this embodiment
of new beginnings, is figuratively connected with both the geography and the optimism of Eden as the expectations of its citizens
"soar into Shinar aspiration." But a calculatedly casual reference to
the sons of Noah (who also ruined their opportunity to start afresh)
sets up a pattern of reference and allusion that undercuts the optimism and foreshadows the decay of the young state (BT, 355–56).
Now, if we also recall that the harbor of Vivenza was marked by a
helmeted goddess of liberty whose base bore the noble assertion,
"In this republican land all men are born free and equal"—and the
cynical afterthought "Except the tribe of Hamo"—we see what Melville means by his reference to the sons of Noah. Just as the bell-
tower is a conscious variation of the Tower of Babel, Noah and his
sons represent another fallen ideal. Ham, in particular, whose Canaanite descendants were cursed to be servants of servants unto
their brethren, is a relevant prototype for this story of master and
slave.

This pattern by which the proud and mighty are inevitably top-
pled, already announced in each of the three epigraphs of "The Bell-
Tower", is repeated again in the image of the ruined tower in the
first sentence, and still again in the same sentence by the references
to "Anak and the Titan." Melville persistently reads history as mythology and mythology as history, and both provide the symbolic
shorthand for treating his own society. His *Anak* refers to one of a

race of aboriginal (some say Canaanite) giants annihilated by the Hebrews, and "the Titan" reminds us of those children of Heaven and Earth, who overthrew Uranus and raised Cronus to power. (An old mistake comes to Melville's aid here, for Cronus, who was originally identified with the wealth of the harvest, was later confused with Chronos or Time. Not only does our Father Time with his harvest scythe merge these identities, but Melville's bell-tower, he tells us, unites for the first time the hitherto separate functions of bell and clock. It is the epitome of a society enriched by its harvest of commerce and ready, like the wise Dr. Franklin whom Melville satirizes in *Israel Potter*, to yoke bell-tower and clock-tower, religion and business, in a monument to profit).

Several more of Melville's allusions reinforce the theme of slavery with its implication that masters will fall beneath the onslaught of their slaves. The proud, god-rivaling artisan–inventor Bannadonna first refers to his mechanical bell-ringer as Haman. This name is more descriptive than restrictive, for Bannadonna the creator does not think his creation a fully developed being—rather a kind of "half-man," constructed explicitly to perform certain mechanical-muscular labors. We think also of the Persian minister who would enslave the Jews and was undone by Esther, and whose ambition led him to the gallows he had himself constructed. In addition the name resembles the earlier *Ham* and its derivative *Hamo*, which Melville had clearly associated with Negro slavery in the United States.

More specific is the suggestion of one of the magistrates that the first of Bannadonna's twelve representations of the hours in the elaborate clockwork resembled Deborah, the prophetess, in a Florentine painting. The implicit warning is again ignored, but we are left with a further reminder of a rebellion of the enslaved. It was Deborah who predicted that Sisera, captain of the Canaanite forces, would fall at the hand of a woman. And Jael, after putting Sisera at his ease, hammered a tent peg into his head, sparking the Israelites to cast off their bondage and destroy their former masters. In this story, as in that of Esther, a woman was a direct agent of the villain's destruction; and in a sense this was also true of Bannadonna, who was so engrossed in removing the individuality from the appearance of the first of his twelve feminine figures that he was unaware that the time had come for his mechanical slave to hammer out the hour.

This mechanical slave fashioned by the head and hand of Bannadonna is the most intentionally ambiguous of the several symbolic figures in the story. Because he is hooded and his true nature masked until he crushes the skull of his creator, he is frequently referred to as "the domino" (a term that has overtones of mastery or authority and could also fit the figuratively cowled and masked blacks of "Benito Cereno"), but his intended name was Talus. Again, mythological ambiguity serves Melville's purpose, for there were two known as Talus, one human and the other mechanical. Daedalus, who is certainly a prototype of Bannadonna, was jealous at the ingenuity and skill of his nephew Talus and threw this potential rival to his death. The other Talus was a brazen giant given by Hephaestus to Minos. This man of metal, with his vein of blood, guarded Crete from intruders and regularly circled the island three times a day, a clockwork watchman.[4]

In suggesting that Bannadonna's manacled serf is suspiciously pliant and capable of independent movement and of drawing breath, Melville is writing a species of science fiction, but something more too. For there is the uncertainty whether Talus–Haman is a machine with human attributes, or a human viewed in a mechanistic, subhuman way. After all, human life had gone into the design: Bannadonna had killed a recalcitrant workman and unintentionally cast his flesh into the molten mass. The godlike inventor, in making this creature in the image of man, intended "a supplement to the Six Days' Work; stocking the earth with a new serf, more useful than the ox, swifter than the dolphin, stronger than the lion, more cunning than the ape, for industry an ant, more fiery than serpents, and yet in patience, another ass"—the perfect slave (BT, 368). This creature possessed strength, locomotion, and "the appearance, at least, of intelligence and will," but as Bannadonna assured the visiting magistrates whom he had segregated from his slave with a coarse piece of

---

4. Both the first epigraph with its reference to slaves plotting revenge and some of the actual description of Bannadonna's robot are reminiscent of Caliban, who also plotted to smash the head of his master, Prospero. Melville may have avoided any mention of *The Tempest* because Caliban's revolt was so utterly unsuccessful.

canvas, this creature, despite his human appearance, had no soul. Melville, certainly, had encountered similar explanations and justifications in the arguments of mid–nineteenth-century proponents of slavery. In Chapter 162 of *Mardi*, his caricature of John C. Calhoun asserts that though the ancestors of his slaves may have had souls, "Souls have. been bred out of their descendants; as the instinct of scent is killed in pointers." This slave driver (named *Nulli*, reminiscent not only of Calhoun's constitutional interpretations but of a negative, life-denying quality suggested in *Bannadonna*, too) nevertheless insists that his serfs were better fed, clothed, and cared for than workers in other areas.

Bannadonna is simultaneously a proud creator of lifelike artificial forces and a relentless enemy of the natural life force. His dedication is an affirmation of utility and a denial of spiritual vitality. As Fenton's analysis of this story demonstrates, the primary application of this moral seems to be to the industrial Northeast, where public support of technological progress made it a common mission. Melville's fears on this score, expressed a few months earlier in his "Tartarus of Maids," formed the hideous paradox of machines taking on human functions and young girls being treated as so many cold, white, mechanical slaves. In that story machine production obviated human reproduction. In "The Bell-Tower" he is concerned with essentially the same paradox. Bannadonna's name suggests that he dispenses with woman, and his highest creation is a perversion of natural procreation in "stocking the earth with a new serf." His aim is "to solve nature, to steal into her, to intrigue beyond her," suggesting that his science is a means of using nature in distinctly unnatural ways—to outstrip natural law in its physical and biological dimensions and to subvert natural law in its political applications (BT, 369–70).

Richard Chase has suggested some of the sexual significance of "The Bell-Tower," but more in pschoanalytical than in cultural terms.[5] Rather than a symbol of Melville's psychic state, it seems likely that this tower is the symbol of an aspiring society supremely

5. Richard Chase, *Herman Melville: A Critical Study* (New York: Macmillan, 1949), 122–25.

confident of its productive power. It is an erection devoid of humanity and love, a perverse parody of artistic creativity and natural pro-
creativity. For Melville the values implicit in the tower and in its
crowning mechanism were not only cause for concern but threat to
human survival. The repeated references to the initial flaw in the
bell and the ultimate collapse of the structure are Melville's assertion of the essential impotence of the rational, utilitarian view of
matter and of man. His reference in the third epigraph to man's attempt "to conquer a larger liberty," which results only in extending
the empire of necessity, points directly to what he felt was man's
loss of freedom and authority and his inability to determine his own
course, particularly in American society. It applied then as well as
now to a world in which mankind was becoming increasingly enslaved by, and more than occasionally the victim of, the complex
products of human knowledge, skill, and ambition.

The flawed bell in this story also has a haunting similarity to that
familiar icon of American freedom, the Liberty Bell in Philadelphia.
Melville clearly intends the flaw in his story to stand for a moral
weakness in the political structure, the weakness of a society that in-
corporated in its laws the subordinate status of its black population.
In the literal terms of the story the source of the flaw was Bannadonna's wanton act of gross inhumanity, the murder of one of his
workmen. The community, in forgiving this violation, is tacitly linked
to the criminal policy that humanity is expendable in the course of
gratifying personal ambition and marking national achievement. All
of Bannadonna's careful attempts to conceal the blemish in his casting are necessarily superficial; the profound fault remains, even if
unseen by the admiring populace. The symbolism here approaches
but does not equal the blatancy of that in Chapter 158 of *Mardi*
where a collared menial with red stripes on his back hoists a national
standard similarly striped.

From the start Melville has used a pattern of images and allusions
which draw attention to the cruelty, folly, and danger of slavery. Although he was concerned, like Emerson or Thoreau at nearly the
same time, with the kind of bondage developing in the North, he
gave his story a second thrust, pointing it at another more flagrant

denial of humanity.[6] The cold and inhuman rationalization which insisted on the soulless inferiority of the enslaved Negro constituted a flaw in the original design of American liberty and in 1855 could well have appeared the irremediable weakness in the fabric of the Republic. In this there is an echo of what Thomas Jefferson feared when in his *Notes on Virginia* he looked ahead to the three main consequences of slavery: the debasement and moral enslavement of the master; the alienation of the slave who can feel no loyalty to or reverence for the nation which proscribed his manhood; and the inevitable upheaval which would be precipitated, under the doctrine of natural rights, by God if not by man. And there is in no lesser sense an announcement of what William Faulkner felt when he looked back at the flawed past of southern society and sought for possible means of atonement.

The equation of the kind of wage slavery described in "The Tartarus of Maids" with the subhuman protagonist in "The Bell-Tower" or between "Bartleby" (who rebels against another kind of economic compulsion) and the slavery situation in "Benito Cereno" constitutes Melville's own version of "the hireling and the slave" argument used in the 1850s by such aggressive apologists for southern society as George Fitzhugh and William J. Grayson. Melville had announced

6. Emerson's "Works and Days," delivered as a lecture in early 1857 and published in *Society and Solitude* in 1870, dramatically suggests that even on the eve of the Civil War, the atmosphere of Doomsday was conveyed by the degree to which men had become enslaved by their technology. To a remarkable degree the imagery which he uses to stress the quality of the time parallels that of Melville's "The Bell-Tower." He begins by asserting that all machines are modeled after man: "The human body is the magazine of inventions, the patent office, where are the models from which every hint was taken." He then stresses that these machines have effected a kind of renaissance—a sense "that life seems made over new." This new power may serve in a menial capacity "and bring a bowl of gruel to a sick man's bed," or it "can twist beams of iron like candy-braids"; replacing man's muscles, "it already walks about the field like a man, and will do anything required of it"; and duplicating his mental powers, it will "calculate interest and logarithms" and "draw bills and answers in chancery." When he describes the ocean telegraph, he draws, perhaps unconsciously, from the reservoir of gothic imagery from which Hawthorne, Poe, and Melville also drew: so astonishing is this performance that it is "as if the intellect were taking the brute earth into training, and shooting the first thrills of life and thought through the unwilling brain." But this man-made monster can turn on his maker, for "machinery is aggressive," and "all tools are in one sense edge tools and dangerous." Ultimately, "the machine unmakes the man . . . . the machine is so perfect, the engineer is nobody." Edward Waldo Emerson (ed.), *The Complete Works of Ralph Waldo Emerson* (12 vols.; Cambridge: Riverside Press, 1904), VII, 157–65.

this argument as early as *Mardi* and returned to it as late as *Clarel*, where the unreconstructed Ungar takes his stand against the loss of faith, the lack of taste, and the brutal leveling forces of an industrial America. But despite his use of an argument which was itself a rationalization favoring slavery, Melville never seems the least sympathetic to slavery. Instead he seems to see domination and subjugation as a lamentable fact of human existence; and any of the forces which subject man to a condition of physical or intellectual subservience—whether naval discipline, economic pressures, ideas of class and caste, or any official truth—thereby coerce his will and render him a slave. Against this Melville took his stand, though it was often screened from public view by a multitude of symbolic means.

"Benito Cereno"

"Benito Cereno" is a story whose time has come. By that I mean that the concepts essential to understanding the story are now more prevalent than ever before in American society, assuring the existence of a sizable, potentially receptive audience. Even so, I suspect that the guidance offered in the innumerable college classrooms where students encounter this much-anthologized story for the first time is as varied as the views expressed in the five decades of criticism on "Benito Cereno." But the story itself is too important a work of art and an account of cultural confrontation for one to be detoured into a detailed discussion of the criticism, illuminating as much of it is, misguided as some of it turns out to be.[7]

7. The range of allegorical interpretation runs from identification of Cereno as Melville the writer suffering the attacks of hostile critics, to Cereno as metaphorical embodiment of Charles V betrayed by black deeds of the Church in Spain, to Cereno as representative of Spanish colonial policy and the slave-holding establishment. Babo thus ranges from malicious literary critic, or sadistic agent of the Spanish Inquisition, or overt devil, to heroic freedom-fighter. While there is greater consensus regarding the character of Delano as the representative American, there are some significant differences in assessing his relative strengths and limitations.

Much of the relevant criticism is included or listed in two collections with a similar purpose. Both reprint the pertinent chapter from Amasa Delano's account of the experience underlying "Benito Cereno" and both contain selected and annotated bibliographies: (1) Seymour L. Gross (ed.), *A Benito Cereno Handbook* (Belmont, Calif.: Wadsworth, 1965), and (2) John P. Runden (ed.), *Melville's Benito Cereno* (Boston: D. C. Heath, 1965). Some important subsequent articles are listed in James Woodress (ed.), *Eight American Authors* (New York: W. W. Norton, 1971), and in the recent annual compilations of *American Literary Scholarship* (Durham, N.C.: Duke University Press).

Yet the story is itself the chief cause of such critical variance; the values and preconceptions of critics are only contributing causes. There is some basis for charges of murkiness or structural incoherence, but I suspect that Melville's "failure" to clarify stems more from insight than from oversight. The story is a remarkable study in the problems of perception—a subject for which Melville schooled himself in his reading of Shakespeare and Hawthorne, both of whom, Melville asserted, were largely misunderstood by their audiences. In this sense "Benito Cereno" has its deep source in *Lear* or *Othello* rather than Amasa Delano's *A Narrative of Voyages and Travels, in the Northern and Southern Hemispheres* (1817). Like Dwight's *Travels*, which Melville disparaged in his review of Hawthorne's *Mosses*, Delano's account obscured almost as much as it revealed, and Melville's exploration of individual consciousness and cultural differences raises problems that Delano never recognized.

But Delano's *Narrative* does have an apparent clarity and focus that "Benito Cereno" does not have; in fact, the reader who dislikes the lack of certainty in Melville's story might actually prefer the more assured, less ambiguous style of the original. For Melville quite literally makes his reader the victim of the perceptual and conceptual difficulties that beset his protagonists, challenging that reader either to abide within the conceptual worlds of the representatives of American and Spanish cultures or to join him in trying to discern the "truth that comes in with darkness," which neither Delano nor Cereno is capable of penetrating. Like the many-ended intricacies of the Spanish sailor's knot that totally confounds Captain Delano, Melville knots character, setting, symbol, and incident into a cultural puzzle, defying solution. When questioned about the purpose of the knot, the old sailor answered, "For someone else to undo" (BC, 296). The answer constitutes Melville's challenge to readers of "Benito Cereno." He was aware that most would drop the knot as meaningless, some would solve it by cutting, and only a few would really struggle to unravel the intricacies.

There should be no further need to document by reference to primary text or published criticism the evidence for concluding that Amasa Delano embodies prominent New World—specifically North American—attitudes and that Benito Cereno represents a waning

Old World culture. But only gradually did there appear any realization that Babo, leader of the rebellious slaves, is a militant spokesman for what are now called, however imprecisely at times, Third
World views—here referring to the condition of implicit inferiority
that comes of being non-American, non-European, and nonwhite.

For the greatest part of its length, the third-person narrative is
limited and controlled by the consciousness—the values, preconceptions, and outlook—of Amasa Delano, a generous, tolerant, as-
suredly practical man. In Melville's story he is even a more com-
petent ship's captain than in his own memoir, where he mentions
problems of morale and discipline on his own ship and occasionally
lapses into a tone of self-pity. While Melville tells his audience that
Delano is "a person of a singularly undistrustful good-nature, not
liable . . . to indulge in personal alarms, any way involving the im-
putation of malign evil in man," he also tries to alert a segment of his
audience with a line of awkwardly ironic exposition thrown away on
most readers: "Whether in view of what humanity is capable, such a
trait implies, along with a benevolent heart, more than ordinary
quickness and accuracy of perception, may be left to the wise to
determine" (BC, 256).

That such wise readers existed in significant numbers to support
the kind of writer Melville tried to be in the 1850s, he had good
reason to doubt. Writing about Melville's relationship to the Harpers, "a firm which had religious connections with Methodism," the
late William Charvat described "the problem faced by many American writers of that time—a reading audience so mixed that it was difficult to predict public reactions to deviations from common beliefs
and accepted standards of decorum." Charvat went on to say that
Melville never was able to assume an audience grouping with "de-
finable degrees of tolerance and sophistication," because the stratification which gives writers a degree of freedom in our time did not
begin in America until well after 1850.[8] Yet more than any other of
Melville's stories, "Benito Cereno" requires a reader willing to re-
read the story, ready to reexamine the circumstances and able to re-
think their meaning—a reader who can abandon the comfort of his

8. William Charvat, *The Profession of Authorship in America, 1800–1870*, ed. Matthew J.
Bruccoli (Columbus: Ohio State University Press, 1968), 211.

social assumptions, relinquish the security of conventional wisdom, liberate himself from the confines of his culture, and gain the perspective of differing points of view.

Even within that segment of recent or current readers who catch the cue concerning accuracy of perception, its significance has been perceived differently. Numerous readers whose critical reputations, enlightened social attitudes, and political liberalism are unquestionably solid (F. O. Matthiessen, one case in point) have faulted Melville for his ascription of evil to Babo and the blacks and alleged his underlying insensitivity to the injustice of slavery. They have reacted to the story as if it were a unilateral denunciation of "Black Power" by Benito Cereno, its pitiable victim, instead of a complex illustration of that "great power of blackness" which Melville discorned in the works of Shakespeare or Hawthorne and which most readers missed or misunderstood, "for it is, mostly insinuated to those who may best understand it, and account for it; it is not obtruded upon every one alike" (HHM, 131). That "power of blackness" not only referred to the presence of evil in the world and its universal permeation of human personality in a Calvinistic sense; it also recognized gross imperfection in human societies and institutions along with the widespread inability of participants to perceive inequity or iniquity and their ingrained hostility to anyone who presumed to point out so unpopular a truth.

"Let any clergyman try to preach the Truth from its very stronghold, the pulpit, and they would ride him out of his church on his own pulpit bannister," Melville complained to Hawthorne in the famous "Dollars damn me" letter of June, 1851, and further appraising his potential audience, he added, "What I feel most moved to write, that is banned. . . . Yet, altogether, write the *other* way I cannot." Aware that mid–nineteenth-century Americans, especially successful ones like the narrator in "Bartleby" or Amasa Delano himself, had a disproportionately high opinion of themselves, Melville was drawn to expose arrogance and its demeaning or even dehumanizing effect on human relationships. As a writer, Melville had to go under to get by the public's ban on this kind of truth, concealing it in the account of the consequences of a slave rebellion at sea.

Also smuggled in covertly is an image of a Negro leader, unprecedented in American literature. Exploiting the stereotyped behavior familiar to an American audience, Babo plays two roles simultaneously, while his true character goes unremarked by the other protagonists, whose "accuracy of perception" is effectively blocked by those stereotypes. From Amasa Delano's standpoint Babo is a simple, devoted, subhuman servant, who clearly knows his place; like a dog he is capable of returning love and loyalty even to a capricious, hardhearted master. Fulfilling Delano's expectations, Babo projects an image of fidelity that easily wins the American's admiration and confidence. To Benito Cereno, however, he seems a heartless savage, an amoral monster inspired by pure evil. It was not until the 1950s that there appeared among some few members of Melville's most appreciative readership the beginnings of a new estimate of Babo; but it was the acceleration of the civil rights movement, the rise of black consciousness, and the published works of Malcolm X, Frantz Fañon, and Eldridge Cleaver that more fully prepared white readers of "Benito Cereno" to approximate the standpoint of Babo, discuss his motivation, and appreciate his intelligence and ingenuity. But even through the 1950s some contended that Melville had made changes in Amasa Delano's memoir intended to blacken the blacks and whiten the whites and that he deserves censure for pushing a proslavery position to cash in on a ready market by capitalizing on anti-Negro fears and feelings. (Careful reading hardly supports such a view. Furthermore, the newly appointed editor of *Putnam's* in 1855 was Frederick Law Olmstead, whose antislavery views strongly influenced editorial policy. *Putnam's* published both "The Bell-Tower" and "Benito Cereno" during the year of Olmstead's editorship.) Even now there are readers, black as well as white, who see an attempt to get Melville off the hook of racism in any suggestion that Babo is an underground hero because of his creative use of symbols to further the blacks' quest for freedom, his remarkable performance as actor–director of the theatrical deception, and his refusal to yield to the combined force of Old and New World law and religion.

Audience receptiveness toward the character of a militant black artist–activist, directing the slumbering forces in that area of black concentration which Melville was perhaps the first to label "the ghetto," must have been low in mid–nineteenth-century America. Readers in the 1970s are better able to recognize the crippling deficiencies of Delano and Cereno and see Babo as the most fully developed example of manhood in the story—which itself becomes a kind of underground revenge tragedy of a "bad dude" who was "offed" because he "had it all together" and, for a time at least, directed artful cunning and purposeful violence against Old and New World oppressors. As the legal deposition makes clear, though Babo himself never articulates it, there is a Cleaver-like logic behind his decision to kill Alexandro Aranda after the rebellion had succeeded. The murder, preparation of the skeleton, and its use as replacement for the figurehead of Christopher Columbus—whose name and deeds signify the Old World's religious, political, and cultural imperialism— this murder and its horrifying, symbolic warning to the surviving whites that they too may follow their leader, temporal or spiritual, is itself a political act, fully rational and justifiable from Babo's standpoint. For as long as Aranda lived, the blacks could not be legally free; in the eyes of Old World or New World representatives they were his property. In fact the validity of the slave owner's rights even in the northern states was affirmed by the mid-1850s when Melville submitted the story. The celebrated cases of Thomas Sims and Anthony Burns, fugitive slaves returned by federal law to southern masters, reversed earlier decisions including the U.S. Supreme Court judgment freeing the black insurgents who had won control of the Spanish ship *Amistad*, some fifteen years earlier.

Melville's audience should have known of and been conditioned by these historical and legal aspects of the slavery question. The majority probably agreed with these legal vindications of property rights and were not at all prepared to encounter in a magazine story a challenge to, rather than a confirmation of, what they already believed. They might also have recognized some similarity between Alexandro Aranda's benevolence toward his slaves—leaving them unchained aboard the *San Dominick* because he was confident of their tractability—and the case of Nat Turner, who turned the opportunities offered by a "generous" master into the staging ground for massive insurrection. Melville consciously enlarged the role of Aranda from the original narrative to emphasize the liberal master's underestimation of the slaves' desire for freedom. He just as consciously changed the ship's name and set the date back to 1799 to coincide with the insurrection on Santo Domingo, the site not only of one of Columbus' first landings but also of the first European settlement and of the first large-scale import of African labor into the New World. These latter changes alone are enough to challenge the views of critics who would censure Melville for his insensitivity to slavery as well as those who say that the issue of race and slavery is only incidental to Melville's concern with abstract evil.

Aranda's benevolent despotism and costly miscalculation are replicated in the genial condescension and bland overconfidence of Amasa Delano in regard to blacks. Don Alexandro misjudged, as it were, the moral, political, and psychological nature of the knot he helped fashion, and the error cost him his life. Amasa Delano is blind to the intertwined issues of domination and subjugation, civilization and the primitive, authority and liberty, and associated strands of cultural difference. He is locked into his preconceptions as securely as Atufal, the proud giant, seems locked into his chains, but paradoxically, even after the mystery is unlocked for Delano, he has still not solved the knot. Defeated, like Aranda, by its complexity, he nevertheless survives—ironically protected by the degree of his misperception. He is a man for whom believing is seeing, and in a setting where the sea is "like waved lead," the sky "a gray surtout," he is still confident of his standing with God and his knowledge of men. Trying to penetrate the opacities and rationalize the deceptions, Delano wanders the decks of the *San Dominick* with all the ingenousness of a midshipman experiencing the Encantadas for the first time. Lacking the moral and mental instrumentalities, insensitive to irony and ambiguity, he tries to follow the navigational charts through waters more troubled than he could possibly imagine. He trusts his liberal sympathies, his tolerant generosity, and his self-righteous certainties to guide him. Melville counted on most readers moving through the opacities of his story in the same way.

Delano cannot conceive of how a good man could do bad; he sees suffering and misery as resulting providentially from vice; and in a cultural corollary to the work ethic, he links the lack of competence, precision, and order aboard the *San Dominick* to the moral default of Old World Spain, where position is due more to noble birth than ability or achievement. Stock responses and often contradictory stereotypes betray him repeatedly as he misconstrues or only partially recognizes the symbolic import of sword, flag, or chains. These have traditional associations which he can share, but he cannot approach the full meaning of the shrouded figurehead, rotting balustrade, or enigmatic sternpiece. The latter, carved with the castle and lion of Spain, bears "a dark satyr in a mask, holding his foot on the prostrate neck of a writhing figure, likewise masked" (BC, 259). Delano cannot even associate this master-slave symbol with his idea of the relationship between Cereno and Babo. After the legal deposition more fully acquaints him (and us) with Cereno's viewpoint and experience, he can listen to, but not share, Cereno's reversal of the symbolized roles. Delano's firm belief in Negro simplemindedness, his acceptance of the legend of the loyal body servant, his acquiescence with the concept of slave as extension of the master's will, and his generous acceptance of the burden of white paternalism drain the symbol of its initial meaning as well as its ironic reversal, and abort the possibility of his recognizing his own participation in this account of the controvertibility of roles and the ambiguity of evil. And very likely most of Melville's readers, sharing many of Delano's assumptions, see no deeper into the events than he can. It is in an ironic sense that Melville describes Delano "with scales dropped from his eyes," for the full epiphanic meaning of the sternpiece is provided by Delano's clutching the terrified Spaniard with his left hand while "his right foot . . . ground the prostrate negro" into the bottom of the small boat—a heraldic representation of America triumphant over decadent Europe and backward Africa (BC, 327–28). Unwittingly but effectively, Delano constitutes Melville's discerning announcement of New World imperialism replacing the enfeebled authority of Old World imperial force.

For the audience to recognize the full extent of Delano's shallowness and perceptual limitations would involve many of them unwillingly in mocking themselves and acknowledging the arrogance of their own assumptions. Most would rather ignore the irony of Delano's tenuous cloak of self-assurance as he half imagines his danger in the hands of the pitiably impotent Spaniard whom he misconstrues as a cruel master and capricious pirate: "Who would murder Amasa Delano? His conscience is clean. There is some one above" (BC, 298). In all likelihood, more readers were guilty of the same arrogance of innocence as Amasa Delano: the genteel presumptousness that the internalized concepts of his culture enabled him to comprehend the world and speak with certainty of God's will and the inner nature of other men and women. These cultural concepts were to divine design like print and seal, assuring that the world of man and nature was programed into lawful patterns and orderly processes. Founded on extravagant promise, this New World faith was expressed in expectation not in recollection. In his summary comments to Benito Cereno, Delano stresses the power of "yon bright sun" to forget, of "the blue sea, and the blue sky" to restore themselves, of "these mild trades" to heal—nature constantly nourishing, sustaining, restoring (BC, 352). Without having read Emerson, Delano knew that the world existed for man; without Thoreau's guidance he lived in the infinite expectation of the dawn.

In contrast to Delano's gospel of faith, hope, and confidence, Cereno speaks from the painful depths of his experience—a gospel of memory that relives the agony without the resurrection. In moral terms, the story is a virtual standoff: the American's technical competence and intellectual infantilism matched against the Spaniard's physical enervation and pathetic incapacity. Only Babo—resourceful in life, stubbornly silent at his trial, unabashed even in death—combines all the human attributes of a tragic hero. But he could not be cast in such a role from a New World or an Old World perspective, and in Melville's time the Third World lacked an adequate voice or a significant vote.

We can assume that many readers also shared Delano's covert prejudices against Spain and the Spanish presence in the New World, linking anti-Catholic sentiments and antimonarchist feelings with Spanish decadence, colonial maladministration, and resistance to progress—the Protestant ethic become foreign policy and justifying American responsibility for removing incompetent authority in a foreign principality. Similarly, they could share his recurrent suspicions of Benito Cereno as sinister conspirator or torpid invalid unfit to command, while almost simultaneously trying to expel these fears through an openhanded, democratic diminution and acceptance of ethnic differences: "These Spaniards are all an odd set; the very word Spaniard has a curious, conspirator, Guy-Fawkish twang to it. And yet, I dare say, Spaniards in the main are as good folks as any in Duxbury, Massachusetts" (BC, 300). It is highly unlikely that Melville's audience could recognize that either of Delano's assumptions —one expressed in clearly prejudicial terms, the other in specious egalitarianism—impeded effective communication. Despite his knowledge of Spanish, Delano could neither understand anyone of Cereno's background, nor imagine his predicament. In fact, applied social science labors to make explicit in 1975 what was so implicit to Melville about intercultural communication in 1855. Consider the following passage taken from a recent Department of State publication and based on research performed under contract with the Department of the Army:

> It is virtually impossible for anyone to communicate with other people without making assumptions about them. We may make these assumptions knowingly or, more commonly, without being aware of making them. Ease of communication is determined, in part, by the extent to which such assumptions are correct. When false assumptions interfere with communication, we may recognize that this is happening. We may sometimes discover later that it has occurred. Frequently, we never become aware of it.
>
> Our assumptions about other people can be traced to a variety of causal factors. Of particular importance in intercultural encounters are assumptions that are the result of our own cultural conditioning. The effects of that conditioning on our thought processes can be quite subtle, making it difficult to recognize the resulting assumptions for what they are. Often such assumptions manifest themselves as *projected cognitive similarity*—that is, when we implicitly assume that the other person's ideas and thought processes are similar to what ours would be if we were in their place. [9]

Toward Babo, Delano does not attempt the social and psychological equivalency of "projected cognitive similarity"; but in regard to Benito Cereno, it is Captain Delano's tranquilizer, beclouding his perception of what the Spaniard is going through and the meaning of what he has been through.

9. Alfred J. Kraemer, "Cultural Self-Awareness and Communication," *International Educational and Cultural Exchange*, X, (Winter, 1975), 13.

Many readers, however, construe Benito Cereno's physical and psychological trauma, his tortured recognition of evil, as the central meaning of the story, and some even go so far as to identify Cereno with Melville, who they feel was similarly appalled by the immediacy of evil. This identification further assumes the author's approbation of Cereno's outlook and ignores his effeteness, impotence, and inability to confront the world as it is. His monastic withdrawal, as R. H. Fogle has pointed out, is no more adequate or admirable a way of dealing with the world than is the carefree bachelor approach of Amasa Delano. The two men are as opposed to each other in their conceptions of the world as the two sides of a Galapagos tortoise, and their confrontation leads only to surface communication. They remain forever blocked from any benefit of each other's strength or insight, morally or psychologically crippled by their own incompleteness. If Amasa Delano, unscarred by pain and misery, lives in an ambiance of benign expectation, Benito Cereno lives with the agony of his experience, his memory the ceaseless nightmare of his present existence. The American is an historical amnesiac untroubled by the past; the Spaniard a much-troubled victim of physical and spiritual trauma.

From its original figurehead, honoring the agent of Spain who discovered the New World, to Benito Cereno's unhappy retreat and death in the monastery of Mount Agonia, to the legalized barbarism of Babo's execution the drama on the *San Dominick* has telescoped three centuries of Spanish history. Melville's view of these circumstances anticipates that of Carlos Fuentes, who argues that the forces "that killed the promise of freedom and love and joy in Spain," that produced Spanish decadence and impotence, "began in the instant of Spanish glory." Connecting the climactic discovery of the New World and the crest of the Inquisition in 1492, he asserts that the misguided attempt to strengthen "national unity, Catholic faith, and purity of blood out of love for Christ and his Holy Mother" inevitably launched Spain on a course of degeneracy, withdrawal, and isolation: "The hollow imperial gesture, by which Spain defeated herself, fatally cut herself off from the human, cultural and economic resources that fled with the expulsion of the Jews and the defeat of the Arabs." Of course, this view asserts more than Melville includes,

but Fuentes' image of a nation fruitlessly "fighting against the Reformation," living with a self-imposed "quarantine . . . against the
diseases of modernity," worshiping the symbols of "honor, purity,
and orthodoxy," fashioning "verbal masks . . . to uphold appearances" while its aristocratic dynasties faded "into insanity, hemo-
philia, syphillis, frivolity and . . . idiocy," can deepen a contemporary reader's understanding of Cereno's weakness, withdrawal, and
death.[10]

Fuentes' phrases effectively gloss Melville's imagistic description
of the *San Dominick* as "a whitewashed monastery" with "Black
Friars pacing the cloisters." (The Dominicans, or Black Friars, were
prominent sponsors of the Inquisition). Other details such as the
"slovenly neglect," the "Dry Bones" and "hearse-like" aspect of the
ship, the state-cabin windows "hermetically closed and calked," the
numerous signs of "faded grandeur," further fit into Fuentes' argument. Even the Spanish captain's behavior and appearance—his
"saturnine mood of ill-health," "his national formality," his "mental
disorder," his "unstrung," "half-lunatic" state of mind—exemplify
Fuentes' charges against the Spanish aristocracy (BC, 257–65). The
fading grandeur and structural rot of the *San Dominick* contrasts
with the power and pride once conveyed by its heraldic castle and
lion, and Don Benito is as much a relic as that fading crest, leaning
weakly on contrivance and appearance to stiffen the semblance of
authority.

With this view of Spanish history a modern reader blessed with
greater sophistication in regard to verbal masks and legalistic deceit
might more readily see the lengthy legal deposition as a contrived
cover-up rather than a revelation. The deposition clearly expresses
the values and reinforces the status quo of the Spanish colonial
establishment—ignoring Spanish injustices and black aspiration,
glossing over the civilized savagery of the Spanish to condemn black
barbarities—and views that somewhat indiscriminate massacre of
blacks and Spaniards by Delano's SWAT force ("nearly a score of
negroes were killed," none of the Americans) as a fortunate victory.
Thus, the legalistic expression of the establishment view, in its in-

10. Fuentes' remarks appeared in the course of a review of *Count Julian*, by Juan Goyti-
solo, in the *New York Times Book Review*, LXXIX, (May 5, 1974), 5.

tent to reveal the "true history of the *San Dominick's* voyage (BC, 333), communicates a socially acceptable fiction—a device Melville also employs at the end of *Billy Budd* where the historical record is left with an account of how the mutinous foreigner Budd stabbed the patriotic Claggart and was duly executed for his crime.

The deposition follows the narrative as if to unlock its mysteries, clarify its deceptions, and offer reassurance about the quality of justice. But the more attentive reader recognizes that the complexities of the knot have not been solved, even though Melville has served up a key to fit the padlocked narrative. Like Atufal's shackles, the locked-up truth in the narrative remains enchained only as long as the victim, or victimized reader, participates in the deception. The deposition thus wraps the reader in new coils of deception as it seems to unwrap the old. The key in this instance is that no man is merely a spectator, that significant art compels participation and engagement before it yields enlightenment, and that the reader in his approach to experience (including the experience of art) ultimately has the means to his own liberation.

Modern readers might also have some more associations with which to construct a context for "Benito Cereno." If they knew that the leader of the *Amistad* mutineers was a black known as Cinque or Cinquez, they could confront the ironic emergence in the 1970s of a black insurrectionist who took that name in espousing his violent, prison-spawned version of liberation. Such an irony not only underscores Santayana's dictum about those ignorant of the past doomed to relive it, but also points up how close to savagery the civilized authorities of Chicago or Los Angeles can be in dealing with the violence of the Panthers or the Symbionese.

I was myself surprised to discover that the real Amasa Delano—whose name echoes through recent American history in the annals of one of our near-dynastic families, as well as the site of a domestic Third World confrontation in the California grape fields—should have been an early pioneer of Pan-American foreign policy and crosscultural understanding. And in another compounding of ironic associations, I thought of how a prominent American official has had his goodwill missions to Latin America marred by the jumble of painful reality and unlikely mythic allusion, replaying on the stage of an Attica prison yard the drama of the *San Dominick*. "Benito Cereno" is truly a story whose time has come, whose currency will not soon pass, and whose present readers must be encouraged to use their own knowledge and experience in undoing the knot that Melville's contemporaries were less equipped to handle.

5

◎◎◎

CONFIDENCE
IN
CHRISTIANITY

"The Lightning-Rod Man"

The story of gods calling upon simple country folk and subsequently rewarding them in keeping with the kind of hospitality they have shown is an ancient device in didactic fiction. "The Lightning-Rod Man" is in this tradition, but with some important differences that make it more a fable for Melville's time than a retelling of an ancient tale. For purposes of history, Melville renamed the Berkshires "the Acroceaunian hills,"[1] and the narrator addresses his vaguely unpleasant and presumptuous caller, who has appeared in the midst of a violent thunderstorm, as "Jupiter Tonans," both appellations taking us back to Greek and Roman times (LRM, 213–14). But the particular pitch of this hard-selling peddler and the product he dispenses bring us up quickly to eighteenth-century America, so neatly dichotomized by Jonathan Edwards and Benjamin Franklin, and to the later projection of tendencies they represented into mid–nineteenth-century America. It is not necessary for Melville to have read Jonathan Edwards' *Personal Narrative*, since he had so many graphic opportunities for acquaintance with the Calvinistic version

---

1. The name literally means "the high-thundering hills," and Tonans identifies Jupiter or Zeus as the Thunderer. In the "Introduction" to *The Complete Stories of Herman Melville*, Jay Leyda points out that the title of Chapter III in the Sixth Book of Cotton Mather's *Magnalia Christi Americana* is "Ceraunius. Relating remarkables done by thunder." Leyda also cites the following admonition from Mather's discussion of what the thunder said: "IV. A fourth voice of the glorious God in the thunder, is *make your peace with God immediately, lest by the stroke of his thunder he take you away in his wrath*," xxvii.

of Jupiter Tonans in his own upbringing, but it adds to our contextual background for the story to consider this passage from Edwards' spiritual autobiography:

> Before, I used to be uncommonly terrified with thunder, and to be struck with terror when I saw a thunder storm rising; but now, on the contrary, it rejoiced me. I felt God, so to speak, at the first appearance of a thunder storm; and used to take the opportunity, at such times, to fix myself in order to view the clouds, and see the lightnings play, and hear the majestic and awful voice of God's thunder.

Although Melville has mentioned both Edwards and Franklin elsewhere in his writings, I am not trying to insist that he had them in mind in this story, but rather that he was concerned with the sort of fervent and fearful religious revivalism best exemplified in the Great Awakening, and also with the security and faith in the products of science and technological progress fostered by the Enlightenment. The lightning-rod man is a walking metaphor in which hellfire-and-brimstone religion is the tenor, and an easy faith in Dr. Franklin's device for neutralizing the destructive force of nature is the vehicle. Or to put it in different terms, the lightning-rod man, so dependent on the concept of a God of awful wrath, is peddling an old-fashioned product, but science and the rhetoric of rationalism have provided him with a more up-to-date and attractive package, a new pitch for the fear and superstition of the past. And anyone who buys his product puts his confidence in what is clearly a confidence game.

Hershel Parker has placed "The Lightning-Rod Man" in the genre of the essentially comic encounter between the sly salesman and his hoped-for, usually rural, and often resistant victim.[2] It seems quite plausible that Melville cast this story in an established American comic genre (combining it with the aforementioned pagan fable of encounter between mortal and supernatural beings) as a protective and diversionary tactic. Both editor and publisher of *Putnam's Monthly* had written Melville in May, 1854, explaining why they could not accept "The Two Temples," which, they felt, would be too offensive to religious sensibilities. This fact ought to have discouraged Melville from submitting another satirical attack on a particular

2. Hershel Parker, "Melville's Salesman Story," *Studies in Short Fiction*, I (Fall, 1963), 154–56.

mode of Christian worship—to the same periodical, at that—unless, of course, he thought he could get away with it, eluding the probably hostile criticism by diverting the understanding of most readers. In addition to Melville's practice of combining in a single work a story to please himself and a more innocuous one to please the publisher and the public, I am suggesting that the comic form might have been Melville's self-protective lightning-rod intended to divert "the scattered bolts" and disarm the potential "charge of spearpoints" descending, as the narrator says, "on my low shingled roof" (LRM, 213). Parker's discovery that "The Lightning-Rod Man" was reprinted in an 1858 anthology of humor strengthens this possibility.

The important thing in the story, however, is not what protection Melville may have devised, but the kind of protection offered by the doleful stranger and the quality of his guarantee. In technique and in meaning the story seems to me closely allied to *The Confidence-Man*. Like the mysterious protagonist of the novel, the lightning-rod man seems a larger-than-human personality engaged in a familiar human activity—enriching himself by fleecing his fellows. His protection racket is an archetypal confidence game; his copper shaft an attempt to symbolize the comfort and security promised in the familiar reference in the Twenty-third Psalm to "Thy rod and thy staff." And almost as if the story were a simpler and shorter version of *The Confidence-Man*, the key ideas of security and safety serve the same thematic function as confidence and trust in the novel.

The opening paragraph of "The Lightning-Rod Man" depicts the narrator standing securely on his own ample hearthstone, warming himself while the storm rages magnificently outside. Every aspect of the storm is described in terms sharp and skewer-like: "bolts boomed," "Zigzag irradiations," "swift slants of sharp rain," and the aforementioned "charge of spear points" on the armor of his domestic security. This motif is repeated in the shape and character of the "strange-looking walking-stick" in the hand of the gloomy and threatening dealer in life and death who emerges from the storm (LRM, 213). He seems akin to that dark stranger who, similarly equipped with a strange walking-stick, guided young Goodman Brown on his dark adventure. Before Melville's story is finished, the bullying visitor who here meets unaccustomed resistance will aim his three-tined instrument of protection like a harpoon or lance at the heart of the stubborn and unawed narrator.

The narrator is at first a friendly and gracious host, inviting the stranger in to dry off on the hearth. But the stranger rejects this act of grace, with the admonition "not for worlds!" His conversation is sprinkled with similarly unplayful examples of wordplay—phrases like "For Heaven's sake," "Good Heavens," and "Merciful Heaven" (when it is presumably for man's sake and safety that he tries to ward off the merciless bolts from heaven), verbs like *conjure* and *command*, and such adjectives as *pagan* and *profane*. In appearance the stranger seems an escapee from some gothic tale with his "lean, gloomy figure," his "hair dark and lank, mattedly streaked over his brow," "sunken pitfalls of eyes . . . ringed by indigo halos" (LRM, 213–15). He may be the devil himself, though cloaked in piety, or the agent of a wrathful God, but his gospel is a peculiarly American blend of science and salvation.

He tries to instill fear in the good-humored and self-reliant narrator, but with little success. After refusing the comfort of the hearth himself, he insists that it is the most dangerous spot during a storm because "the heated air and soot are conductors." The walls are also dangerous conductors, so the safest spot is the center of the room. Furthermore "wet clothes are better conductors than the body; and so, if the lightning strikes, it might pass down the wet clothes without touching the body." His spuriously scientific advice is to cringe in wet clothes on a rug in the middle of the room, insulated by attic and cellar. But the greatest safety lies in the protection of his rod. Promising the solid security of a rock of ages, he offers to "make a Gibraltar" out of the mountain cottage, while "Himalayas of concussions" thunder outside. He has references which testify to the number of conversions he has made through fear, and the narrator wonders whether the intentional selection of stormy weather—"an hour peculiarly favorable for producing impressions favorable to your trade"—doesn't make a confidence game out of these conversions (LRM, 215–19).

Not all of the references encourage faith in this seller of protection against the awful acts of God. A steeple bearing one of his rods was blasted by lightning a week before, but the stranger blames a work-

man for faulty installation: "Not my fault, but his." This is an interesting excuse for one who drops so many clues attesting to divinity.
When questioned about a girl in Montreal "struck at her bed-side
with a rosary in her hands," he ostensibly blames the iron, rather
than copper rods, used there; but his tirade seems subtly anti-
Catholic: "Those Canadians are fools," he says. "Some of them knob
the rod at the top, which risks a deadly explosion, instead of imper-
ceptibly carrying down the current into the earth, as this sort of rod
does. *Mine* is the only true rod. Look at it. Only one dollar a foot."
This is a cheap price for salvation, but the excessive jealousy and
wrath at those who choose other rods make the narrator wonder
whether his guest's lack of faith in other rods "might make one dis-
trustful with respect to yourself." Melville seems to be suggesting
that this modern protection racket is an updated selling of indul-
gences, a situation badly in need of reform. Before he finally rejects
the stranger's brand of security based on fearful subservience, the
narrator calls him a Tetzel, that ecclesiastical confidence man whose
notorious abuses helped spark the Reformation (LRM, 216–21).

A stray remark about lightning flashing "from the earth to the
clouds" suddenly inspires the narrator with some kind of perverse
confidence and encouragement. He dismisses the pseudoscientific
explanation offered by the stranger, preferring to believe in the
brave man's response to the bullying forces in the universe—a determined "No! in Thunder," such as Melville attributed to Hawthorne. He now considers all the fearful ploys of the lightning-rod
man as foolish superstitions, and in challenging this representative
of hellfire-and-brimstone evagelism, he questions the idea or concept of god that renders men fearful. He has become one of those
tall men that the stranger says the lightning sometimes "selects" for
its conductor and victim. The lightning-rod man with his hard sell
and his "Sinners in the Hands of an Angry God" tone threatens that
anyone rejecting his word will become "a heap of charred offal, like a
haltered horse burnt in his stall; and all in one flash!" (LRM, 219–20).
But the narrator scornfully risks the danger of natural forces and rejects the self-abasing fear that left so many "burnt-over areas" in
New England and New York, those areas most deeply affected by
the revivalist spirit.

His new confidence does not deny God, nor even the idea of pre-destination, but rather the kind of God who can be bought or bribed by self-abnegation: "The hairs of our heads are numbered, and the days of our lives. In thunder as in sunshine, I stand at ease in the hands of my God. False negotiator, away!" Apparently identifying this unacceptable idea of God with the wrathful God of the Old Testament, he continues: "See, the scroll of the storm is rolled back; the house is unharmed; and in the blue heavens I read in the rainbow, that the Diety will not, of purpose, make war on man's earth" (LRM, 221).

This mood of positive optimism marking the end of "The Lightning-Rod Man" is unique in Melville's short stories. It is a mood that Melville more often treats with irony rather than advocacy. The narrator is confident that his concept of a benevolent force, much like Emerson's Oversoul, constitutes a new and better dispensation. It is a personal revelation that enables him to reject the burden of the past whether in the jealous tyranny of the Old Testament God or the overly zealous, fear-based evangelism of post-Puritan America. It provides him with a sense of dignity, if not quite divinity, as a man, and this the stranger cannot bear. Screaming "Impious wretch!" he springs at the narrator; his protective rod and supporting staff become a "tri-forked thing" with which he can punish the skeptic and "publish your infidel notion"—the same kind of publication provided Lemsford's poems by the authorities in *White-Jacket*, who shot them from a cannon (LRM, 221).

Able to act on his faith, the narrator scornfully asserts his independence and self-reliance by throwing "the dark lightning-king" out of the door along with the fragments of his specimen rod, now a broken and useless shadow of a sceptre. In considerably scaled-down but nevertheless impressive terms, this disarming account of man's smashing the tyrant's sceptre and dispelling the fear of divine retribution deepens the mythological implications even as it suggests some distinctively American theological and political applications. Having freed himself, however, he has not freed mankind, by any means, for the lightning-rod man "still dwells in the land; still travels in storm-time, and drives a brave trade with the fears of man" (LRM, 221). His pitch, presumably, is still effective among those who, easily convinced of their own sinfulness, cower before a God of retribution, hoping that their new convenant with the lightning-rod man will enable them to escape "the lightning of His terrible swift sword" and that their newly installed security system carries a permanent warranty.

"The Apple-Tree Table"

"The Apple-Tree Table" is another overtly comic, covertly defiant story submitted to *Putnam's Monthly*, whose editor and publisher had both written to Melville cautioning him to avoid probable or possible offense to religious sensibilities. The content of "The Apple-Tree Table" put Melville in a familiar bind and evoked the same strategy as in "The Lightning-Rod Man." It was the same predicament he complained of to Hawthorne in that same "Dollars damn me" letter of June, 1851: "What I feel most moved to write, that is banned,—it will not pay. Yet, altogether, write the *other* way I cannot." Melville stated the case accurately, as his subsequent contributions to *Putnam's* bear out. Just as "The Lightning-Rod Man" and "Jimmy Rose" examine aspects of Christianity in more subtle and covert terms than "The Two Temples," "The Apple-Tree Table" is a clever elaboration of the recurrent controversy inside and outside Christianity regarding the existence of the soul and the hope of immortality.

In "The Bell-Tower" Melville used an Italian Renaissance setting to shade his allegory while anatomizing the dilemma of slavery; in "The Lightning-Rod Man" the comic frame of an encounter between an overly aggressive salesman and his surprisingly resistant, would-be victim diverted many readers from the possibility that Melville was satirizing the hard-sell tactics and spurious doctrine of some religious fundamentalists. In "The Apple-Tree Table" he again hides the meaning which might distress or offend some readers behind a facade, or more accurately, within circumstances embodying many of the most familiar elements of that too-familiar genre, the situation comedy, and thereby escapes the ban. The characters include the harassed, well-intentioned father whose occasional tippling is exaggerated into addiction by a domineering wife; a pair of squealing, highly impressionable daughters; and a superstitious servant, whose language-twisting tendencies heighten the caricature of credulity. Given this cast and the stock situation which draws comedy out of the incongruous combination of the eager will to believe and the almost instinctive fear of the supernatural, it is not surprising that most of Melville's readers did not look beneath his tale of a table. They were too diverted by the visual aspects of the story—which verge on slapstick—to note that Melville was calling into question the orthodox Christian belief in the immortality of the soul or the Transcendentalist belief in mystical rebirth. Even Thoreau, who could never be accused of writing to please his audience, concluded *Walden*, his most extended piece of social criticism and individualistic heresy, with the reassuring tale of the "strong and beautiful bug which came out of the dry leaf of an old table of apple-tree wood," a tale projecting the drama of and strengthening man's "faith in a resurrection and immortality." In Melville's view of the same situation, Thoreau's bug becomes, *sotto voce*, Melville's humbug.[3]

Although Melville may have been stimulated to write "The Apple-Tree Table" by Thoreau's anecdote, the germ of the story occurs in Chapter 69 of *Mardi*, published five years before *Walden*. There Yoomy the poet uses the example of butterfly and larva to reinforce his belief that death might be "a birth to be wrought in man"; but Babbalanja the philosopher rejects such an interpretation, insisting that "the analogy has an unsatisfactory end":

> From its chrysalis state the silkworm but becomes a moth that very quickly expires. Its longest existence is as a worm. All vanity, vanity, Yoomy, to seek in Nature for positive warranty to these aspirations of ours. Through all her provinces, Nature seems to promise immortality to life but destruction to beings.

3. The best extended comment on "The Apple-Tree Table" is Frank Davidson's "Melville, Thoreau, and 'The Apple-Tree Table,'" *American Literature*, XXV (January, 1954), 479–89. Davidson discusses the possibility not only that Melville was spurred into using the apple tree story, which he found in a guidebook to the Berkshires, by Thoreau's highly metaphorical use of the same details, but also that the story reflects the development of Melville's religious thought, the table specifically symbolizing Calvinism much as Oliver Wendell Holmes's "The Deacon's Masterpiece" does. While I agree that the story is an imaginative projection of Melville's thoughts on religion, I see the subject as the immortality of the soul rather than religion in general or Calvinism in particular and the table as simply the field wherein specific phenomena give rise to varying hypostheses and conclusions which are really dependent on the viewer's own perspective.

The characters in "The Apple-Tree Table" are members of the same family which figures in "Jimmy Rose" and "I and My Chimney." In each story the father (who in "Jimmy Rose" identifies himself as William Ford) serves as narrator in describing a domestic crisis which turns out to have important social and philosophical overtones. One theme common to all three stories is the conflict between religious mystery and scientific explanation or between that which is sacred through historical and mythical associations and the contemporary, matter-of-fact, utilitarian view which debunks myth and devalues its once-potent symbols.

The mention of the "Fox Girls" in the story is related to this theme and is designed to underscore Melville's meaning by reminding readers of current controversy concerning "Original Spiritual Manifestations." The "Fox Girls," who enjoyed sensational success as spirit rappers in the early 1850s, had begun their spiritualist career in upstate New York in 1848, and achieved international notoriety through discussions of their claims in American and British journals in 1853. In the same year Judge Edmonds of the New York supreme court strongly supported the Fox sisters in a lengthy treatise on spiritualism, adding judicial respectability to the earlier support of such public figures as Horace Greeley. Significantly, Maggie and Katie Fox had begun their mysterious communication by addressing requests to "Mr. Splitfoot," a circumstance that fits neatly with the playful satanism of Melville's satire on spiritualism. Ultimately Katie Fox revealed that they had functioned as a successful pair of confidence women, deceiving thousands of gullible and more than a few skeptical observers. Their talent, she revealed, lay not in communicating with the spirit world through raps but in convincing their audience that the sounds they secretly produced by cracking the joints of their toes were of supernatural origin. The most devoted of their followers, however, were not seriously shaken in their faith, for they insisted that the confession, not the earlier claims, constituted the fraud.[4] They represent a popular vulgarization of what I believe to be Melville's main line of thought in "The Apple-

4. Alice Felt Tyler, *Freedom's Ferment* (Minneapolis: University of Minnesota Press, 1949), 82–83. For more detailed discussion of "The Apple-Tree Table" as a topical satire on spiritualism, see Carolyn L. Karcher, "The Spiritual Lesson of Melville's 'The Apple-Tree Table,'" *American Quarterly*, XXIII (Spring, 1971), 101–109.

Tree Table"—the tension between natural history and supernatural mystery.

Much more to the point is the reference in the opening paragraph to the "ghostly, dismantled old quarto," found in the long-locked garret with the peculiar old table. The book turns out to be Cotton Mather's natural and supernatural miscellanea, *Magnalia Christi Americana*, and the table itself looks as if it "might have belonged to Friar Bacon" (ATT, 409). Both Cotton Mather and Roger Bacon, of course, were men trained in theology and learned in science, who, nevertheless, placed considerable credence in the possibility of other-worldly communication. Melville's audience would no doubt be aware of Mather's obsession with witchcraft; they would be less likely to know that Bacon for a time was under ecclesiastical censure for his alleged interest in the black arts.

The narrator, in several other instances, mentions the name of Democritus, as a means no doubt of suggesting a view of spiritual phenomena more skeptical than that of Bacon or Mather. Democritus not only formulated the first theory of atomic structure of matter and insisted on experimental principles of verification; he also believed in the existence of the soul—but with an important difference. He held that the soul, like the body, was made up of atoms, but that these atoms of soul were physically and functionally different from the normal atoms of matter and structurally intercalated between, say, the normal atoms of heart or brain. Thus man had a soul, but the soul did not survive the death of the body, and life after death was a feeble fable. Through these historical allusions Melville establishes the ideological poles of his argument, without stating it explicitly and thereby marring the mood of a very funny story.

To maintain this surface mood of comedy, a mood very much akin to Washington Irving's playful use of gothic elements in stories with submerged social and political reference, Melville sets his story in the dusty and disused, reportedly haunted garret "of a very old house in an old-fashioned quarter of one of the oldest towns in America" (ATT, 409). (One more degree of antiquity would have pushed the setting back to Europe, but Melville must have felt that the Puritan past, supported by a few medieval references, was far enough). The narrator is a genial, pragmatic man, who although he considers the rumor of supernatural activity in the house absurd, does nothing to contradict it—in fact, the effect of the rumor was to lower his purchase price. Now after five years of occupancy, he has found the key and can explore the haunted garret.

The very atmosphere of the insect-ridden garret reinforces the story thematically, but not without a degree of mockery, for the narrator's experience there strongly suggests the reality of resurrection from the grave, whereas the later developments seem to challenge this belief and to equate the faith based on symbolic analogies, on correspondences, with wishful thinking. Proceeding toward the sole source of light, the narrator makes his way up "something like a Gothic pulpit-stairway, leading to a pulpit-like platform, from which a still narrower ladder—a sort of Jacob's ladder—led some ways higher to the lofty scuttle," from which the light came through a small pane of glass. The area is infested with scurrying and flying life and the dead husks of past life. It is unmistakably suggestive of mortality: "Indeed, the whole stairs, and platform, and ladder, were festooned, and carpeted, and canopied with cobwebs; which in funereal accumulations, hung, too, from the groined, murky ceiling, like the Carolina moss in the cypress forest. In these cobwebs swung, as in aerial catacombs, myriads of all tribes of mummied insects." Breaking open this scuttle, the narrator thrusts his head through to the open air and reports his exultation in the poetic formulae of rebirth: "As from the gloom of the grave and the companionship of worms, man shall at last rapturously rise into the living greenness and glory immortal" (ATT, 410–11). This is the hopeful hypothesis which underlies the story and which is quietly but definitely dispelled at the end.

Although he has identified himself as one who does not yield to rumors of supernatural phenomena, the narrator has quite opposite associations when he examines the assortment of furniture in the garret. An old desk, obviously a haven for mice, exudes "subterranean squeakings," some old, elaborately carved chairs "seemed fit to seat a conclave of conjurors." A lidless old chest contains a stack of mildewing documents, "one of which . . . looked as if it might have been the original bond that Doctor Faust gave to Mephistopheles." This last allusion reminds us not only of the value of man's immortal soul, but also of the dark, romantic view of the character and source of science—a point which is further emphasized by the next reference to "a broken telescope, and a celestial globe staved in." In addition to bearing the moldy copy of Cotton Mather's *Magnalia*, the table itself stands on "three cloven feet" (ATT, 412). Despite all these unpromising associations, the narrator sees its possible usefulness as a breakfast and tea table, a gaming table, and a reading table, and so moves it from its exile in the attic to a more prominent spot in the parlor.

At a turn of the stairs, carrying the table with its hinged top flat against his chest and concealing him from anyone below, the narrator unknowingly nudges his daughter Julia, who, turning to see who has taken such liberties, sees not her father, but one cobweb-covered, cloven hoof thrust out of the darkness. She screams in terror: this bit of slapstick sets off the situation comedy. Both sisters shun the table, or are ill at ease when induced to sit at it for breakfast or tea, after it has been refinished and installed in the parlor. Julia, in particular, continues to avoid looking at the base of the table. To their mother, such superstitious behavior is worse than folly; it is weakness, and she feels it her maternal duty to eliminate it.

The narrator, meanwhile, has taken to reading Cotton Mather while seated at the table on long winter evenings. In the course of what is obviously a satire on ghost stories and gothic tales, he frightens himself by imagining the possible supernatural import of every late night sight and sound, much like Ichabod Crane who had used the same guidebook. When he tells his wife of the strange ticking sound emanating from the table in the parlor, she blames the dram he has downed. Resolved the next morning "to put Cotton Mather permanently aside," he bathes vigorously, as if to wash off the morbidity, and descends to breakfast (ATT, 418). Instead of a pleasant Sunday morning breakfast, he finds his daughters distraught and insisting that the table has been repossessed, as it were, by spirits, and his wife rummaging through the carpet under the table in search of the source of the sound. Investigation of the carpet and the flooring beneath produces nothing, but in the meantime Biddy, the Irish maid, has removed the table to the farthest corner of the woodshed.

For comic purposes much of the focus now shifts to Biddy, whose overreactions to circumstances hinting at the supernatural remind us of the similarly stereotyped role of the Irish immigrant in mid–nineteenth-century popular fiction and that of the frightened and fanciful Negro in Hollywood films of a generation ago. The threat of the table is enough to cause Biddy to don hat and shawl and ask for her wages. Bullied by her no-nonsense mistress into staying, she calls upon the "Holy Vargin" to protect her from spirits. After another round of humorous exchange involving all members of the family, the narrator decides to stay awake after the others have retired—thus following the example of Democritus, who, threatened by supposedly ghostly noises as he studied in the silence of the tombs, "affirmed them a humbug, unworthy the least attention." True to his model, he manages on this night, though after considerable trepidation, to solve the mystery. The ticking proves to be the sound of an insect hatched from an egg long ago laid in the wood of tree from which the table was made, and now, warmed by the fire and the urn so often upon it, the insect struggles to emerge from the varnished wood. When it does, the narrator has the presence of mind to clap a tumbler over it, while indulging in the kind of irreverent wordplay that runs through the story: "Now, for the soul of me, I could not . . . comprehend the phenomenon. A live bug come out of a dead table?" But the next scene is again Biddy's, for befitting her stock role, she comes upon the tumbler while cleaning the room, sees within it what she calls "a 'bomnable bug," and consigns this lowly symbol of highest possibility to the flames (ATT, 420–27).

More low comedy follows as the girls react excessively to the idea of there having been a bug in one of "our tumblers," and the wife chides her husband severely for having brought a bug into the house. When the ticking resumes, the enlightened wife wants to rub the table with roach powder, but prevented from doing it, she manages to close the existing hole with cement. But there is obviously a second miracle about to occur, and the narrator continues his vigil through part of the night, all the next day, and into the night again, accompanied now by wife and daughters who want to witness the happening. Still following the situation comedy formula, the girls scream when a popping sound comes from under the table, but their mother matter-of-factly tells them that it is only cider bottles popping in the cellar, a spirituous rather than a spiritual phenomenon. As the others drop off to sleep, the narrator takes scientific-sounding notes, such as "Four o'clock. No sign of the bug. Ticking regular, but not spirited." All but the eminently rational wife scream and cower when there is a sharp rapping at the door, and she again has to reassure them—only the baker bringing the bread (ATT, 426–32).

An instant later they discover that the great event they have been watching for is occurring. All of them, the two flighty daughters included, are charmed by the emergence of the radiantly beautiful bug. Deciding to seek the advice of someone better informed than his family, the narrator takes his wife's suggestion to consult Professor Johnson, the naturalist, rather than follow Julia's urging to bring in Madame Pazzi, the conjuress. The learned man will not grant Julia's insistence that spirits are responsible for this rebirth. His prosy and unexciting explanation treats the incident as interesting but not unique. The eggs had been "laid inside the bark of the living tree" and then lain dormant and insulated for years, as the tree continued to grow. By his computation the egg lay in the tree some ninety years and in the tabletop for about eighty years (ATT, 434). (The total then given is one hundred and fifty years, with no way of telling whether the error was inadvertent or intended to cast doubt on the care and accuracy of Professor Johnson).

Apparently defeated in her attempt to verify the supernatural character of this marvelous resurrection, Julia, nevertheless, attaches a spiritual meaning to the incident, seeing in it an analogy (as did Yoomy as well as Thoreau) promising a "glorified resurrection for the spirit of man." The transcendental message she has read in the event has strengthened her belief in the spirit world but made it more benign: "I still believe in spirits, only now I believe in them with delight, when before I thought of them with terror" (ATT, 435). She has managed to turn the naturalist's crushing assembly of fact into a transcendental triumph over the fear of evil and the unknown.

Frank Davidson, in his analysis of "The Apple-Tree Table," contends that Melville's ending is inconclusive, that neither author nor narrator takes a stand on the religious controversy represented in the story. While it is true that the man of science is not attractively presented in his coldness and insensitivity, it seems obvious that Julia's version of the events is far too fanciful—especially when we discover that this marvelously reborn creature "did not long enjoy its radiant life; it expired the next day" (ATT, 435). Babbalanja's view is still Melville's last word on the subject.

Slightly more conclusive than the intentionally understated account of the bug's brief life is the final comparison between the two spots of sealing wax which mark the holes made by the two bugs in the tabletop and the two markings which indicate "the spots where the cannon balls struck Brattle Street Church" (ATT, 435). Consistent with his view that Melville meant the table to symbolize Calvinism, Davidson finds it important that the Brattle Street Church was the first to break with the orthodoxy of the Mathers and foster more liberal tendencies. While I find this suggestion quite plausible, I cannot overlook the fact that the cannon balls struck and damaged a structure as closely identified with Christianity in general as with Calvinism in particular; undoubtedly, the scars on the church mark a degree of hostility to doctrine. By implication it seems that the similar scars in the table, while they were not externally inflicted, also mark a degree of hostility to widely held doctrine, specifically toward ideas of rebirth and the immortality of the soul.

Far more readily than Thoreau, Melville saw the comic absurdity of documenting immortality with an anecdote of entomological entombment. Melville's story seems to suggest that to force a correspondence between the birth of a bug and the emergence of the soul is sentimental at best and silly at worst. Although he might have been influenced by Thoreau's use of this event, Melville's mood seems much closer to that of Democritus who, working in the cool and quiet of the tombs, decided that ghostly fears and spiritual promises were based on the kind of pranks that people play on themselves or on others.

"Jimmy Rose"

If "The Apple-Tree Table" can be interpreted as a comic expression of Melville's skeptical attitude toward immortality, "Jimmy Rose" shows Melville at the opposite end of his arc, full of sadness and regret that the promise of immortality or of spiritual rebirth cannot more effectively survive in mid–nineteenth-century America. It is a sentiment he recorded quite pointedly in his journal of the trip he took to Europe and the Middle East in late 1856 and early 1857, shortly after completion of *The Piazza Tales*: "Heartily wish Niebuhr and Strauss to the dogs—The deuce take their penetration and acumen. They have robbed us of the bloom. If they have undeceived anyone—no thanks to them." [5] Directed at two of the historians who took a "scientific" approach to religious history and fashioned what was known as the Higher Criticism, Melville's curse could stand as epigraph to "Jimmy Rose."

Compared to most of Melville's stories, "Jimmy Rose" has suffered from relative neglect; no one seems to have felt that it was particularly significant in regard to theme or technique. To R. H. Fogle, Jimmy Rose was one of several minor studies in failure, a watered-down Job scorned by God and man. R. W. B. Lewis guardedly ventured that "'Jimmy Rose' may be not much more than an anecdote." James W. Gargano saw "Jimmy Rose" as the story of a man who lived by false standards, rejected self-knowledge, and continued to falsify reality. Conversely, Ralph M. Tutt viewed "Jimmy Rose" as the story of a displaced aristocrat, perhaps a conservative southerner who cannot maintain his accustomed status in the shifting currents of northern society, but a man who has maintained his identity and integrity at the risk of being thought an eccentric. In his final sentence, however, Tutt suggests that Melville's purpose was not to engender sympathy for Jimmy Rose *per se*, but to expose the "obtuseness of a society oriented primarily to material values" and re-

---

5. Herman Melville, *Journal up the Straits, October 11, 1856–May 5, 1857*, ed. R. M. Weaver (New York: The Colophon, 1935), 107–108. The references are to Barthold Georg Niebuhr and David Friedrich Strauss.

veal a "tragic flaw in the American character."[6] I think that this is
the direction in which further interpretation of the story must move.

Not that any of the aforementioned interpretations of "Jimmy
Rose" is invalid, but they are all, in one way or another, partial read-
ings and do not adequately recognize the degree to which this story,
like most of Melville's short fiction, presents a continuing examination and objectification of crucial aspects of the American character
and American society. In almost every case these stories grow out of
Melville's response to the unsettled, and unsettling, conditions of
America in the middle of the nineteenth century.

How does "Jimmy Rose" illustrate this principle? Clearly it is
about the rapidity of social change which can quite suddenly remove
a man from his customary and presumably secure place in his community, or more slowly, but no less completely, turn once-hallowed
institutions and the values they represent into hollow mockeries. On
the one hand, "Jimmy Rose," as an expression of resistance to muta-
bility, is kin to the resurrected but socially dislocated Rip Van
Winkle who must in an instant adjust to the new iconography of democracy wherein George Washington has replaced George III (St.
George having long ago had his day). On the other hand, the fallen
businessman whose worldly empire had "burst"—a "clean smash"—
is as closely identified with his particular edifice as Poe's Roderick
Usher was with his cracked and crumbling mansion (JR, 246). His financial crack-up and the cruel rebuffs which follow it might have
driven a lesser man than Jimmy Rose to madness or suicide, but he
survives and apparently adjusts to the humiliating and servile role
he must assume in order to be tolerated by the people who have enjoyed his grace and hospitality on innumerable occasions. It is in the
changes wrought in Jimmy Rose, in the architectural and ornamental
modifications and transformations of his house, and in the specific
vocabulary and general character of the narrator that Melville's
meaning resides.

6. Richard Harter Fogle, *Melville's Shorter Tales* (Norman: University of Oklahoma Press,
1960) 61–62; R. W. B. Lewis, *Herman Melville* (New York: Dell, 1962), 17; James W. Gargano, "Melville's 'Jimmy Rose,'" *Western Humanities Review*, XVI (Summer, 1962), 276–80;
Ralph M. Tutt, "'Jimmy Rose'—Melville's Displaced Noble," *Emerson Society Quarterly*, No.
33 (1963), 28–32.

Melville introduces us to the dominant theme of the story in the opening paragraphs, well in advance of our acquaintance with Jimmy Rose himself; and in these passages describing the "great old house," the narrator makes known his own character, tastes, and values. This narrator is as important to the meaning of the story as the lawyer–narrator is in "Bartleby," and the house of Jimmy Rose is as important a setting as the Wall Street law office in "Bartleby." Just as the conservative and initially complacent narrator in "Bartleby" explains that we first must know him, his business, and his general surroundings before we can understand the chief character in the story, the well-to-do William Ford, who is our only source of information about Jimmy Rose, proceeds in the same way and concludes with a similar prayer-like injunction that links the once-proud but now-forlorn Jimmy Rose with the rueful condition of humanity.

The house, then, is Melville's first focus. It stands in "one of the lower wards, once the haunt of style and fashion, full of gay parlors and bridal chambers; but now, for the most part, transformed into counting rooms and warehouses." This process of social change is not merely a matter of commercial and utilitarian interests pushing out the earlier qualities of tasteful leisure and refinement. When "bales and boxes usurp the place of sofas" and "daybooks and ledgers are spread where once the breakfast toast was buttered," we sense the threat to gay dalliance and pleasant domesticity alike (JR, 241).

Although the "lower ward" has changed drastically, the house has resisted change and seems a monument to departed days, recalling ruined English abbeys or "the ancient tombs of Templars." But it has not been impervious to the passage of time, and there are modifications in its exterior and decay in its interior decoration, though the massive substructure remains remarkably sound. Since the supporting timbers are so substantial as to make a walk in the ample cellars seem "much like walking along a line-of-battle ship's deck," we can be reasonably sure that some kind of world in itself, some large human organization or institution is being suggested here (JR, 242). But which one?

The exterior changes suggest an answer, and the interior decoration ascertains it. Removed from the outside was "a fine old pulpit-

like porch crowning the summit of six lofty steps, and set off with a
broad-brimmed sounding-board overshadowing the whole." The
suggestion, of course, is of a church from which pronouncements
could be made with authority and impunity. Also removed and replaced with more modern Venetian blinds were "the original heavy
window-shutters (each pierced with a crescent in the upper panel to
admit an Oriental and moony light of a sultry morning in July)" (JR,
242). This could be a realistically observed architectural detail in old
New York houses, or it could be also symbolic amplification and reinforcement of the change undergone by the church in America.
Melville's interest in comparative religion could easily have suggested the crescent shape and the moony light as a symbol antitheti-
cal to the practical and empirical mood of enlightened America.[7] As
explained by Sir James G. Frazer, some Egyptians identified the
moon with Osiris, whose enemy was the sun, "because the moon,
with her humid and generative light, is favorable to the propagation
of animals and the growth of plants; while the sun with his fierce fire
scorches and burns up all growing things, renders the greater part of
the earth uninhabitable by reason of his blaze, and often overpowers
the moon herself."[8] Since the narrator also comments on the rich
antique color of the massive timbers, suggesting to him an Indian
origin, the oriental references are, perhaps, more than casual; and
quite noticeable but somewhat puzzling and inaccessible inside the
house are carvings "of queer horticultural and zoological devices"
(JR, 242). Melville seems to be setting the stage for the appearance
of an ancient fertility god in the most unlikely circumstances, but it
is still too early to jump to conclusions about the role or identity of
Jimmy Rose.

One reason the narrator is so fond of the house, which he unexpectedly but appropriately falls heir to, is its age. It is ninety
years old. Let us suppose that the story takes place about 1850; that
would date the house around 1760, an artifact of the colonial or pre-
Revolutionary past. So, in a sense, is the narrator. He still discusses

---

7. H. Bruce Franklin in *The Wake of the Gods: Melville's Mythology* (Stanford, Calif.:
Stanford University Press, 1963) discusses the remarkably ample materials in comparative religion and mythology known to Melville and the uses he made of this information.

8. James G. Frazer, *The Golden Bough* (12 vols.; London, 1955), VI, 129.

financial matters in shillings and pounds and, even more revealingly, admits his fears that his wife is too young for him. (She wanted to destroy the aging and democratically inappropriate decor in the house.) The narrator is distinctly French in his tastes and outlook, his family and their servant girl no less distinctly American. But significantly he is not Jacobin French, but definitely *ancien régime* in his values. Part of his own attachment to the house stems from his feeling that "the graft of modernness had not taken in its ancient stock," and part from the suggestion of French aristocratic values in the decor. The covering of the walls "preserved the patterns of the times of Louis XVI"; the paper "could only have come from Paris—genuine Versailles paper—the sort of paper that might have hung in Marie Antoinette's boudoir." The gaudy illustrations included "the most imposing Parisian-looking birds: parrots, macaws, and peacocks, but mostly peacocks. Real Prince Esterhazys of birds: all rubies, diamonds, and Orders of the Golden Fleece." He makes a point of his preference for the word *parlor*, for which his daughters substitute *drawing-room*; even his vocabulary reveals his identification with French refinement rather than American bluntness. The residents of the house before Mr. Ford inherited it had used the grand parlor of the peacocks for vulgar, utilitarian purposes—keeping their fuel and drying their clothes there—and did nothing to keep leaks from marring the "princely plumage" of these noble birds. For this reason he terms them "irreverent tenants," linking them with the despoilers of shrines and enemies of tradition. When his wife and daughters want to replace the grandeur of the peacocks, "to destroy the whole hen-roost, as Biddy called it," with "nice, genteel, cream-colored paper," the narrator is adamant and will "permit no violation of the old parlor" (JR, 242–44). Oriented toward European concepts of quality and value, this narrator is fighting a quiet crusade against the infidel threats of change; he is engaged in a kind of rearguard action against what America is coming to mean.

Even more central to the story than the gaudy peacocks of the French court are the "massive festoons of roses" on the walls, which make the parlor seem an arbored garden. To the narrator the roses suggest the original owner, "the gentle Jimmy Rose," whose "princely business" enabled him to live in a style appropriate to the magnificence of the house. But again Biddy's judgment on this bit of decor underscores the lack of respect that the New World holds for the Old. She may have been only a servant, but she was irrepressibly American in not knowing her place and daring to say that these fading symbols of courtly refinement were *onions* (JR, 243). And her vernacular denigration of this anomalous grandeur in mid–nineteenth-century America ("a hen-roost with onions"—Huck Finn could hardly have stressed more effectively the discrepancy between the world of the cultivated ideal and that of hard-nosed fact) sums up the experience of the unfortunate Jimmy Rose too.

Since Melville apparently tried to suggest that the house was not only a monument to leisure and opulence but an ancient and hallowed institution preserving religious, military, and class distinctions, the rose becomes a very fortunate and evocative means of relating the house and its most memorable inhabitant. It has been a crucial symbol in Christianity and the imaginative literature linked to Christianity, but its symbolic function long antedates Christianity. Its meaning in mythology was as important, if not more important to Melville's purposes, I suspect, than its Christian symbolism. But let me suggest a matter of scholarly curiosity that coincides remarkably in time and temper with Melville's story before turning to the mythological ramifications.

The passage from Melville's *Journal up the Straits* damning Niebuhr and Strauss indicates his awareness of the historians who were looking dispassionately at the life of Jesus and the origins of Christianity. To Melville this belated phase of the Enlightenment was a costly addition to knowledge, for in their scientific approach to matters of sacred mystery, "they have robbed us of the bloom." To make the life of Jesus the subject of historical research is to treat the supernatural as an eminently natural occurrence. Biddy had no faith in transcendental symbols, and she saw onions in a hen-roost. So did contemporary biblical scholars. Much controversy over whether the text of the Authorized Version of the Bible was correctly translated from Greek preceded the publication in 1855 of the Revised Version of the Bible. In this latest version the Hebrew word *habasseleth*, originally translated as "rose" was reinterpreted as the Arab *basal* or "onion."[9] Here again is that fall from splendor, the Rose of Sharon become a homely onion.

The symbolism of the rose—its origins and its uses in modern British literature—has been discussed by Barbara Seward. She feels that "the great resurgence of symbolism during the romantic era [particularly of rose symbolism] has been in large part the complicated result of a diminishing faith in measurable values, a reaction against rational and positivist attitudes, and a need to find transcendental outlets for man's baffled emotional and spiritual desires."[10] Although she is thinking of English Romantics, Miss Seward's statement well applies to Melville also. (We might remember his exclamation to Hawthorne in that famous letter of June, 1851. After expressing admiration for "Ethan Brand," Hawthorne's own parable about the destructive fires of change and the sad legacy of the Enlightened intellect, Melville confessed, "I stand for the heart. To the dogs with the head. I had rather be a fool with a heart than Jupiter Olympus with his head.") More specifically, Miss Seward continues, "The ubiquitous rose . . . for the nineteenth century . . . became the symbol of a multiplicity of subjective values that might redeem the sensitive individual in a presumably insensate world; for the twentieth century it has become the symbol of any and all affirmative values that might redeem the insensate world itself."[11] Jimmy Rose, at midcentury, apparently has the first effect on the sensitive and somewhat dislocated and backward-looking narrator, but even he despairs that Jimmy, a partial redeemer (who at the end may not have redeemed himself), could have any effect on the mechanism, the materialism, or the utilitarianism of the insensate "lower ward," which is in terms of meaning and value a reduction of mid–nineteenth-century America.

Jimmy Rose is an anomaly in this practical, no-nonsense, progressive America. In his prime he was a handsome, healthy, manly, gentle, and gracious person, "by nature a great ladies' man, and like most deep adorers of the sex, never tied up his freedom of general worship by making one willful sacrifice of himself at the altar" (JR,

9. James Hastings, *A Dictionary of the Bible* (New York: Scribner, 1909), 313.
10. Barbara Seward, *The Symbolic Rose* (New York: Columbia University Press, 1960), 5.

244). And so too, our pre-Christian mythologies tell us, were Adonis, Osiris, and Dionysius, all of whom were associated with the rose and annual rituals of resurrection.[12] It was in a different but not totally unrelated sense, of course, that women sought the body of Christ, and again the symbolic promise of the rose triumphs over the pain of the thorns. In his next sentence, Melville compares Jimmy Rose to Cosimo de' Medici, that monumental figure of the Florentine Renaissance—ostensibly to describe the grand style in which Jimmy entertained but also to remind us subtly of the idea of floral rebirth, so it does not seem unlikely that Melville wanted us to see Jimmy Rose as a figure larger than life and deeply rooted in the timeless spiritual experience of mankind. But Jimmy did not survive unchanged in the transplant to American soil.

The American Jimmy Rose is a citizen of an enlightened republic affirming the equality of men, with presumably no place in its social arrangement for so dubious a being as an aristocrat, much less a demigod. As long as Jimmy has a fortune to draw upon and a penchant for lavish entertainment, he has admiring friends and undeniable status in society. His services are much in demand, like those of a minister of an upper-class church, to add the proper tone and flourish on numerous public occasions; and the words of praise and blessing come readily to his lips—perhaps too readily, for after Jimmy had fulsomely presented a brace of pistols to a successful gen-

11. *Ibid.*

12. Since Miss Seward's introductory chapter presents what she found in Frazer's works and other sources of information about classical mythology and literature, it is very convenient to use her summary to document the connection between the rose and ideas of fertility and rebirth, ideas which she suggests produce "associations with love, beauty, life, joy, creation, and eternity" (6). Miss Seward cites the belief that the red rose sprang from the blood of the slain Adonis, whose retreat to the underworld and seasonal emergence marked the renewal of vegetation (8).Others associate the rose only indirectly with Adonis (whose flower is the anemone); rather, they cite its origin in Aphrodite's having scratched herself and bled on a white rose in her haste to get to Adonis, who had been rent and slain by a wild boar—but the rose still signifies love, loss, and the hopeful promise of rebirth. In the case of Osiris, the lotus or rose was linked again with love and the generative principle, for it was the flower sacred to Isis, the feminine agent in this life cycle (10–11). With Dionysius the rose takes on additional meanings of natural passion and ecstasy, as well as fecundity, and "could be linked with Aphrodite's as the flower of a compound joy that encompassed wine, love, beauty, song, spring, and youth" (14). In its Christian transmutation, of course, the rose lost much of its sensual emphasis and became more specifically a symbol of spiritual love and of martyrdom linked to both Christ and the Virgin; nevertheless, it could also continue to express sensual aspects as in courtly love and *carpe diem.*

eral, the narrator seems momentarily critical. However, the speaker is Melville, who for the moment has put his sentiments into the narrator's words: "Ah, Jimmy, Jimmy! Thou didst excel in compliments. But it was inwrought with thy inmost texture to be affluent in all things which give pleasure. And who shall reproach thee with borrowed wit on this occasion . . . ? Plagiarize otherwise as they may, not often are the men of this world plagiarists in praise" (JR, 245). We are reminded not only of Jimmy as a source of all pleasurable things but also of the degree to which he would repeat the sentiments the crowd wanted to hear and honor even the specialists in slaughter. He was a plagiarist in the sense that Bartleby, who refused to copy at his employer's command, was not. In seeking to please his audience, Jimmy was untrue to himself, and to this degree, responisble for his subsequent fall, his bankruptcy of the spirit.

It is significant that this crowd which enjoyed Jimmy's fine feasts appreciated them on the level of the senses and never as ceremony. Yet the description of Jimmy's unsurpassed hospitality cuts a little deeper, combining the qualities of a good host in the social sense with those of the Host in the ecclesiastical sense: "His uncommon cheeriness; the splendor of his dress; his sparkling wit; radiant chandeliers; infinite fund of small talk; French furniture; glowing welcomes to his guests; his bounteous heart and board; his noble graces and his glorious wine; what wonder if all these drew crowds to Jimmy's hospitable abode?" What is suggested by this combination of cheer, splendor, radiance, infinity (but of small talk!), generous heart, "noble graces," and "glorious wine" is further emphasized by the toast offered "by a brocaded lady": "Our noble host; the bloom on his cheek, may it last long as the bloom in his heart!" The assembled guests toss down this toast "gaily and frankly," and Jimmy, proud and grateful, also drinks in the scene, "angelically glancing round at the sparkling faces, and equally sparkling, and equally feeling, decanters" (JR, 244–45). This last puzzling reference to the "equally sparkling, and equally feeling, decanters" is, I suppose, bitter irony, since we do know that the guests sparkle at the entertainment without realizing that there was once a deeper reason for such revelry, and that the decanters of "glorious wine" were once true vessels of feeling and of glory. The merry faces and the fine crystal

decanters, both divested of understanding, feeling, or spiritual significance, and the crowd-pleasing source of these entertainments,
the too easily satisfied Jimmy Rose, all give reason for Melville's
damning Niebuhr and Strauss: "They have robbed us of the bloom."
It seems clear from this story, however, that the Higher Criticism is
simply a scholarly exemplification of values that thoroughly permeate "the lower wards."

At this point in the story, the narrator recites for the first time the
refrain which is repeated thrice more in the remaining pages: "Ah!
poor, poor Jimmy—God guard us all—poor Jimmy Rose!" These
words are the only indication that the narrator has penetrated any
distance at all into the mystery of Jimmy Rose, for this refrain serves
as his Rosary as he passes along the episodes of the story as if they
were beads.[13]

In a sense, then, Jimmy Rose had descended considerably from
glory and splendor, even before everyone learned of his bankruptcy,
a smash due to the loss of two vessels bearing imports from China.
Again, I suppose, Melville means for his not-very-perceptive narrator to tell us that the original sources of Jimmy's wealth and
importance—the religions of the Orient—no longer provided the
goods. The narrator gets the news from one of Jimmy's many adoring
guests (the first to have drunk to the aforementioned toast at Jimmy's
last supper), who laments that they will no longer share that "rare
wine Jimmy gave us the other night." "Jimmy's burst," he continues,
"Clean smash, I assure you," but this man's loss is momentary, for
he invites the narrator to split a bottle of claret and spend a merry
evening at "Cato's" (JR, 246). Ironically, again, there is a reminder

---

13. Melville has in other places, such as *Billy Budd* and "After the Pleasure Party," used
the same constellation of images, associating *bud, bloom, rose, bead,* and *Rosary,* the terms
having varying natural and supernatural intensity. Several other Melville poems clearly associate the rose with Christian symbolism, such as these lines from a short lyric entitled "Without
Price": "Thy meat shall turn to roses red, / Thy bread to roses white." Another poem "The
Avatar" also strengthens the plausibility of my suggestions concerning "Jimmy Rose" as an
abortive avatar or a failed Christ:

> Bloom or repute for graft or seed
> In flowers the flower gods never heed,
> The Rose-God once came down and took
> Form in a rose? Nay, but indeed
> The meeker form and humbler look
> Of Sweet-Briar, a wilding weed.

of the essential meaninglessness of modern society where a Stoic philosopher and Dante's guide through Purgatory can run a place of pleasure, just as the "Socrates" in "The Paradise of Bachelors" dispensed the comforting means of clouding one's mind.

Following his smash, Jimmy, now abandoned by his old friends or fleeing their open hostility, retreats into an old, untenanted, tomblike house, which was one of his properties. Shunning all men, even threatening the narrator who comes in sympathy, Jimmy goes underground and emerges much later a transformed man. When the narrator next meets him, twenty-five years later, he is a shell of his former self, but "the old Persian roses bloomed in his cheeks." Jimmy, who had been a lord among men and referred to as "master," is now a pauper, and despite attempts to conceal his threadbare condition, he seems to fool no one. The narrator suggests that Jimmy had been half-mad during his retreat and explains his reemergence by suggesting "it at last seemed irreligious to Jimmy even to shun mankind" (JR, 248–49).

But Jimmy now depends on the hospitality of others, and it is meager in contrast to his own formerly prodigious grace and hospitality. The tea and toast that he hopes awaits him at the home of some old acquaintance (Jimmy is apparently most successful in his ill-concealed begging on Sundays) is a mockery of the wine and venison which Jimmy had so often provided, a parody of the comradeship and the communion of his former state. Worst of all, Jimmy must further demean himself in his beggary: he smiles perpetually. By whatever means, real or artificial ("no son of man might tell"), he maintains the roses in his cheeks; he keeps up with current trivia to renew his fund of small talk; and his extravagant compliments are his own alms for the rich (JR, 250–52). Whether or not Melville knew that the rose, from its earlier association with Aphrodite or Venus, came to be a mark of the prostitute, this is what Jimmy has become.[14]

In a way Jimmy resembles Ezra Pound's image of the artist brought to his knees by a crass and unconcerned society in "Hugh Selwyn Mauberly." Pound's poet provides "an image of the age's ac-

---

14. Melville, was, of course, familiar with Hawthorne's *Scarlet Letter*, in which the rose symbolism is of major importance, ranging from its transcendental message of individual renewal in nature to its Puritan association with sexual license.

celerated grimace" and is forced into falsehood and degeneracy, as
"Christ follows Dionysus" and "Caliban casts out Ariel." In a stanza
that comes very close to what Melville was suggesting in Jimmy
Rose's guests' superficial savoring of the venison and gross consumption of "rare wine," Pound points to the commercial exploitation of
spiritually evocative and religiously significant symbols:

> Faun's flesh is not to us
> Nor the saint's vision.
> We have the Press for wafer,
> Franchise for circumcision.

Jimmy Rose is both symptom and victim of the time's malady. He
was somewhat short of fulfilling his godlike potentialities before his
financial fall; he seems like the dregs of his former self, drained of his
dignity, radiance, and glory, after he emerges from his tomblike
house. The bloom and its promise are deceptive. His cheeks are
painted promises, and none knows it better than Jimmy. His last act,
as soon as the gentle girl nursing him in his illness leaves his attic, is
to hurl the books she has brought as far away as he can, muttering,
"Why will she bring me this sad old stuff? Does she take me for a
pauper? Thinks she to salve a gentleman's heart with Poor Man's
Plaster?" (JR, 253). Now, this "Poor Man's Plaster" consists of the
books "sent by serious-minded well-wishers to invalids in a serious
crisis," no doubt books of religious encouragement, sources of faith,
promises of the Kingdom of Heaven. And Jimmy rejects them as
worthless. He has finally been robbed of his bloom, but he faces the
unpleasant truth honestly, if bitterly. A type of Christ and an heir to
the mysteries of the East, Jimmy at the end can find no cheer, man-
age no smile, and muster no faith. He is only a disillusioned man
whose painted allure, grand gestures, and beautiful phrases of praise
have become shallow appearance at best, the soul of hypocrisy at
worst. "Poor, poor Jimmy—God guard us all—poor Jimmy Rose!"
So remote was Jimmy Rose, even at his best from his original role or
identity, and so distant is the Christian church from its original
meaning, that this seems a far more pessimistic story than most
readers have realized.

If I have perhaps overemphasized Melville's symbolic techniques in this analysis, let us not forget that they were for him a means to an end. In this case his end was an appraisal of Christianity—its character, concerns, and contributions—in America. If I read "Jimmy Rose" correctly, Melville found it too often servile, self-seeking, and backward-looking, barely tolerated by an increasingly materialistic and mechanistic society which begrudged even its feeble support. And yet he mourned its passing, for Christianity and the church offered one of the few opportunities for contact, however sporadic or diluted, with the glory and terror of metaphysical mystery. To lose any institution which countered the onslaught of scientific materialism was to lose part of the essential vitality and hope that fed the imagination. For the church to prostitute its principles to please society was bad enough; that it had to do so in order to survive in a society permeated by a utilitarian ethic was worse. Faced with the difficult task of telling so unpleasant a truth, Melville chose to hide it in symbol and suggestion, even from the narrator himself. Of Melville himself, it seems safe to say that, like the narrator's lament for the fallen Jimmy Rose, he fervently wished it were otherwise.

6

⊚⊚⊚

ILLUSORY FAILURES
AND THE FAILURE OF
ILLUSION

"The Fiddler"

Both "The Fiddler" and "The Happy Failure" seem, on the surface at least, to praise the abandonment of ambition and to advocate accommodation to human limitations. Both stories further seem to imply the folly of seeking fame and the wisdom of achieving a balanced and realistic view of the world and oneself. Because two of the three characters in "The Fiddler" are versions of the artist, there is even more of a temptation than in "The Happy Failure" to read the story as fictionalized autobiography, equating the poet–narrator, depressed by the damning criticism of his latest effort, with Melville himself, still stung by the unenthusiastic reception of *Pierre*, and even suggesting that the artist–musician, who has made his peace with a fickle public and feels no need to torment himself, represents what Melville's family would have liked him to be. Quite uniformly the few critics who have found the story worth more than a contemptuous or apologetic comment have seen Helmstone, the narrator, as Melville's own self-caricature and Hautboy, the fiddler, as the artist who has come back from defeat.[1]

1. Richard Chase, *Herman Melville: A Critical Study* (New York: Macmillan, 1949), 173–75; Edward H. Rosenberry, *Melville and the Comic Spirit* (Cambridge: Harvard University Press, 1955), 144–45; Richard Harter Fogle, *Melville's Shorter Tales* (Norman: University of Oklahoma Press, 1960), 59–61; and W. R. Thompson, "Melville's 'The Fiddler': A Study in Dissolution," *Texas Studies in Literature and Language*, II (Winter, 1961), 492–500. Thompson's is the only extensive analysis of "The Fiddler," and to his credit he sees Hautboy not as an example of the artist's triumph over adversity but of the artist's capitulation and surrender to society.

Such an interpretation, however, ignores much of the tone of the story and deals only partially with the imagery. Just as "The Happy Failure" contains elements that challenge the surface moral of the story and just as Jimmy Rose's resurrection is extremely equivocal, the amiable, gracious, cheerful fiddler of Melville's story may be fashioning a dirge as he dashes off his carefree, easy pieces.

There are only three characters in the story and Melville has given them all tag names. The narrator, a pretentious poet, full of self-pity because critics were less than enthusiastic about his work, is named Helmstone—suggesting a sinking direction, not an anchor but still a drag. He is moody, desperate, discontented; four times he describes himself as "sneering with spleen" or "splenetic." Another of those narrators lacking or at least very limited in self-knowledge, he indicts himself as he recites to himself "that sublime passage in my poem, in which Cleothemes the Argive vindicates the justice of the war" (Fid., 234–35). Without revealing to us an actual line of Helmstone's poetry, Melville vindicates the cruelest of the critics, for the poem apparently is an extended cliché. As a would-be artist, Helmstone has produced a pompous, genteel imitation of classical tradition. His poem is subservient to authority in style and in content as well. His spokesman, who justifies the war, seems to be some kind of official apologist for the temporal authorities of the state and his vindication of death in service to a political cause bespeaks a narrow and expedient morality.

Imagining his own public recital of this passage, or even an enactment of the whole poem, Helmstone envisions the audience demonstrating its preference for a circus clown. In his excessive self-pity, he reveals himself as a pretentious buffoon, a literary clown, ridiculous at best, bathetic at worst. Spiteful and morose, he sides with cynicism and despair not because his "tragic poem" has achieved any genuinely tragic sense of life but because he has not won personal acclaim. He is a caricature of the alienated artist; significantly less than a fully developed creative intelligence, he is the *lowest* common denominator of the writer in America. If the reader sympathizes with Helmstone, he has allowed himself to be gulled by self-pity and to suspend critical discernment for sentimentality.

The character of Standard, the narrator's old friend who intro-

duces him to Hautboy, is an obvious embodiment of average tastes
and sentiments. He comes on strongly as a hale, boisterous, thought-
less sort of person who unwittingly strikes upon an ironic truth, as in
the following exchange, early in the story:

> "Well met, Helmstone, my boy! Ah! what's the matter? Haven't been
> committing murder? Ain't flying justice? You look wild!"
> "You have seen it, then?" said I, of course referring to the criticism.
> "Oh yes; I was there at the morning performance. Great clown, I as-
> sure you" (Fid., 233).

The confusion between the criticism of Helmstone's poetry and the
circus performance cuts both ways and exposes the values of each
character. Even the reference to murder takes on greater significance in relation to Helmstone's poem and to the imagery later in
the story which spells out the death of art and the degradation of the
artist in America. The reference to "flying justice" has more immediate relevance to Helmstone's attempt to escape the judgment leveled
at his poem. (Helmstone refers to the mistake as "mortifying," an
unfunny pun that conveys his conscious embarrassment and unconscious loss of vigor and vitality). Standard, whose name also suggests
the level at which art must aim (as in his great appreciation of the
clown) and the criterion employed in judging artistic achievement,
introduces Helmstone to Hautboy and subsequently acts as Hautboy's agent and publicist.

He persuades Helmstone of Hautboy's talent, virtue, and wisdom,
ultimately making the narrator Hautboy's disciple. His catechistic
mode of questioning the narrator to lead him to a realization of Hautboy's greatness is twice described as being accompanied by "drumming on the slab"—*slab* in one sense describing the marble table of
the restaurant to which they have adjourned, and in another sense
reinforcing the motif of death in the story (Fid., 236, 237). Standard
is Hautboy's drummer, his advance man, and by the end of the story
he has been so successful a salesman that the narrator keeps perfect
pace with his companions and steps to the music they all hear, styl-
istically polished but essentially insignificant. In this sense, Standard
functions like the iceman of O'Neill's play—bringing death as he
seems to supply a basis for life. His own values lead to a kind of murder, a crime he refers to only in jest.

Hautboy's name offers even more room for conjecture, but the possibilities seem to coalesce. His physical attributes are first mentioned, with more attention subsequently to his psychological and emotional propensities:

> His person was short and full, with a juvenile, animated cast to it. His complexion rurally ruddy; his eye sincere, cheery, and gray. His hair alone betrayed that he was not an overgrown boy. From his hair I set him down as forty or more (Fid., 233).

We see that Hautboy does not live up to his name in physical stature, but by the end of the story he will seem a lofty lesson in strength and wisdom to the narrator. There are other paradoxes also which link his name to his character or appearance. Only his hair counters the youthful exuberance of his nature and reveals that he is an *old boy*. Numerous references to his gleeful good humor document his perpetually high spirits and lend some plausibility to the phonetic possibilities of *Oh boy* or *Ho boy* as variants of Hautboy: he is "graceful with genuine good nature"; his "face shone with gladness"; he exhibits "clear, honest cheeriness," a "ruddy radiance" and laughing eye; his voice is "lifted in jubilant delight" (Fid., 234–35). Hautboy seems to exist continually on a sort of emotional "high."

Not only does Hautboy seem "graceful" in his behavior, but there also seems to be a moral or spiritual graciousness in his appreciative nature. The narrator is moved to comment that "it seemed mere loyalty to human nature to accept an invitation from so unmistakably kind and honest a heart," and that "such genuine enjoyment as his struck me to the soul with a sense of the reality of the thing called happiness." When he is most pleased by the accomplished clown they are watching, Hautboy turns to his companions "to see if his rare pleasure was shared." The narrator is so in awe of such uncomplicated joy that he hints at something more: "the marvelous juvenility of Hautboy assumed a sort of divine and immortal air, like that of some forever youthful god of Greece" (Fid., 234). In these passages Melville is subtly endowing social circumstances and human attributes with quasispiritual significance, particularly stressing a pattern of relatedness between joy, cheer, grace, and gratefulness—motifs also present in such stories as "Jimmy Rose," "The Two Temples," and "Poor Man's Pudding and Rich Man's Crumbs."

In this context the first syllable of Hautboy's name could well refer to the increasingly exalted significance the narrator finds in his example and achievement. At first he admires the fiddler's "good sense and good humor," then he praises "the excellent judgment" that enabled Hautboy "to hit the exact line between enthusiasm and apathy." At this stage the narrator, while admiring Hautboy, can still insist to Standard, "Your cheery Hautboy, after all, is no pattern, no lesson for you and me." Only because he thinks Hautboy devoid of ambition and artistic talent, much less genius, can he believe him capable of such serene accommodation to the way of the world:

> It was plain that while Hautboy saw the world pretty much as it was, yet he did not theoretically espouse its bright side nor its dark side. Rejecting all solutions, he but acknowledged facts. What was sad in the world he did not superficially gainsay; what was glad in it he did not cynically slur; and all which was to him personally enjoyable, he gratefully took to his heart (Fid., 235–37).

Here is a man with no rebellious attitudes, no vain strivings, no consuming urge for reform, no passionate commitments, and no susceptibility to alienation from his surrounding society.[2]

When Hautboy leaves to keep another engagement, Standard begins "drumming on the slab" and asks the narrator, "What do you think of your new acquaintance?" Helmstone's reply suggests that his progress from downhearted doubter to dedicated believer has already begun: "Standard, I owe you a thousand thanks for introducing me to one of the most singular men I have ever seen. It needed the optical sight of such a man to believe in the possibility of his existence." Questioned further about his feelings toward Hautboy, Helmstone adds, "I hugely love and admire him . . . I wish I were Hautboy." Standard's reply again emphasizes the uniqueness of Hautboy: "That's a pity, now. There's only one Hautboy in the world." The narrator is certain that anyone with such "wonderful cheerfulness" must be "unpossessed of genius" and therefore "eternally blessed." However, he thinks Hautboy, apart from that cheer-

2. Hautboy's name is also the word from which we derive *oboe*, a bit of etymology Melville could not have overlooked. Thus, by the end of the story Helmstone has chosen to lean on a man whose name denotes a slender, graceful, reed instrument.

fulness, wholly mundane, "with average abilities; options clear, because circumscribed; passions docile, because they are feeble. . . . Nothing tempts him beyond common limit. . . . Acquiescent and calm from the cradle to the grave, he obviously slides through the crowd" (Fid., 236–37).

All this sets the stage for the narrator's discovery that Hautboy had been a famous prodigy, that he still retained much of that talent, and that he might after all present a pattern for the artist in American society. Of course, this is not the first time that Melville turned to the subject of the artist in America, imbued that subject with religious significance, and developed the possibility of the genuine artist presenting a pattern or example of fulfillment and salvation for the aspiring one. In "Hawthorne and His Mosses," that strange review with many of the narrative and dramatic elements of fiction, Melville erected Hawthorne into the savior of American literature and a pattern of artistic liberation for Melville himself. In an odd way the strategy employed in this revealing essay parallels the circumstances in "The Fiddler," and a close look at some of the characteristics attributed to Hawthorne, the genuine artist who has established art in America, helps show up Hautboy as the false artist establishing a pattern that will submerge art in America.[3]

Like Hautboy, Hawthorne was a man the world thought pleasant, mild, and harmless, but whom Melville found capable of attaining unsuspected heights: a "man in whom humour and love, like mountain peaks, soar to such a rapt height, as to receive the irradiations of the upper skies." Melville saw Hawthorne as a god among men, walking as meekly and unrecognized among his fellow Americans as Christ among the Jews, and he was led to observe that rarely if ever does outward appearance convey spiritual greatness: "Not even in our Saviour, did his visible frame betoken anything of the augustness of the nature within. Else, how could those Jewish eyewitnesses

3. My purpose here is not to assert the identification of Hautboy with Hawthorne, although the later connection of Hautboy with *vine* (one of Melville's code words for Hawthorne) might strengthen the possibility of such a conjecture. Nor do I mean to suggest that Melville in 1854 still upholds Hawthorne as a model of artistic achievement. His enthusiasm for Hawthorne had waned by then, but I do not think that Melville had repudiated his portrait of the American artist, for which Hawthorne had been the model in 1850. Hautboy does not resemble the portrait, and, in all likelihood, Melville's revised estimate of Hawthorne no longer does either.

fail to see heaven in his glance." (HHM, 128, 124). In a highly ironic, almost parodistic way Melville's narrator, the unsuccessful poet in "The Fiddler," discovers unsuspected spiritual dimensions in the good-natured, but unprepossessing figure of Hautboy.

Where Hautboy presents an example of unrelieved, sunny, good humor, avoiding any pessimistic extreme, Hawthorne impressed Melville with his greater depths and intensity: "For in spite of all the Indian-summer sunlight on the hither side of Hawthorne's soul, the other side—like the dark half of the physical sphere—is shrouded in a blackness, ten times black." What Melville called "this great power of blackness" distinguished the real artist from the shallower facsimile; and with Hawthorne, though "you may be witched by his sunlight [and] . . . bright gildings . . . there is the blackness of darkness beyond." A good part of Hautboy's appeal lies also in his evident serenity and leisurely good sense, and this too, if we take the portrait of Hawthorne as the paradigm of the artist, disqualifies Hautboy. Comparing Hawthorne to Shakespeare, Melville insisted that the true artist projects a sense of his inner torment into his characters, but that this mode of suggesting unpleasant truths does not win public admiration. Even in the case of Shakespeare "much of the blind, unbridled admiration . . . has been lavished upon the least part of him" (HHM, 129–30).

These sentiments might seem at first to corroborate Helmstone's condemnation of an unappreciative public, but he, like Hautboy, is devalued by comparison with Melville's characterization of the real artist. Helmstone's own description of his epic poem revealed it as imitative, artificial, and given to rant; Melville's prescription for an American artist called for "a man who is bound to carry republican progressiveness into Literature as well as into Life," who would "condemn all imitation, though it comes to us graceful and fragrant as the morning." In exalting Hawthorne as "the literary Shiloh of America," Melville further praised him for refraining "from all the popularising noise and show of broad farce, and blood-besmeared tragedy" (HHM, 132, 136, 142, 131). By contrast, Hautboy's enthusiastic reaction to the circus clown shows his appreciation of "popularising noise" and "broad farce," and Helmstone's epic poem betrays a weakness for "blood-besmeared tragedy." Thus, both

Helmstone and Hautboy in their claims to the status of artist seldom rise above the level of superficial cliché—the level so amply represented by the character of Standard.

It is Standard who, when Hautboy returns, persuades him to perform in the off-Broadway loft where he lives. On a "dented old fiddle" Hautboy "played away right merrily at 'Yankee Doodle' and other off-handed, dashing, and disdainfully carefree airs." Despite the triteness of the tunes, the narrator says "I was transfixed by something miraculously superior in the style." Without hesitation, he accepts these easy pieces as sublime artistry; enchanted by Hautboy, his discontent vanished, he says, "My whole splenetic soul capitulated to the magical fiddle." Standard suggests an analogy with the fable of Orpheus and his lyre, and the narrator readily assents to the subhuman role it casts him in (Fid., 239). In several senses, he is ready to capitulate, and that I think, is the underlying theme of this story in which Melville has tried to tell a kind of truth, "even though it be covertly, and by snatches" (HHM, 131).

Hautboy's repertoire recalls the passage from the essay on Hawthorne in which Melville characterizes an unnamed author, apparently representing Washington Irving, as a "popular and amiable" imitator of foreign models who avoids "all topics but smooth ones." Many of the qualities of Irving, an easygoing, graceful stylist, are shared by Hautboy, whose choice of tunes hardly tasks his talent and strongly suggests that he too prefers smooth technical performance to intellectual challenge. When Melville first sketched such an inadequate representative of art, he advised "Let us believe it, then once for all, that there is no hope for us in these smooth pleasing writers that know their powers" (HHM, 135). Helmstone, the narrator in "The Fiddler," however, decides that in such an example lies his only hope.

He reaches this decision despite the unconscious warning in Standard's response to continuing questions about Hautboy's identity. It is a warning concealed in the attempt to force faith on a kind of doubting Thomas: "Why, haven't you seen him? And didn't you yourself lay his whole anatomy open on the marble slab at Taylor's? What more can you possibly learn? Doubtless, your own masterly insight has already put you in possession of all" (Fid., 239). Helmstone learns some of the facts of Hautboy's former, more fortunate life, but he does not learn that Hautboy's present happiness and serenity have been attained through a considerable sacrifice—his rebirth attained through the death of his creative drives.[4]

Standard identifies Hautboy as "an extraordinary genius" who rose to early fame, "who has been an object of wonder to the wisest, been caressed by the loveliest, [and] received the open homage of thousands of the rabble." And as Melville said of Christ and of Hawthorne, Standard says of Hautboy: "Today he walks Broadway and no man knows him." He whispers Hautboy's true name into Helmstone's ear along with the suggestion that in his relative anonymity "he is happier than a king." Helmstone recognizes the name, remembers his own enthusiastic applause of that name in a theater years ago, and manages to obliterate his depression over the rejection of his poem. He looks to Hautboy as a savior and to his example as a solution. Determined to become a disciple, he destroys his manuscripts, buys a fiddle, and goes "to take regular lessons of Hautboy" (Fid., 239–40).

The final image in the story seems to suggest that following Hautboy's pattern is a dubious or ambiguous solution; as the narrator says: "I behold in Hautboy the vine and the rose climbing the shattered shafts of his tumbled temple of Fame" (Fid., 240). One meaning reinforces the idea of rising above misfortune, but subsidiary meanings suggest the vine and rose rising to mask a ruin or even to mark a grave. The narrator has found a faith, but Standard may well have led him to a false messiah. Melville had admired Hawthorne for being "a seeker, not a finder yet" (HHM, 138). What must he have thought of the example of Hautboy, who long ago gave up the quest and settled for modest comforts and an untroubled mind?

The best answer, it seems to me, is that Hautboy represents a costly compromise between the artist and society, a cheapening and vulgarization of the ideal Melville had described in his review of Hawthorne—figuratively, the death of creativity. If there is an autobiographical element in the story, it lies in Melville's very pessimistic projection of the possibilities for the artist in America (a mood quite similar again to that of his "Dollars damn me" letter to Haw-

4. Thompson, "'The Fiddler,'" 496, cites and analyzes the death imagery in this story.

thorne) and his fear of the power of popular taste to level aspiration and disregard significant achievement, to make heroes and forget them as quickly. Seen in this light, "The Fiddler" is an indirect and muted protest against the process of cultural "Standardization" which Melville saw as the ruin of art in America but which he somewhat ineffectively expressed in this story.

"The Happy Failure"

Many readers, including some of the more eminent Melville scholars, have been quite uncertain about "The Happy Failure" and have, for good reason, passed over it quickly. The reason, I hasten to add, lies in Melville's own failure to fuse his weighty implications with an adequate narrative and symbolic structure. Because of the discrepancy between the portentous burden and the slight vehicle, the story seems either to be unnecessarily opaque or actively to undercut its thematic suggestions.

"The Happy Failure" is basically a parable of the human condition, or, in view of the explicit reference to Aesop near the end of the story, Melville's attempt at writing a fable for his time. Several traditional literary or cultural ideas are suggested by Melville's strategy, and these in turn are allied to the few published comments that the story has occasioned. First, it is a variation on the theme of "the vanity of human wishes," an idea underlying Leon Howard's autobiographical approach to "The Happy Failure." Howard sees the story as a thinly veiled rationalization of Melville's own pride, hope, and disappointment, especially poignant after the commercial and artistic failure of *Pierre*. Second, it is a considerably scaled down version of *felix culpa*, an ultimately fortunate failure which R. H. Fogle views as the necessary means of restoring an old man's humanity. Third, it is a jocular deflation of the American dream of success, the view underlying Charles G. Hoffman's treatment of the story as a light satire on commercialism.[5] It is all of these and more besides.

5. Leon Howard, "The Mystery of Melville's Short Stories," *Americana Austriaca* (Vienna: W. Braumüller Universitats Verlag, 1966), 208; Fogle, *Melville's Shorter Tales*, 58–59; Charles G. Hoffman, "The Shorter Fiction of Herman Melville," *South Atlantic Quarterly*, LII (July, 1953), 425. More recently there has appeared a longer examination of the story, but in general it extends the lines of inquiry suggested by Hoffman, Fogle, and Howard: Richard D. Lynde, "Melville's Success in 'The Happy Failure,'" *College Language Association Journal*, XVIII (December, 1969), 119–30.

But just as none of the critics has managed to bring together all of Melville's meanings in this story, the author himself fell short of bringing all his means together, and the story undoubtedly deserves its lesser status among his short fiction. Nevertheless even his lesser works deserve to be understood whether they merit admiration or not. In view of the cultural and intellectual gravity and the technical virtuosity of some of his short stories, I cannot believe that any of them ought to be reduced to the status of providing a gloss to problems of Melville biography.

The story has three characters: an elderly man, who has high hopes for the "Great Hydraulic-Hydrostatic Apparatus" to which he has devoted the last ten years; his equally old black servant, who despite the northern setting (the subtitle is "A Story of the River Hudson"), is at least in some respects a slave; and the old man's nephew, who is a young boy in the events of the story but who narrates it from a later, more mature point of view. Of these three the narrator's uncle is the major character, but in a sense the most important thing in the story is the mysterious, sphinx-like, black box and the machinery it contains. The box, which never fulfills its intended function—the creation of a new paradise by "draining swamps and marshes, and converting them, at the rate of one acre the hour, into fields more fertile than those of the Genessee"—serves nevertheless as the agency of moral illumination by which each character is able to define his humanity and reestablish his human ties (HF, 225).

The narrator's first dim perception of the box makes it seem "one of the gates of Gaza," so much does it weigh down the staggering old black man who bears it on his back. Not only does the reference to Gaza introduce the note of impending self-destruction but the circumstance also reveals the tyrannical impatience of the uncle, who "roars" commands like "stump along, Yorpy!" and calls his servant a "grizzle-headed cherub" and his nephew a "simpleton." A closer look at Yorpy's burden shows it to be "a huge, shabby, oblong box, hermetically sealed . . . a forlorn-looking, lack-lustre, old ash-box." Further commands to Yorpy tell him to "hold on to the box like grim death." Yorpy's retort, in a South African dialect which provides significant wordplay, like that of Black Guinea in *The Confidence-Man*, is "Duyvel take de pox! . . . De pox has been my cuss for de ten long 'ear." Thus, on the first two pages of the story one pattern of imagery links the box with a heavy burden, a biblical ruin, a deadly affliction, a curse, and a coffin (HF, 223–24). Its deepest association is with mortality itself.

In the uncle's mind, however, the box has assumed a different character. Not only is it the means by which he will make his million; it also, like the Ark of the Covenant, bears the hope of his "ever-lasting fortune," "the glory" of his highest possibilities, and his claim to "immortal renown" (HF, 224). In his quest for fame, he hopes to succeed where so powerful a figure as the Roman emperor Appius Claudius failed when he tried to drain the Pontine marshes. His faith in his invention is his own monomania and megalomania; it is also his faith in "what can be done in the present enlightened age." He believes that science and technology are not merely agents of progress but the means to salvation. He has a passion to distinguish himself from the rest of mankind by "pulling hard for it [glory]— against the stream," rather than following "the natural tendency of man, in the mass . . . to go down with the universal current into oblivion" (HF, 224). Linked by allusion and association to "grim death," the box represents for the elderly uncle his best hope for fame, fortune, and glory. The word *glory* or such variations as *glorify* appear ten times in only four pages, strengthening the association of the box with the hope of immortality, but setting up in modest terms a drama of the fall of man. (Some symbolic entities, certainly, can radiate such paradoxical meanings, but Melville, I feel, expected too much when he tried in a few pages to make a black box carry almost as much meaning as a white whale).[6]

The uncle is guilty of hubris, and like other Melville characters who assume godlike power, he seems frantic in his need for secrecy. Having reached Quash Island (the name of which also foreshadows shattered hopes and voided dreams), his fear of premature discovery makes him seem increasingly paranoid. A far-off horseman, no more than a speck on a lofty cliffside, or the imagined figure of a boy in a

6. Dorothee M. Finklestein has suggested that the uncle's invention derives from the hydraulic machine invented by the Italian Egyptologist and pyramid explorer Giovanni Battista Belzoni. Since the box is also described as "sphinx-like" in the opening paragraphs of Melville's story, this suggestion, which is also associated with ideas of immortality, seems quite likely. Finklestein, *Melville's Orienda* (New Haven: Yale University Press, 1961), pp. 122–23.

tree on the opposite bank appear to be spies. In the uncle's mind the imagined figure is likened to Zacchaeus, an allusion that further casts him in a godlike role and sets him up for a fall. The incident wholly reverses the meaning in the original parable wherein Jesus blesses Zacchaeus and makes him pure and righteous: "For the Son of man came to seek and to save the lost" (Luke 19:10). The uncle's words are "never mind; I defy the boy," thus defying the moral established by Jesus and asserting the primacy of his own personal ambition (HF, 227).

As he directs the transfer of the box from the boat to the marshy island, the uncle cautions Yorpy to be careful with his burden: "That's more precious than a box of gold." Borne down into the shallows, Yorpy growls in reply, "Heavy as de gelt," incorporating another pun like the "box-pox" pairing, the sequence this time following a gold–gelt–guilt progression, and adding further to the moral burden of the box.

A good portion of the uncle's guilt lies in his treatment of Yorpy. He assumes that Yorpy cannot possess more intellect than a child and uses him as a beast of burden in human form. These racist conceptions are intensified by the reference to Yorpy's "black hoof," a satyr-like as well as satanic identification and a familiar nineteenth-century American stereotype of the Negro (HF, 229). In the case of the uncle it seems clear that his dehumanized conception of Yorpy grew in proportion to his own slavish devotion to the black box and its promise of enduring glory.

Melville seems to have tried to link a threatening image of technology (the "convoluted metal pipes and syringes . . . inextricably interwreathed together in one gigantic coil . . . looked like a huge nest of anacondas and adders" [HF, 228]), the idea of dehumanization, and the specter of Negro slavery in this story as he did more effectively in "The Bell-Tower," which was published a year later. Just as the mechanism in "The Bell-Tower" fails to fulfill its god-rivaling creator's hopes, the mechanism in "The Happy Failure" does not work either, and in both stories master and slave are deprived of a full range of human characteristics and sympathies. There are also echoes of some of Hawthorne's themes, such as the rejection of technological means for attaining salvation in "The Celestial Railroad" and the folly of seeking earthly immortality in "The Ambitious Guest."

When his Great Hydraulic-Hydrostatic Apparatus balks, the uncle kicks into the machinery, rips out the "anacondas and adders," and flings them into the water—destroying the work of ten years' single-minded concentration. The boy begs him to stop, to put it together, to try again, saying, "While there is life there is hope." The uncle, however, revises this statement: "While there is life hereafter there is despair" (HF, 230). There is no punctuation to link *hereafter* to the first clause or to the second; the word slides both ways and so does the meaning—the greater emphasis, however, falling on the realization of man's finite nature and the unyielding boundary of death.

Nevertheless, the old man picks up some of the pieces, fits them again into the box, and enlists Yorpy and the boy to tip the box into working position again. The result is reflected in the uncle's face: "It seemed pinched, shriveled into mouldy whiteness, like a mildewed grape." Continuing his recollected narrative, the boy says, "I dropped the box, and sprang toward him just in time to prevent his fall" (HF, 231). I suspect that this last phrase is an important note in the story, that it is a story of a failure that produces a lesser fall while averting the greater fall that success or the monomaniacal pursuit of success might have produced.

Abandoning the box, Yorpy and the boy help the old man into the boat, and as the current sweeps them swiftly down the River Hudson, the boy recalls how his uncle had so recently cited "the universal drift of the mass of humanity toward utter oblivion." Figuratively, they seem headed for despair and death, until the uncle does the one thing that changes their course. After complaining that "there's not much left in an old world for an old man to invent," and urging his nephew "never try to invent anything but—happiness," he calls for the only act that makes anyone in the story happy: he asks them to return for the box. But it is not to try to make a further claim to fame, glory, and immortality; it is because "it will make a good woodbox," and because "faithful old Yorpy can sell the old iron for tobacco money." This sentimental gesture, this first instance of thinking of someone else, seems to be the act of grace that saves the old man's

humanity, and simultaneously it affirms Yorpy's humanity as well
(HF, 231). He is like an Ethan Brand who takes the opportunity to
desist from a destructive course, but Melville's story is so much
slighter that even the comparison seems disproportionate.

Long maligned and much mistreated, Yorpy is overjoyed at the
change: "Dear massa! dear old massa! dat be very fust time in de ten
long 'ear yoo hab mention kindly old Yorpy. I tank yoo, dear old
massa; I tank yoo so kindly. Yoo is yourself again in de ten long 'ear."
And in further realization of what he had made of himself and what a
burdensome role he had forced on Yorpy, the uncle converts Yorpy's
phrase about the "long 'ears" into "long ears enough . . . Aesopian
ears" (HF, 231). Not only has he been vain, suspicious, and insensitive to others, but the asinine lengths to which he had gone to claim
a spurious glory were like the attempt of the ass in Aesop's fable to
don the lionskin and pass himself off as a lion. His long ears made
him an ass when he tried to be king; the uncle's quest for power and
glory comes to the same end.

In his newly established humanity, however, the old man no
longer roars commands but exhibits a painful understanding of the
tragedy so narrowly averted: "Boy, I'm glad I've failed. I say, boy,
failure has made a good old man of me. It was horrible at first, but
I'm glad I've failed, Praise be to God for the failure!" And the boy,
looking back on this strange experience, recalls it as a kind of conversion: "His face kindled with a strange, rapt earnestness. I have never
forgotten that look. If the event made my uncle a good old man, as
he called it, it made me a wise young one. Example did for me the
work of experience." Thus all three characters in the story are in different ways humanized by the circumstances (HF, 231–32).

When, some years later, "after peaceful days of autumnal content," the uncle died quietly, old Yorpy was still there to close his
eyes—having served earlier, like Lear's Fool, to open his eyes.
Looking for the last time at the uncle's face, the boy imagines again
"his deep, fervent cry—'Praise be to God for the failure!'" (HF,
232). The failure is man—in his all-too-human fallibility—and his
greatest challenge lies not in reaching the distant prospect of fame,
perfection, or glory, but in recognizing the limitations inherent in
the human condition. Having lusted after a kind of immortality, the

uncle has been an example of ironic triumph, finding his salvation in the mortality he had sought to evade.

While I think I have summarized much of Melville's accessible meaning in "The Happy Failure," I cannot leave the story without suggesting the possibility of a deeper cynicism which a few of my better students perceive in the story, or perhaps bring to it. To them the uncle's smug resignation is a "cop-out," Yorpy's satisfaction at being promoted from a beast of burden to a faithful old house dog is a clear disappointment, and the narrator's grateful affirmation of a philosophy insulated from the unhappy extremes of experience is a too-benign embrace of oblivion. In the light of such an interpretation, the River Hudson becomes the enduring victor and all men rather helpless chips that "go down with the universal current into oblivion" or fill the recesses of a shabby, oblong, old wood-box. If Melville were capable of conning the reader into agreement with Hautboy's compromise, there may be a similarly cynical trickiness in "The Happy Failure" too.

"Cock-A-Doodle-Doo!"

"Cock-A-Doodle-Doo!" is the most complex and ambitious of the stories in this chapter—stories in which the narrator pegs his hopes on the spiritual buoyancy of some belief or illusion. "Cock-A-Doodle-Doo!" is the longest investigation into the power of illusion and the strongest rejection of such total reliance on willful belief. But Melville describes the circumstances, using image and allusion to tilt the reader toward a conclusion without drawing that conclusion for him. Thus some critics view the story as an outstanding example of comic writing, while others treat it with utter seriousness, even sententiousness.[7] And yet, none of these critics is really wrong.

7. There has been no shortage of comment on "Cock-A-Doodle-Doo!," but the extremes of interpretation and the certainty with which some of these views have been urged seem to call for a better balanced analysis of the story and for a more satisfactory integration with the body of Melville's short fiction. Significant comment began with Egbert S. Oliver's argument that Melville's story satirizes Thoreau's position in *A Week on the Concord and Merrimack Rivers—* "'Cock-A-Doodle-Doo!' and Transcendental Hocus-Pocus," *New England Quarterly*, XXI (June, 1948), 204–16. The view that Melville's story is a parody of transcendentalism—whether the focus is Thoreau, Emerson, or resounding optimism in general—pervades most of the subsequent comment, such as William Bysshe Stein's two essays, the first, "Melville Roasts Thoreau's Cock," in *Modern Language Notes*, LXXIV (March, 1959), 218–19, and the second, "Melville's Cock and the Bell of St. Paul," in the *Emerson Society Quarterly*, No. 27 (1962), 5–

The central symbol, a rooster, named Trumpet by his owner and
Signor Beneventano by the narrator, is a convincing annunciation of
the magnificence inherent in each day, his voice a clarion call to
eliminate evil, overcome the maladies of mortality, and deny death
itself. But like the brilliant bug of Melville's "The Apple-Tree Table,"
that dubious symbol of immortality reborn after a century and a
half's dormancy, the triumphant cock fails to survive the circumstances of the story. In this regard, the story is an extended variation
on the old joke about the operation being a success despite the patient's death; here the message of immortality was received, and believed, despite the death of the sender. It is an unfunny joke, neither
comic nor, as Sidney Moss interpreted it, "comedic," but at best
tragicomic and dependent on incongruence, anomaly, inconsistency,
and imbalance.

It is a relentlessly paradoxical story, a fictional argument containing in itself thesis and antithesis and—since it was Melville's second
published story—foreshadowing the technique of opposing panels in
Melville's diptychs. It is about harsh reality and comforting illusion,
brutal facts and facile faith; it opposes the burdens of life and the

---

10, and pertinent sections in Leon Howard, *Herman Melville: A Biography* (Berkley: University of California Press, 1951) and Edward H. Rosenberry, *Melville and The Comic Spirit*
(Cambridge: Harvard University Press, 1955). A strong dissent from this view appears in Sidney P. Moss's article, "'Cock-A-Doodle-Doo!' and Some Legends in Melville Scholarship,"
American Literature, XL (May, 1968), 192–210. Moss feels not only that Melville's antitran-
scendentalist attitudes have been greatly exaggerated but also that "Cock-A-Doodle-Doo!"
voices a genuine opposition to life-denying forces, an exultation in the possibilities of life, and
an affirmation of resurrection and rebirth. In his view neither the narrator nor apparently
Merrymusk suffers any illness or disequilibrium: "Only those who cannot hear the cock have
organic ill" (193). Since Merrymusk, his wife, and his four children all hear the "never-say-die"
crow of the cock before they do in fact die, there seems to be more faith than science in Moss's
literary pathology.

Stein's second essay moves from the view that the narrator "is a burlesque Thoreau" to the
view that St. Paul and his version of Christianity comprise the most impressive target of Melville's satire. Fogle in *Melville's Shorter Tales* (28–35) also feels that the theme of Christian
hope is central to the story, but he is not certain whether it is more effectively affirmed or undermined. His uncertainty, I think, is the result of the central division or ambivalence in the
story.

Another facet of the story is emphasized by Richard Chase, who says that it "deals with the
artist's need for the sense of power and the guilt-feelings which accompany it." He also was the
first to recognize not only that Melville drew from the phraseology of Wordsworth's "Resolution and Independence" but that "the whole meaning is similar to that of the poem," (*Herman
Melville*, 163). I wonder, however, whether Melville's story, while similar to Wordsworth's
poem, does not in the end invert the meaning of the poem.

creative release of art as well as the limitations of existence and the spiritual liberation of religion. Most analyses have emphasized one or the other elements of these paradoxes, and as I have suggested, they suffer from incompleteness rather than error.

Several have actually recognized that "Cock-A-Doodle-Doo!" has resemblances to "Bartleby," both stories having been published in 1853, but the tendency has been to view "Bartleby" as a dramatization of negation and "Cock-A-Doodle-Doo!" as a dramatization of affirmation. The resemblances are actually closer than that. A good part of the meaning of each story lies in how the narrator views the circumstances and how he is transformed by his experience. I am amazed that most who have discussed "Cock-A-Doodle-Doo!" find the narrator sound in mind and body despite his admission at the end of the story that since these events "never . . . have I felt the doleful dumps, but under all circumstances crow late and early with a continual crow. COCK-A-DOODLE-DOO!—OO!—OO!—OO!" (CDD, 147). There is pain and sickness beneath the surface exultation of this man mimicing a rooster, and his aggressive self-confidence has been achieved at considerable cost. His triumphant crow blends into a howl, and I think that like "Bartleby" this story is a study of dementia, but with some important differences.

Whereas the narrator of "Bartleby" grew in sensitivity and human sympathy, the narrator of "Cock-A-Doodle-Doo!" is dehumanized, metamorphosed into an absurd, grotesque objectification of what he has come to believe. Whereas Bartleby succumbed to seemingly impenetrable obstacles and crushing limitations of social circumstance and the human condition, the narrator of Melville's second short story is the victim of his need and will to believe that none of those obstacles or limitations exist, despite the pressure they exert on him at the start of the story. Walled in by the various aspects of his existence, Bartleby lapses into negativism and autistic withdrawal, while asserting a heightened sense of his own presumptuous individuality —the symptoms of a pitiable catatonic schizophrenic who can no longer function productively. The narrator of the second story, a man who sees in all his surroundings "tokens of a divided empire" (CDD, 119), begins in a mood of deep depression and exhibits unmistakable symptoms of paranoia until he is shocked into apparent soundness by the invigorating crow of an unseen cock. His mood swings to the opposite extreme. He develops a heightened sense of his own powers and possibilities; acts aggressively against his persecutors, real and imagined; and egotistically defies custom and convention. With no impairment in his intelligence and with a possible increase in the power of creative imagination, this narrator has become a functioning schizophrenic, a living representation of the oppositions and imbalance which shape the circumstances and advance the themes in this complex story.[8]

There is not much in the previously published criticism of this story that supports my view of the narrator as a man whose faith in certain illusions carries him into the area of delusion and madness, but there are suggestions that approach this view. W. B. Stein calls the narrator an ironist, a fool, a buffoon, and a victim. R. H. Fogle recognizes some puzzling contradictions. The message of Christianity is central, "yet doubt is cast upon it." The rooster is a symbol of awakened hope, but "has jarring connotations." Fogle does not, however, look to the state of mind of the narrator, but to that of the author, whose lack of control and balance produced a story that "means what it says but betrays something else. Intended as a trumpet call of affirmation, it reveals in its dissonances the note of underlying despair."[9] He has detected the strain of paradox and contradiction, but charges it to ineptness or accident rather than intention or

---

8. To distinguish schizophrenia from the layman's notion that it involves multiple personality as in *The Three Faces of Eve*, I would like to cite the following statement from the work of a pioneer student of schizophrenia: "The psychic complexes do not combine in a conglomeration of strivings with a unified resultant as they do in a healthy person; rather, one set of complexes dominates the personality for a time, while other groups of ideas or drives are 'split off' and seem either partly or completely impotent." Eugene Bleuler, *Dementia Praecox, or the Group of Schizophrenias*, trans. J. Zinkin (New York: International Universities Press, 1950), 9.

Offering a taxonomy of various types of schizophrenia, a contemporary psychiatrist cites the following symptoms as most characteristic of paranoid schizophrenia:
  a. Premorbid suspicious character; onset later in life
  b. Marked ideas of reference, delusions of persecution
  c. Frequent accusatory and auditory hallucinations
  d. Hostile and unpleasant manner
  e. Loosening of associations, hypochondriacal preoccupations, neologisms
  f. Aloof and unpredictable assaultiveness
  g. Well-preserved intellectual functioning outside of psychotic core.
From C. Peter Rosenbaum, *The Meaning of Madness: Symptomatology, Sociology, Biology, and Therapy of the Schizophrenias* (New York: Science House, 1970), 23.

9. Stein, "Melville's Cock" ESQ, 5, 6, 9; Fogle, *Melville's Shorter Tales*, 34–35.

design. I hope that closer attention to the story and its links to other Melville stories will strengthen my assertions about the narrator and reveal Melville in a position of greater control over his means and his meanings.

"Cock-A-Doodle-Doo!" introduced the kind of narrator–protagonist who reappeared as the disgruntled poet in "The Fiddler" and the devotee of the visual picturesque and theatrical pretense in "The Piazza." In each of these, the narrator is a would-be artist or at least a quester for that beauty which he associates with hope, truth, divinity, and occasionally the promise of immortality. In different ways his imagination commits him to the pursuit of illusion, whether through art, literature, theater, or religion; and if the illusion gains ascendance over unacceptable reality, there is the danger of delusion and madness. "The Piazza" is probably the closest parallel for the way in which the narrator obliterates the distinction between appearance and reality but stops short of madness because he recognizes how his kind of illusion has become distorted delusion in someone else. He subsequently acknowledges his illusions and draws aesthetic solace from them, but he cannot save the young girl who in her isolation and misery has permitted delusion to dominate her world and herself. The narrator in "Cock-A-Doodle-Doo!" has a similar chance to recognize his danger, to see that gross delusion can lead to derangement and death, but he does not take it and follows the lure of his imagination beyond the point of possible return.

There is no balance in his view of the world at the beginning of the story. His mood is one of total dismay, and his mind turns morbidly to incidents that can only depress him further: political despotisms which survived the abortive revolutions of midcentury Europe, mounting casualties from locomotive and steamer accidents, and a variety of personal difficulties and debts. "Too full of hypoes to sleep," he walks into the countryside, which he describes in an inversion of romantic images that deserves to be called the *unpicturesque*. The language produces associations of discomfort, disease, decay, and death. The morning has "a cool and misty, damp, disagreeable air." The country, carcasslike, "looked underdone, its raw juices squirting out." In what seems almost like a parody of Emerson's account of the mystical exhilaration which he felt as he crossed a puddle-dotted common at twilight, the narrator tells how he made his way up a hill, "spitefully thrusting my crab-stick into the oozy sod." His posture, he says, "brought my head pretty well earthward, as if I were in the act of butting it against the world. I marked the fact, but only grinned at it with a ghastly grin" (CDD, 119). Emerson had insisted, in similar circumstances that "the air is a cordial of incredible virtue"; Melville's narrator, in the mood of his paranoid hyperbole, finds it permeated with poison.

Signs of fragmentation and discord predominate:

> All round me were tokens of a divided empire. The old grass and the new grass were striving together. In the low wet swales the verdure peeped out in vivid green; beyond, on the mountains, lay light patches of snow, strangely relieved against their russet sides; all the humped hills looked like brindled kine in the shivers [a nervous disease characterized by chills and muscular spasms]. The woods were strewn with dry dead boughs, snapped off by the riotous winds of March, while the young trees skirting the woods were just beginning to show the first yellowish tinge of the nascent spray (CDD, 119–20).

Death is stronger than life, disease more prominent than vigor, decay more apparent than growth in his world. His seat for a moment is "a great rotting log" not far from "a lagging, fever-and-agueish river." In the low spots "shreds of vapor listlessly wandered in the air, like abandoned or helmless nations or ships." Over the next village "there rested a great flat canopy of haze, like a pall . . . the condensed smoke of the chimneys, with the condensed, exhaled breath of the villagers, prevented from dispersion by the imprisoning hills." This stifling smog "was too heavy and lifeless to mount of itself," and his morbid imagination convinces him that the pall is "doubtless hiding many a man with the mumps, and many a queasy child." In his pocket is a medicine he means to send to the poor Irishman's baby, stricken with scarlet fever.[10] Others have "the varioloid, and

---

10. The route by which the narrator goes from his inability to pay his debts to self-pity and resentment at the unjust nature of his physical ailments provides an interesting set of associations, very close to the "Klang-associations," punning, and other verbal manipulations characteristic of many schizophrenics. In the "Klang-association" ideas follow one another because of similarities of sound not because of logical links (Rosenbaum, *The Meaning of Madness*, 5). Thus the narrator unloads a chain of morbid grievances set off by the shifting meanings of *drug*: "I can't pay this horrid man; and yet they say money was never so plentiful—a drug in the market; but blame me if I can get any of the drug, though there never was a sick man more in need

the chicken-pox," or the "measles, mumps, croup . . . cholera-morbus, and summer-complaint." In addition to his hypochondriacal tendencies, he fears recurrent dyspepsia and suffers twinges of rheumatism (from having given up his berth "to a sick lady" and spending a rainy night on deck) which he personifies in a further fantasy of persecution: "Twinge! Shoot away, ye rheumatics! Ye couldn't lay on worse if I were some villain who had murdered the lady instead of befriending her" (CDD, 120–22).

The reference to "many a man, with the mumps" also has a possible connotation of imminent sexual sterility or debility, for immediately following the remark is a description of two highly fatal accidents. One was caused by "a thick-headed engineer, who knew not a valve from a flue"; the other "where two infatuate trains ran pell-mell into each other, and climbed and clawed each other's backs; and one locomotive was found fairly shelled, like a chick, inside of a passenger car in the antagonist train; and near a score of noble hearts, a bride and her groom, and an innocent little infant, were all disembarked into the grim bulk of Charon, who ferried them over, all baggageless, to some clinkered iron-foundry or other." The grotesque parody of copulation and gestation, the mingled images of hopeful beginnings and violent endings, challenge the nineteenth-century faith in technological progress and suggest that the "great improvements of the age" are transforming the country into a sterile, mechanistic, surrealistic hell (CDD, 120–21).[11]

---

of that particular sort of medicine. It's a lie; money ain't plentiful—feel of my pocket. Ha! here's a powder I was going to send to the sick baby in yonder hovel." He then lists all the afflictions "rife in the country" and laments that "many of the poor little ones, after going through all this trouble, snap off short" their recovery from these illnesses "and all else, in vain!" So far his course has taken him from his economic needs to what is available in excess ("drug in the market") and therefore of little consequence, to his physiological needs (drug as medicine in general), to the medicine in his (penniless) pocket, to a catalogue of currently contagious diseases, to the ironic inevitability of death for many who survive as well as for those who succumb to these diseases. He completes the chain of associations by dwelling again on delusions of his own persecution (122).

The paragraph resembles the associative technique developed by Sterne in *Tristram Shandy* (which Melville's narrator is currently reading) and anticipates the stream-of-consciousness techniques developed by Joyce in the twentieth century. For some readers its major importance is purely a matter of literary technique; however, the morbidity motif seems to me too prominent to be merely an example of wit and virtuosity.

11. There is a considerable phallic wordplay in the story, as Stein makes abundantly clear in his two essays.

Imagining himself "Dictator of North America," the narrator fashions a revealing fantasy of assault and revenge upon the establishment, those "thousand villains and asses who have the management of railroads and steamboats, and innumerable other vital things in the world." His fear of impotence now become a fancied omnipotence, he satanically envisions a sadistic punishment for those who have been running things: "I'd string them up! and hang, draw, and quarter; fry, roast, and boil; stew, grill, and devil them, like so many turkey-legs—the rascally numskulls of stokers; I'd set them to stokering in Tartarus—I would" (CDD, 121). But this is only a momentary fantasy born of frustration; the narrator feels himself more bedeviled than devilish. (Melville, of course, did much more with the social, moral, and organic implications of technology in his "Tartarus of Maids," published some sixteen months later).

Even the local railroad is doing the devil's work and exacting a high toll. To the narrator it is a mechanical "Moloch," an insatiable "iron fiend," crying "more! more! more!" as it "comes straight-bent through these vernal woods, like the Asiatic cholera cantering on a camel!" There is a strong element of auditory hallucination and bizarre hyperbole in transforming the sound of the locomotive into an "old dragon," announced by "snort! puff! scream!" as it fulfills its mission of "chartered murderer," "death monopolizer," "judge, jury, and hangman all together" (CDD, 121).

He feels victimized even more by another representative of life-disrupting forces, "that smaller dunning fiend, my creditor." In this "dollars-damn-me" mood, he sees the dun possessing machine-like features and a mechanical persistence: "a lantern-jawed rascal, who seems to run on a railroad track . . . and duns me even on Sunday, all the way to church and back . . . and sits in the same pew with me, and pretending to be polite and hand me the prayer-book . . . pokes his pesky bill under my nose in the midst of my devotions and so shoves himself between me and salvation" (CDD, 121–22).

As his mood affects not only his view of himself and other men, it produces a highly colored symbolic misperception. It makes even the young calves into ambulatory facsimiles of inanimate objects. After a hard winter they appear with "sharp bones sticking out like elbows; all quilted with a strange stuff dried on their flanks like layers of pancakes." With their hair worn off in places, the calves look like "six abominable old hair-trunks wandering about here in this pasture." But before this life-denying, debovinizing misperception can go farther, he hears the triumphant, inspiring cockcrow, warming, invigorating, "full of pluck, full of fire, full of fun, full of glee. It plainly says–'*Never say die!*'" (CDD, 122–23). And from this moment begins his metamorphosis.

Sidney Moss, who views the story as a genuine affirmation of life rather than a satire on extremes of pessimism and of optimism, emphasizes that the narrator "has been a calf to fall into despondency and madness," and sees nothing anomalous or bizarre when in response to the next crow of the cock "he finds himself flapping his elbows and crowing too."[12] But what the narrator really says under the spell of the cock's crow can convey something other than a healthful optimism: "Unwittingly, I found that I had been addressing the two-year-olds—the calves—in my enthusiasm; which shows how one's true nature will betray itself at times in the most unconscious way" (CDD, 123). If the influence of the cock makes him talk to calves, crow like a rooster, and flap his elbows—just for openers —we cannot easily conclude that he has found the source of health and vigor. In his search for, discovery of, and surrender to the source of inspiration, he becomes a very strange bird himself.

I do not plan to argue that "Cock-A-Doodle-Doo!" is in any but the loosest sense autobiographical. I do not see the story as evidence that Melville himself was in a state of incipient or advanced schizophrenia, or that either the narrator or Merrymusk, the only other male character, is a projection of Melville himself.[13] Rather, the story is an important example of Melville's continuing attention to a

---

12. Moss, "'Cock-A-Doodle-Doo!'" 207.

13. Richard Chase identifies both characters as "pictures of Melville" (*Herman Melville*, 165). Leon Howard views Merrymusk as the hero of the story who chooses death by "patient starvation rather than accept the values of the everyday world," and because Merrymusk is an ex-sailor, Howard sees him as a representation of Melville ("The Mystery of Melville's Short Stories," 207). I do not think the evidence warrants either conclusion. The story strongly suggests illness as the reason for the death of Merrymusk and his family, with malnutrition as a symbolic contributing factor. The fact that he had been a sailor seems to have been introduced to explain how "he caught the fever, and came nigh dying" (137), fits with the underlying morbidity of the story, and suggests that a long-delayed relapse might account for his death. Howard is more precise in opposing Merrymusk to "the values of the everyday world," for Merrymusk suffers the delusion that all health and sustenance are assured by the cock's crow.

theme that permeates much of his work—the nature of art and the role of the artist.

In pursuing this theme, he is led to investigate the necessity and the danger of certain features of illusion, with its mixture of idealism, deception, and delusion. It is present in *Mardi*, particularly in the conclusion when Taji chooses to pursue his idealized and illusory Yillah, rather than content himself with what he calls "a life of dying."[14] It is not far beneath the surface in *Redburn*, especially in regard to Redburn's imaginative deficiency and the Redburn–Harry Bolton relationship. Central also in "Hawthorne and His Mosses," probably Melville's most hopeful view of the possibilities for the artist in America, it is one of the strands in the many lines that run through *Moby Dick*. More readily identifiable in *Pierre* and in "Bartleby," it is nevertheless implicit in "The Two Temples," "The Bell-Tower," "The Fiddler," "The Piazza," and *The Confidence-Man*. At times Melville examines this problem as an abstract, philosophical matter—at other times in a significantly American social context. Sometimes the metaphor for art is literature; but it may also be theater, painting, music, or sculpture, and often there are analogies to religion. "Cock-A-Doodle-Doo!," however, is Melville's most prolonged look at the psychic imbalance to which the artist is particularly susceptible because the force of his commitment can so readily make the values of art superior to those of life, the charm of illusion preferable to mundane realities.

When the narrator first hears the cock's crow, his world brightens, the sun reappears, the mists are dispersed. The clamorous and triumphant sound is contrapuntal to the earlier sound of the locomotive and even stronger in its hallucinatory power: "Bless me—it makes my blood bound—I feel wild. What? jumping on this rotten log here, to flap my elbows and to crow too?"[15] His concern with the

14. Herman Melville, *Mardi* (Evanston and Chicago: Northwestern University Press–Newberry Library, 1970), 654.

15. The language here and elsewhere in the story does seem to parody Thoreau or Emerson, but these were not by any means the major sources of primitivism and pantheism available to Melville. Near the end of the "Dollars damn me" letter, he describes his reaction to such ideas in Goethe: "*'Live in the all.'* That is to say, your separate identity is but a wretched one, —good; but get out of yourself, spread and expand yourself, and bring to yourself the tinglings of life that are felt in the flowers and the woods. . . . What nonsense!" Having rejected this romantic hypothesis and then in a postscript anticipating Hawthorne's rejection of it, Melville

cock's power to sustain his jubilation through the day (and thereby to sustain the narrator's new-found elation) is reflected in several lines he adapted from a couplet by Wordsworth (another major source of Melville's "all feeling"):

> . . . Of fine mornings,
> We fine lusty cocks begin our crow in gladness;
> But when eve does come we don't crow quite so much,
> For then cometh despondency and madness (CDD, 124).

Superficially, at least, the events of the story seem to reverse the sequence the narrator fears; that is, he seems to begin in madness and end in gladness. But perhaps the narrator is not the best judge of what has happened to him.

There is no doubt that Melville depended on Wordsworth's "Resolution and Independence" for more than the couplet he stretched into three-and-a-half lines. The opening lines of the poem establish the pattern for "Cock-A-Doodle-Doo!"

> There was a roaring in the wind all night;
> The rain came heavily and fell in floods;
> But now the sun is rising calm and bright;
> The birds are singing in the distant woods.

Becoming more specific, Wordsworth mentions the birds whose sounds brighten the day—stock-dove, jay, magpie, and skylark—but no rooster. Perhaps Melville's substitution, however, can be explained as much by American rusticity, or by the crowing cock as a traditional symbol of immortality, as by the Emerson–Thoreau emphasis on the signs and significance of morning.

---

switches back to indicate some sympathy for such an alluring illusion and to cite his awareness of the dangers of letting momentary illusion become persistent delusion: "This 'all' feeling, though, there is some truth in. You must often have felt it, lying on the grass on a warm summer's day. Your legs seem to send out shoots into the earth. Your hair feels like leaves upon your head. This is the *all* feeling. But what plays the mischief with the truth is that men will insist upon the universal application of a temporary feeling or opinion."

Melville asserts his own recognition of harsh reality in a third addendum to the letter: "You must not fail to admire my discretion in paying the postage on this letter." Either he had neglected to so with an earlier letter and Hawthorne chided him for it, or he merely wanted to indicate that he was not so mystical as to entrust even such intimate communication to intuitive transport. Herman Melville to Nathaniel Hawthorne, June 1(?), 1851, in Merrell R. Davis and William H. Gilman (eds.), *The Letters of Herman Melville* (New Haven: Yale University Press, 1960), 130–31.

The mood of elation, however, does not hold for the narrator of Wordsworth's poem: "And fears and fancies thick upon me came; / Dim sadness—and blind thoughts, I knew not, nor could name." He thinks of poets less fortunate than he, "of Chatterton, the marvellous boy" and offers the couplet that Melville altered: "We poets in our youth begin in gladness; / But thereof come in the end despondency and madness." The most apparent change of course is the substitution of *cocks* for *poets* in Melville's version, a substitution that strongly suggests a connection as well as a distinction. The cock in this somewhat ridiculous equation becomes the spokesman for poetry and art, or perhaps more accurately, an emblem of what attractions, satisfactions, and dread liabilities await the artist who insists on "the universal application" of "Live in the all" and "Never say die!"

Wordsworth's poet–narrator next meets the unfortunate old man who provided some of the basis for Melville's Merrymusk. Despite age, pain, and misfortune, this old man remains dignified, cheerful, and firm in mind, as he barely ekes out a pittance by grubbing in the mud of country ponds for leeches. The example of the old man, so admirable in spirit and intellect, points the way for the poet out of his depression and morbidity.[16]

The sound of the cock's crow does the same for Melville's narrator. It gives him a new zest for life, transforms his view of the world, virtually makes him a new man:

---

16. It is possible that Melville was also influenced by Wordsworth's comments on his own poem: "I will explain to you . . . my feelings in writing *that* poem. . . . I describe myself as having been exalted to the highest pitch of delight by the joyousness and beauty of nature; and then as depressed even in the midst of those beautiful objects, to the lowest dejection and despair. A young poet in the midst of the happiness of nature is described as overwhelmed by the thoughts of the miserable reverses which have befallen the happiest of all men, *viz.* poets. I think of this till I am so deeply impressed with it, that I consider the manner in which I was rescued from my dejection and despair almost as an interposition of Providence. A person reading the poem with feelings like mine will have been awed and controlled, expecting something spiritual or supernatural. What is brought forward? A lonely place, 'a pond, by which an old man *was*, far from all house or home:' not *stood*, nor *sat*, but *was*—the figure presented in the most naked simplicity possible. This feeling of spirituality or supernaturalness is again referred to as being strong in my mind in this passage. . . . I cannot conceive a figure more impressive than that of an old man like this, the survivor of a wife and ten children, travelling alone among the mountains and all lonely places, carrying with him his own fortitude and the necessities which an unjust state of society has laid upon him." Christopher Wordsworth (ed), *Memoirs of William Wordsworth*, (2 vols.; London: Edward Moxon, 1851), I, 172–73.

Well, I have an appetite for my breakfast this morning, if I have not had it for a week before. I meant to have only tea and toast; but I'll have coffee and eggs—no, brown stout and a beef-steak. I want something hearty. Ah, here comes the down-train: white cars, flashing through the trees like a vein of silver. How cheerfully the steam-pipe chirps! Gay are the passengers. There waves a handkerchief—going down to the city to eat oysters, and see their friends, and drop in at the circus (CDD, 124–25).

Even the mist and smoke which earlier cast such a morbid pall over the village becomes transfigured in this new light:

Look at the mist yonder; what soft curls and undulations round the hills, and the sun weaving his rays among them. See the azure smoke of the village, like the azure tester over a bridal-bed. How bright the country looks there where the river overflowed the meadows. The old grass has to knock under to the new (CDD, 124–125).

But we must ask ourselves whether Wordsworth's *gladness* might not be synonymous with Melville's inspired *madness*, whether the narrator's mood in which he thinks better of himself, of his world, and of his rekindled appetites, really constitutes a healthy outlook or a manic optimism. He has a newly awakened power to act, and to act violently if necessary, against forces that would darken his day:

Well, I feel the better for this walk. Home now, and walk into that steak and crack that bottle of brown-stout, and by the time that's drank—a quart of stout—by that time I shall feel about as stout as Samson. Come to think of it, that dun may call, though. I'll just visit the woods and cut a club. I'll club him, by Jove, as he duns me this day (CDD, 125).

All of this positive self-assertion constitutes an extreme inversion of the narrator's earlier mood and attitudes. Not only has he poeti-cized the railroad and the factory village (as Emerson required in "The Poet") but he plays upon *stout* (as he had earlier done with *drug*), delights in the multiple meanings and grammatical switches sparked by *club* and *dun*, and substitutes the promise of potency for the earlier imagery of impotence. He is no longer obsessed by the imagery of illness, frustrated union, parodies of copulation and birth, and unexpected death. These have been replaced by pleasant fanta-sies of dalliance and fecundity. Even when the dun does arrive, the narrator's behavior suggests a new-found erotic health, as well as ag-

gressive insolence. Instead of going down to meet him, he has the
dun sent up, since, as he says, "I was reading *Tristram Shandy*, and
could not go down under the circumstances." He has reached one of
the bawdier sections of the book—probably the ambiguous playful-
ness of Uncle Toby's insistence that the Widow Wadman touch the
place where he had been wounded. (Her mind is on anatomy, his on
geography and cartography; hence the misunderstanding.) Melville's
narrator cannot get the dun to share his enjoyment of the book or of
a glass of stout, and in a gesture of contemptuous unconcern starts to
light his pipe with his creditor's bill. He then proceeds to throw the
man out, "tied . . . with a sailor-knot . . . his bill between his teeth."
He further orders his hired boy to draw from a sack of potatoes, and
"pelt this pauper away: he's been begging pence of me, and I know
he can work but he's lazy." This description is a brave inversion of
reality and is humorous only if the reader thinks the narrator does
not really believe his own words but is being consciously ironic. Appropriately enough, his conquest of the dun is marked by "a trumpet-
blast of triumph" from the unseen rooster, and the narrator takes
this as justification for his violence and corroboration "that duns only
came into the world to be kicked, banged, bruised, battered,
choked, walloped, hammered, drowned, clubbed!" (CDD, 126–27).
He has acted out a fantasy of self-justified violence, different only in
degree and focus from his earlier fantasy of revenge against the establishment.[17] The dun, with his talk of chores and debts, repre-

---

17. This act of violence further exemplifies the pattern of the paranoid schizophrenic. Consider Rosenbaum's discussion of this thought disorder:

> Delusions and hallucinations, usually of a persecutory or grandiose nature, are quite fre-
> quent. . . . Intellectual functioning, especially outside the areas of delusional thinking,
> tends to be well preserved. The primary mental mechanism is that of projection: the attri-
> bution of that patient's own repressed thoughts and feelings onto such outside forces as
> other people or hallucinated voices. Paranoid schizophrenia frequently makes a later onset
> than do the other varieties with new cases appearing in patients who are in their thirties or
> forties. To the degree that the patient comes to accept a paranoid explanation of his mental
> condition the prognosis is poor; to the degree that he remains anxious about how "real" his
> paranoid experiences are, the prognosis is better. When a patient accepts a psychotic expla-
> nation for the mystifying and frightening events that have been taking place, his anxiety is
> relieved to a great extent, the state of uncertainty ended. Paranoid schizophrenics usually
> maintain an attitude of great aloofness and contempt for the world. . . . If privately they
> have concluded that a certain person is personally responsible for their discomfort, they
> may assault that person. Such selective assaultiveness stands in marked contrast to the un-
> differentiated destructiveness of a catatonic excitement (*The Meaning of Madness*, 28–29).

sented conscience and conventional justice, a sense of responsibility rooted in the past; the narrator has become an anarchic rebel, denying the past with its debts and its physical and emotional restraints.

As his quest for the source of sustained inspiration continues, he raises the unseen rooster to godlike status, telling himself the sound bespeaks no "foolish, vain-glorious crow of some young sophomorean cock, who knew not the world." Rather he is convinced he hears "the crow of a cock who knew a thing or two; the crow of a cock who had fought the world and got the better of it. . . . It was a wise crow; an invincible crow; a philosophic crow; a crow of all crows." Infused by the meaning he has read into the cock's crow—the illusion that now directs his quest—he is no longer daunted by debts, poverty, political tyranny and injustice, or even fatal accidents: "I felt as if I could meet Death, and invite him to dinner, and toast the Catacombs with him, in pure overflow of self-reliance and a sense of universal security" (CDD, 127–28).

Pursuing the illusion which has, by now, become the source of his delusion, the narrator overlooks a number of implied warnings. He is contemptuous of an "old man mending a tumbledown old rail-fence. The rails were rotting, and . . . crumbled into yellow ochre." Ignoring the analogy to his own faith in illusion, he judges the old farmer to be suffering from "incipient idiocy" and bound for "the asylum" for trying to "make rotten rail-fences stand up on their rotten pins" or mend them "with their own rotten rails." He views this kind of futile self-reliance or equally futile reliance on weak material in the world as "an enterprise to make the heart break." Nearby is a herd of steers "possessed as by devils," and his next encounter is with the owner of ten Shanghai roosters who seem "carrot-colored monsters" (CDD, 130–32). There is little benevolence in these circumstances of nature; rather they hint at meanings that contradict the narrator's "light—elliptical—airy—buoyant" view of the world (CDD, 128). He has become the victim of his own transcendental imagination, too quick in rationalizing contradictions and dismissing fears. Although he begins "to think there was some sort of deception in this mysterious thing" and to wonder whether the "heroic and celestial crow" might be produced by "some wonderful ventriloquist," he very quickly rejects the supposition (CDD, 135).

His obsessive search extends for days, then weeks. He further mortgages his property to pay past debts, continuing to believe in the buoyant exultation of the cock's crow. When he does ultimately find the cock, it is magnificently resplendent, "of a haughty size," standing "haughtily on his haughty legs," in front of the shanty that housed an impoverished woodcutter and his disease-ridden family (CDD, 139). This man, ironically named Merrymusk, is the proud owner of the noble bird and will not sell him for any price. Like the narrator, Merrymusk is sustained in his faith by the awe-inspiring power of the majestic fowl, to whom his ailing children are also devoted.

The narrator calls the fowl "Signor Beneventano," after a singer whose performance he had much admired in the Italian opera.[18] And he sticks to that name even after everyone else refers to the cock as "Trumpet." In so doing he again emphasizes the connection with art, pretense, performance, and artifice, but also undercuts it with a double pun on *blowhard*. A true devotee, he has suspended all disbelief; his illusion has become his reality. So too, Merrymusk, his invalid wife, and their four ailing children, who believe strongly enough in the recurrent affirmations of Trumpet's crow that they are blind to their own obvious misery and deprivation. For them, as for the narrator, "he irradiated the shanty; he glorified its meanness. He glorified the battered chest, and tattered gray coat, and the bunged hat. He glorified the very voices which came in ailing tones from behind the screen." He glorified their miserable circumstances (as Wordsworth had glorified the leech gatherer), drawing strength from the simple religion of this old man who outlived his wife and ten children. Merrymusk's comment—"Better than a 'pothecary, eh? . . . This is Dr. Cock himself"—points up Trumpet's role as healer and reminds us of the drug–disease motif so prominent early in the story (CDD, 141–43). He is their best medicine, their solace, their opiate, the focus of their faith, and the source of their joy; and ultimately—like Christ's association of the cock's crow and subsequent betrayal—he betrays their faith in him.

18. Though taken from Melville's actual experience, the name is etymologically appropriate, combining *bene* (good or well) and *ventare* (to blow hard), as well as suggesting *ventrola* (a weathervane or weathercock).

As a healer, he can minister only to the spirit, crowing in apparent triumph as, in quick succession, each member of the family dies. Yet each dies, insisting in his own way that all is well. Even in the midst of such pathos, the cock still retains the magical power to transform the most sordid circumstances into seeming victory. It is the alchemy of faith, the artfulness of illusion, perpetrated by the priest–actor–artist:

> The pallor of the children was changed to radiance. Their faces shone celestially through grime and dirt. They seemed children of emperors and kings, disguised. The cock sprang upon their bed, shook himself, and crowed, and crowed again, and still and still again. He seemed bent upon crowing the souls of the children out of their wasted bodies. He seemed bent on rejoining instanter this whole family in the upper air. The children seemed to second his endeavors. Far, deep, intense longings for release transfigured them into spirits before my eyes. I saw angels where they lay (CDD, 146).

It is a moment of triumph, the seeming indication of confidence and illusion, a supreme theatrical coup. Again the cock crowed over the dead children: "It was now like a Bravo! like a Hurrah! like a three-times-three! hip! hip! He strode out of the shanty. I followed. He flew upon the apex of the dwelling, spread wide his wings, sounded one supernatural note, and dropped at my feet." Despite the death of the cock and his failure as a healer in any physical sense, the narrator maintains his faith and assumes in a sort of apostolic parody the mantle of Signor Beneventano. He arranges for the stone that marks the mass grave to bear the image of a crowing cock and the words of St. Paul, still denying the finality of death:

> O death, where is thy sting?
> O grave, where is thy victory?

But in the face of the evidence, these rhetorical questions seem a dubious basis for insisting on immortality, an ironic means of simultaneously certifying the victory of faith and illusion and suggesting its hollowness. The more bizarre counterpart of this maddening ambiguity is the final surrealistic spectacle of the narrator warding off despair with his own dubious ululation of triumph and affirmation—"COCK-A-DOODLE-DOO!—OO!—OO!—OO!—OO!" His conversion is complete and he is unmanned by the beatific delusion that he is one with his illusion (CDD, 146–47). Had the narrator been able to finish *Tristram Shandy*, as Melville surely did, he would have known that the last sentence of that novel passes punning judgment on itself as a very good "Cock and bull" story.

It has been a sobering story about a man intoxicated by illusion. Forced to choose between a depressing reality full of tyranny, hypocrisy, and disease and a transcendental view of art and the spiritual liberation it provides, he chose art. His choice led him to make the illusory real and to deny that art is also a kind of lie, faith a kind of imaginative pretense. Melville's purpose was more cautionary than comic, not a devaluation of art or any other realm of transcendant values, but a warning that the extremes of confidence and commitment could betray perception and lead to severe derangement. Fortunately "Cock-A-Doodle-Doo!" was an early formulation rather than Melville's last word on the subject. He continued to weigh the values of illusion and of disillusionment, concluding that it is the unique role of the artist to create the one sort of illusion, which, when understood properly, can help others to face life and the world with fewer illusions. Or to put it more directly, through the "lies" of art, the artist could express the truth that unmasked the lies of the world.

7

◎◎◎

A HOUSE
DIVIDED

"Bartleby"

Inasmuch as "Bartleby" is certainly the most familiar of Melville's short stories, it may seem hard to say something new about this early study of alienation, frustration, and catatonic withdrawal; and the surest guard against originality, I suspect, would be to take account of every commentary on the story. It would be more foolish, however, to try to clear one's mind completely of what others have written about Melville's pitiable and peculiar clerk and the initially complacent but ultimately vulnerable lawyer who narrates the tale.[1]

Despite my having chosen to discuss "Bartleby" at this late stage, I should indicate that it was Melville's first published short story and constitutes a remarkable attempt at a new genre and a considerable recovery from his disappointment over the public reception of *Pierre* in 1852. It was, however, more a recovery in terms of technical virtuosity than in the expression of a more positive outlook, especially in regard to the title character, who, we have been frequently told, confronts the dismal prospects of the aspiring American artist or writer. It was a subject which, quite understandably, never ceased to interest, attract, and challenge Melville—whether in the general

1. Among the numerous commentaries on "Bartleby," I would call attention to two in particular for their skill and thoroughness, and for their relevance to the discussion which follows. They are Leo Marx, "Melville's Parable of the Walls," *Sewanee Review*, LXI (October, 1953), 602–27 (especially valuable for its discussion of Bartleby's condition as Melville's pessimistic view of the fate of the writer in America and an index to his own state of mind); and H. Bruce Franklin, *The Wake of the Gods: Melville's Mythology* (Stanford, Calif: Stanford University Press, 1963), 126–36 (memorable for its convincing argument that Bartleby's ascetic withdrawal recapitulates a strain of Hindu mysticism and much of the significance of Christ, in ethical contrast to the way of Wall Street).

terms of the nature of art, the strengths and liabilities of the artist, or
the particular circumstances of the American scene. If the height of
Melville's faith in what the serious writer could accomplish in America occurred in his enthusiastic review of Hawthorne's *Mosses*, he
reached the depths in *Pierre* and the two short works that followed
in the early 1850s—"Bartleby" and "Cock-A-Doodle-Doo!"

To approach "Bartleby" only as an analogue of the alienated artist
in an insensitive society, however, is to ignore a great deal of the
contextual richness or symbolic suggestiveness of the story. The
stony impersonality of urban America so prominent in the latter
parts of *Pierre* is compressed into the Wall Street law office of "Bartleby," and both stories end with the death of the title character in
the steel and granite isolation of the Tombs—the would-be writer
crushed by the ponderous judgments of a matter-of-fact society. In
each case the character's pathetic end is a compound of his personality (ideals, expectations, delusions, and compulsions) and the pressures of a pragmatic, profit-oriented, and apparently unsympathetic
society. Also in each case the character's psychological demise and
ultimate death follows a breakdown in communication between himself and his society.

When "Bartleby" first appeared (in two installments of *Putnam's
Monthly* in late 1853), the title read "Bartleby, the Scrivener. A
Story of Wall-Street." The shorter form adopted later was very likely
the result of typographical considerations in listing the contents of
Melville's *Piazza Tales*, where all the titles are brief; and since the
Piazza Tales has been the source of most subsequent republications
of the story, the shorter title has become the more familiar. This circumstance is unfortunate because it plays down the social and economic connotations of "Wall-Street" and the degree to which Bartleby was described or identified by his employment in the original
title. Melville's intention, it seems likely, was to use the extended
title to emphasize the highly dramatic, actually expressionistic, Wall
Street setting—a law office where the four employees are literally
and figuratively *walled in* by the circumstances of their employment
and by the social assumptions embodied in their employer and *walled
off* from any hope of mobility of self-fulfillment by the same concept

of class structure. These physical arrangements and social assumptions create an atmosphere of separation and division.

In a less obvious sense than in *White-Jacket*, where the United States ship *Neversink* was a man-of-war representation of an overwhelmingly hierarchical society with distinct class and caste divisions, the Wall Street office is a microcosmic representation of a simpler but similarly structured segment of American society. To Bartleby—who secures employment as a legal copyist, a sort of animated Xerox machine duplicating the documents that reinforce and perpetuate the status quo—the office seems a dead-end existence, denying his unique human individuality, curtailing his freedom of choice, and corroborating his hopelessness. His withdrawal from what his employer would judge to be socially productive activity into his "dead-wall revery" is Bartleby's resentful confirmation of the gross inequities and subtle iniquities of an existence that is servile at best and imprisoning at worst. An illustration of the Marxist concept of alienation, he also fulfills Tocqueville's fearful prediction of the consequences of industrial employment in a burgeoning America (overlooking for the instant that the Wall Street office is not a factory but recognizing that it is as representationally American as the factory in "The Tartarus of Maids"): "It is in vain that laws and manners have been at pains to level all the barriers round such a man and to open to him . . . a thousand different paths to fortune . . . in the midst of universal movement it has rendered him stationary."[2]

Although he somehow obtains a key to the office, Bartleby chooses to remain permanently within an enclosure with no exit, a prisoner who is also his own jailer, so that when he is imprisoned in the Tombs and surrounded by the massive walls, his condition seems changed hardly at all. To his own satisfaction—or more accurately, dissatisfaction—he has proved that democratic theory masks despotic practice, that the supposedly open society can easily be closed off by those in power, and that Christian principle can be stretched to cover exploitative sham. But Melville grants Bartleby only a measure of truth and more than a modicum of distortion and delu-

2. Alexis de Tocqueville, *Democracy in America*, ed. Phillips Bradley (2 vols.; New York: Vintage Books, 1957), II, 169.

sion. He is a character akin to Franz Kafka's Josef K. or Gregor
Samsa, but his story is not as simple as one of Kafka's grotesque alle-
gories. Disenchanted as he often was, Melville did not yet view
American society as the Amerika of some present-day critics.

Technically "Cock-A-Doodle-Doo!" is a more Kafkaesque story
than "Bartleby." For one thing the narrator in the former story becomes more and more subject to his hallucinatory perception of reality, whereas the narrator in "Bartleby" suffers the loss of his comforting preconceptions and brushes against an aspect of reality he could
not earlier have imagined. More important, perhaps, is the fact that
we see nothing from Bartleby's point of view and have to guess at
what ails him, both aided and hindered by the narrator's perception
of Bartleby's symptoms and his interpretation of Bartleby's actions.
As the narrator says in the opening paragraph, "Bartleby was one of
those beings of whom nothing is ascertainable, except from the original sources, and, in his case, those are very small" (BS, 3). Despite
the scarcity of sources, we are given an extensive case history of Bartleby's last days. It is provided entirely by the narrator, who is a very
unlikely and somewhat unwilling evangelist. His account thus has its
inherent limitations, but it is the only gospel we have and it will
have to suffice.

Melville's handling of the point of view in this story is a conscious
and sustained artistic achievement, an exercise in irony unprecedented in American literature. Without apparent strain he manipu-
lates his narrator so that this well-heeled, self-satisfied source both
reveals and obscures the meaning of his troubling experiences. Not
by any means an entirely unreliable narrator, this representative of
conservative business interests is a man of realistically limited perception but capable of considerable moral growth. Melville's most
telling tactic, much like that of Mark Twain in *Huckleberry Finn*,
but more subtle, is to make the narrator's language suggest far more
than the character consciously realizes. Thus his attitudes, his actions and reactions, and most importantly his vocabulary reveal the
meanings that his mind cannot reach; they establish the three dimensions of the story: community, communication, and communion.

To understand these dimensions, we are required to approach
them, at least in part, from Bartleby's point of view, to approximate

his perspective, as "The Piazza," which preceded "Bartleby" in the 1856 volume, instructs us to do. The first dimension (or direction of implicative meaning) involves an idea that is social, political, and economic. The second extends the social function into areas of literary or artistic implication. And the significance of the third is obviously spiritual or religious. These dimensions are related, and partially overlap each other, while still being distinguishable. Yet from our growing intuition of Bartleby's point of view, each seems to have held forth a glowing possibility only to have it disproved by some impenetrable obstacle—physical, social, or metaphysical. The various walls, tangibly representing the obstacles Bartleby has found in his experience, inevitably shape his perspective and deny him any further prospect.

In American society, where promise is so great and expectation so high, Bartleby finds no place to go and no fulfillment in life. He lapses into lethargy, flouts the obligations of a work-money-property-oriented society, stubbornly asserts the negative aspects of his freedom of will, and in abandoning the world of social affairs and human relationships, seems to will his withdrawal from life itself. There is no clear diagnosis of what Bartleby suffers from, but there is enough evidence to construct a complex pathology, demonstrating that Melville found the sources of this condition in the character of the existing society and in the peculiar susceptibilities of the sensitive individual.

The main dimension of the story is concerned with the idea of *community*, or rather the lack of it, within the physical and social divisions of the Wall Street office. The narrator's estimate of himself and his relationship to his subordinates tells us a great deal. The possessive pronoun is prominent as he tells about "myself, my *employés*, my business, my chambers." Like the complacent lawyers in "The Paradise of Bachelors," men insulated from the troubling trials of life who used the law to right no wrongs, the narrator has sought "the cool tranquillity of a snug retreat" where he can "do a snug business among rich men's bonds, and mortgages, and title-deeds." He prides himself for being known as a "safe" man and for possessing such virtues as "prudence" and "method." Morality, justice, sympathy, or passion are outside his value system. He unashamedly loves money and venerates "the late John Jacob Astor," whose name becomes part of the narrator's litany—"for it hath a rounded and orbicular sound to it, and rings like unto bullion." Connotatively *Astor* not only suggests wealth but in combination with *orbicular* it also suggests a heavenly sphere in which the financial luminary Astor is the source of light and emotive power. And the narrator is not merely a well-to-do American or a spokesman for Wall Street, he is rather unabashedly an idolater of the golden bull—now become the almighty dollar. His priesthood of profit and his proprietary air shape his attitude toward the men who work for him. "My *employés*" could be a way of speaking, or it could mean that they have value as means to serve his financial ends (BS, 3–4).

This tendency of the narrator to judge others by their utility to him seems to make him more tolerant of human weakness or eccentricity, but in a very damaging way it mocks the possibility of men joining in a common enterprise founded on self-respect and sympathy. He is a benevolent master of his men and an enlightened employer–exploiter. He can put up with Turkey's excessive drinking, irritability, and carelessness if the elderly clerk remains useful and productive for a predictable part of the day. (Since he pays his copyists on a piecework rate rather than a salary, he can be more tolerant of their unproductive periods.) Turkey cannot be relied on in the afternoon, but Nippers, the other copyist, can be counted on to do his best work then. So between them these two employees (identified like Ginger Nut, the office boy, only by the demeaning nicknames, which turn them into things) produced a good day's work—a situation which the narrator accepts as "a good natural arrangement, under the circumstances" (BS, 10). Their greatest value, their existential purpose, is their service as distinct instrumentalities and not as individual human beings.

Of the two clerks, Nippers is easily the more ambitious, impatient at the routine and menial aspects of his employment and anxious to "be rid of a scrivener's table altogether." But instead of admiring Nippers for his enterprise, the narrator calls it "his diseased ambition"; instead of praising his attempts to raise his social position, the narrator charges him with "a continual discontent" (BS, 8). From the employer's point of view, Nippers is too uppity: he ought to know his place and accept it more graciously. Instead, he envies and in some small way assumes a few perquisites of power. These traits make him seem to his employer an insidious, and even at times satanic, threat to system and authority. Yet because Nippers' eccentricities are evident only when Turkey's are not, both men remain tolerably useful to their employer.

The narrator's essentially selfish standards and the superficial values of Wall Street society underlie his description of his employees' appearance and the acceptability of their dress. He can, for example, more easily overlook Nippers' shortcomings because "he always dressed in a gentlemanly sort of way; and so, incidentally, reflected credit upon my chambers." Turkey's clothes, however, are more apt to be messy and ill-fitting, and so the narrator, in an act of self-serving charity, gives him one of his own more "respectable-looking" coats, assuming that Turkey would show his appreciation by curbing his afternoon rashness. Instead of being more useful and productive and a greater credit to his employer's establishment, Turkey reacts resentfully to what his employer cannot recognize as a demeaning form of charity; and the narrator's explanation further degrades his employee: "Too much oats are bad for horses . . . and precisely as a rash, restive horse is said to feel his oats, so Turkey felt his coat. It made him insolent. He was a man whom prosperity harmed" (BS, 9). The attitude underlying the narrator's remarks is extremely class-oriented; Turkey, like Nippers, is guilty of not knowing his place and not responding properly to what his employer has so graciously bestowed on him. The narrator's reasons for hiring Bartleby so quickly, after merely "a few words touching his qualifications," have to do largely with his appearance and dress—"singularly sedate," "pallidly neat, pitiably respectable"—and the hope that he would be a steadying influence on the uneven tempers of Nippers and Turkey, a model of the neatness, servility, dependence, obedience, gratitude, and contentment the master wants in his scriveners.

The narrator's supreme position in this social microcosm is underscored by his employees' normally deferential attitudes, prefacing their statements with phrases like "with submission, sir" or "excuse me," very much as verbal communication with a reigning monarch would be prefaced with "by your grace." (In marked contrast, how-

ever, is Bartleby's "I prefer not to"—a not so subtle refusal to pay
him court.) The need for a third clerk is occasioned by the increased
business resulting from what the narrator terms "receiving the Master's office" (BS, 11). It is a conveniently abbreviated way of referring to his position as a Master in Chancery, but it further stresses
the social, economic, and psychological relationship between the
narrator and his clerks. Appointment to this office was not only a
very lucrative circumstance, as the narrator points out, but it also
conveyed considerable quasijudicial power. A Master in Chancery
rendered decisions in those matters of equity which the common
law did not cover and the courts were not constituted to settle.
There is irony, of course, in the narrator's being responsible for de-
termining matters of equity—what is fair, just, and impartial—
when his Wall Street ways are so fraught with inequities. A further
irony lies in the legal definition of *equity* which would apply the dic-
tates of conscience or principles of natural justice to settle controver-
sies. Needless to say, the partiality and self-interest of the narrator
are never in doubt and his conscience is merely the internalized dic-
tates of Wall Street. Melville may have had still more in mind in
calling such considerable attention to "the Master's office," for *chancery* can refer to "a wrestling hold that imprisions the head or encir-
cles the neck," and in legal usage the phrase *in chancery* can mean
"in a helpless, hopeless, or embarrassing position." It would not
have been beyond Melville to use such legalistic and lexicographical
puns to stress the subjugation of Wall Street's white-collar proletar-
iat. He could be even more blatant on this score in his indictment of
socially respectable white slavery in "The Tartarus of Maids."

The divisions and confinements that underlie the social relationships are more tangibly embodied in the physical setting. It becomes "a house divided" because such an arrangement fulfills the
narrator's conception of propriety, proprietorship, and utility. It
could easily be the stage setting for a work of twentieth-century ex-
pressionism:

> Ground-glass folding-doors divided my premises into two parts, one of
> which was occupied by my scriveners, the other by myself. According to
> my humor, I threw open these doors, or closed them. I resolved to as-
> sign Bartleby a corner by the folding-doors, but on my side of them so as

to have this quiet man within easy call, in case any trifling thing was to be done. I placed his desk close up to a small side-window. . . . Within three feet of the panes was a wall, and light came down from far above, between two lofty buildings, as from a very small opening in a dome. Still further to a satisfactory arrangement, I procured a high green folding screen, which might entirely isolate Bartleby from my sight, though not to remove him from my voice. And thus, in a manner, privacy and society were conjoined (BS, 11–12).

In these circumstances Bartleby, at least initially, "did an extraordinary quantity of writing," copying through the night as well as day. But it was writing done on command, with as much originality as a machine could muster. When the narrator wants Bartleby to aid in proofreading, he calls with the "natural expectancy of instant compliance," and instead of compliance, Bartleby issues his first "I would prefer not to" (BS, 13). The narrator sits stunned and unbelieving, as Bartleby's assertion of autonomy throws into turmoil the carefully controlled network of assumptions, expectations, and relationships.

In his quiet way Bartleby terrorizes the Wall Street establishment. His understated parody of Satan's *non serviam* implies a greater threat than Nippers' acts of resentment, but only in the dubious light of the Wall Street establishment, which he will not serve, does Bartleby appear a satanic character. From a different perspective there might be a noble madness in the stubborn obstructiveness and passive withdrawal which constitute the developing strategy of his peculiar and paradoxical insurrection.

In one sense it is merely that Bartleby knows his place and will not leave it; in another sense his immobilized behavior seems an act of gross contempt for the conventions of a society oriented to property and profit. His appropriation of private property for personal use—first sleeping in the office and then staging a passive sit-in when directed to leave—strikes at the heart of the system. It also hits the narrator where he lives, as it were: he first feels "disarmed" by Bartleby's quiet rebellion and ultimately feels "unmanned" by the threat to his authority (BS, 14, 21).

However weakened he personally feels, the narrator finds his role forced on him and his will stiffened by the Wall Street society that has served him so well. He must now serve that society and not

Bartleby's crippling eccentricity. By the standards of that society
Bartleby is a perverse nut, and for the narrator to continue to toler-
ate him would be sheer insanity. He is caught between the attitude
of blandly benign accommodation, which has enabled him to turn so
many circumstances to his own benefit, and the social rigidities and
conformist practices of Wall Street, which will permit no such per-
versity or eccentricity as Bartleby's. His decision to oust Bartleby reflects the pressure of the business community, which determines
substantially his status and identity, and his rather bland, apologetic
explanation is that "necessities connected with my business tyran-
nized over all other considerations." On Wall Street, apparently,
good form, conformity, and business forms are the essential means
of communication; thus the narrator's hoped-for farewell to Bartleby
(after giving him an amount in excess of wages due) concludes with
phraseology taken directly from the form of business correspondence: "If, hereafter, in your new place of abode, I can be of any service to you, do not fail to advise me by letter." The message and the
gift preceding it are a form of literal generosity but clearly lacking
the spirit of genuine charity, and in their formality both gift and
message discourage further communication and deny any idea of
community (BS, 29–30).

When Bartleby fails to leave the premises as he has been directed,
the narrator, with unconscious irony, puts the matter on a basis of
business law, asking first, "What earthly right have you to stay here?"
—not realizing that something more than "earthly right" might be
involved. Then he follows with questions that again stress the profit–
property nexus of Wall Street and of the culture at large: "Do you
pay any rent? Do you pay my taxes? Or is this property yours?" Bartleby remains silent; these are not *his* questions, and his seemingly
contemptuous withdrawal infuriates the narrator. In trying pru-
dently to check his anger, he begins to recognize the lack of communal attachments in circumstances like those of his office. He recalls a recent murder case that must have been of note to the New
York business community and wonders whether "the circumstances
of being alone in a solitary office, upstairs, of a building entirely un-
hallowed by humanizing domestic associations" did not help trigger
the act (BS, 33–34).

His innate prudence makes him seek an alternative to anger toward Bartleby, one that will soothe his sensibilities without offending his practical businessman's principles. His first refuge is a form of prudential charity but predicated on self-interest. His second is a kind of pragmatic predestination that glosses his providential relationship to Bartleby. But neither of these theological or philosophical rationalizations enables him to withstand the continuing pressure from his professional peers, and his conscience—more properly his malleable conscientiousness—caves in. Yet thrust Bartleby into the street, he cannot; so he takes the unlikely course of moving his offices to another location, separating himself and leaving Bartleby behind, breaking any possible connection, denying any further responsibility.

While Melville, through artfully constructed narrative, conveys a strong sense of the obstacles to community and the barriers to communication, he also drops hints of further enclosure and division. For one thing the narrator's description of his own power and authority melds into a supremacy that is more than social or economic. In describing Turkey's daily rhythm, he praises him for being "the blandest and most *reverential* of men in the morning," especially, "valuing his morning *services*" and resenting "his afternoon *devotions*" (when he is rash and excessively spirited). This deference and reverence is, of course, directed toward the narrator, who refers to himself as " a *man of peace*" (BS, 6–7). These terms (my italics) might be merely a mildly humorous sort of irony, were it not for the kind of vocabulary used in reference to Bartleby, or as a consequence of Bartleby. His first appearance is referred to as his "advent" (BS, 5). He is "this forlornest of mankind" (BS, 26); and for the puzzled and troubled narrator, he is "not only useless as a necklace, but afflictive to bear" (BS, 29). Several apparently unconscious puns on the word "assumption" spin off the narrator's reaction to Bartleby, and the narrator also speaks of Bartleby's "cadaverous triumph" and his "ascendency" (BS, 31–33). Such a "string" of linked multiple meanings cannot be accidental, and most readers will recognize that these terms have special application in Christian worship.

Moreover, Bartleby is described repeatedly in terms that stress his lack of coloration, his silence, his omnipresence, and his seeming perpetuity—all of which give him a supernatural cast. He is "pallidly neat" upon his first appearance, and later the narrator is "awed into . . . tame compliance" by Bartleby's "pallid haughtiness" (BS, 11, 24). All told, the words *pallid, pale, pallor*, or some similar variation are used fifteen times and *white* and *gray* once each in reference to Bartleby. Words that stress his silence—*quiet, calm, mute, still, noiseless*, as well as *silent* and other synonyms—appear more than twenty times. The emphasis on these attributes is important because of Melville's tendency to associate them with larger-than-life, awe-inspiring forces. To the narrator Bartleby also appears variously as an "apparition," "strange creature," "incubus," "ghost," or "haunt." Unlike other men, he never reads, never drinks beer, tea, or coffee, and seems to eat rarely and then only the spiced wafers called ginger nuts. In what seems an ironic commentary on the sacrament of communion, Bartleby dines on these wafers in solitude. Mystery surrounds his past; and his silence regarding his origins, family, motives, or complaints—Bartleby's own refusal to communicate—pushes the mystery into the present.

But before concluding that Bartleby is Christ (as Bruce Franklin, drawing heavily from the explication of Christian charity in Matthew 25, has done), I would like to suggest that Melville has left room for a natural explanation as well as a supernatural one. Bartleby's symptoms could substantiate a diagnosis of severe mental illness; that is, his condition could be that of a man who is suffering from the delusion that he is Christ and reacting to the indifference, self-absorption, or ridicule of mid–nineteenth-century American society. Or even without the presence of such a delusion, Bartleby's condition could be the consequence of a sensitive individual's reaction to the insensitivity of his surroundings, and a present-day psychoanalyst would find the symptoms forming a familiar composite.

In the taxonomy of schizophrenia provided by one contemporary psychiatrist, for example, we find the following symptoms for the type of catatonic which is characterized by stupor, with "an apparent, but not real, diminution of consciousness":

    i. Negativism, echolalia
   ii. Automatism, dreaminess, grimacing

    iii. Immobility, waxy flexibility
    iv. Refusal to eat[3]

Bartleby's negativism permeates every phase of his behavior, but it can be viewed as a distorted form of autonomy, an attempt at affirming the "I," a passive protest at depersonalization. His repeated response "I prefer not to" differs from the typical echolalia, in which the affected individual repeats the interviewer's or therapist's statements. Bartleby echoes and thereby asserts only himself. Automatism, of course, characterized his action before and after his refusal to work. First he worked day and night, copying "silently, palely, mechanically," then withdrew behind his screen into the dreamy, immobile state that the narrator terms "his dead-wall revery" (BS, 12, 28). The narrator compares Bartleby to a "pale plaster-of-paris bust of Cicero" (BS, 13). Dr. C. Peter Rosenbaum, describing schizophrenic patients in a catatonic stupor, writes that they "adopt strange, uncomfortable-looking, statuelike postures which they maintain for minutes or hours at a time." The narrator supposes that Bartleby's immobility and refusal to work are due to eye strain, "for his eyes looked dull and glazed" (BS, 28). Rosenbaum explains that in such a catatonic condition patients' "faces may portray dreaminess, grimacing, or tics, and frequently one has the impression that they are locked into contact with hallucinations to which . . . they cannot respond." The narrator is depressed by the thought of Bartleby's meager diet and after his removal to the Tombs, tries to provide more amply, but Bartleby refuses to eat and dies "huddled" and "wasted" on the stones "at the base of the wall" (BS, 45). Rosenbaum concludes his description, observing that "such patients may frequently be so immobilized that they neither eat nor maintain sphincter control" and adding that "tube feedings may be necessary to avoid death through inanition."[4] The symptomatology is remarkably similar in these instances, and the similarity is probably more than a matter of coincidence. Perhaps Melville offered a serious diagnosis when he had the twelve-year-old office boy in the story

3. C. Peter Rosenbaum, *The Meaning of Madness* (New York: Science House, 1970), 23.
4. *Ibid.*, 26, 28, 27.

say of Bartleby, "I think, sir, he's a little *luny*" (Melville's italics) (BS, 16).[5]

But "Bartleby" is much more than a case history, and my purpose is not to force such a conjectural psychoanalysis of a fictional figure, whose author, many will hasten to say, antedated the concepts and classifications of contemporary psychoanalysis. (There are too many instances when Melville's imagination led him to treat symbolically what social or behavioral science had not yet articulated for anyone to be long troubled by the thought that Melville could not have known such things. The serious artist is often surrogate psychoanalyst and vicarious victim in one). My purpose here is to propose that Melville could have meant the natural explanation and the supernatural suggestions of Bartleby's behavior to reinforce each other, in a more complex way than his friend Hawthorne had done in offering natural and supernatural alternatives.

To put it more simply, Bartleby is incapacitated by having internalized the schism that frustrates authentic community, intellectual and emotional communication, and spiritual communion. He has become a divided self, a kind of symbolic embodiment of what ails man and society. Obsessed by the imperfection around him, he is also affronted by such inadequate measures to make things right as having to verify copy. There is far more that cannot be made right in the human relationships that exist, in the lack of recognition or reinforcement for individual members of this false community on Wall Street. Having concluded, apparently, that in the kind of existence where vital reinforcement is unavailable, frustration is inevitable,

---

5. The psychodynamics of Bartleby's situation could be better interpreted through some recent post-Freudian developments which stress interpersonal relationships and other factors in the social environment as the cause of personal disturbance, in contradistinction to classical psychoanalysis which would relate the individual's internal conflict to early experience with parental figures. (Melville's narrator makes a point of saying that no such information about Bartleby's origins or early life is available.)

Recent developments in psychoanalytic thought most relevant to a case like Bartleby's include Harry Stack Sullivan's emphasis on the interpersonal situation, R. D. Laing's view of schizophrenia as an attempt to adjust to an apparently irrational or threatening environment, and perhaps most important of all, Gregory Bateson's description of dysfunctional modes of communication that convey paradoxical injunctions and result in personal strategies of response clinically identified as schizophrenia.

Bartleby has no faith in what might possibly sustain him and opts out.[6]

Ironically, he has had an effect and both minor and major changes are in process. Nippers and Turkey, as well as the narrator, come to use the word *prefer* with increasing frequency (while unaware that they use it at all) and thereby show the subtle impact of Bartleby, who also remains unaware of his power to make involuntary converts even among those who oppose him or make him the target of their separate hostilities. He also seems unaware that an important personality change is in process in his employer, whose efforts at charity, at first so prudential and pragmatic, become increasingly suffused with a sense of humanity and compassion. Although he never breaks free completely from his Wall Street proprieties, he shows less need to rationalize his actions or find a utilitarian justification for them. His private reflections reveal not only the growth of tolerance and sympathy, but also the greater profundity of a spiritual conversion:

> For the first time in my life a feeling of overpowering stinging melancholy seized me. Before, I had never experienced aught but a not unpleasing sadness. The bond of a common humanity now drew me irresistibly to gloom. A fraternal melancholy! For both I and Bartleby were sons of Adam. I remembered the bright silks and sparkling faces I had seen that day . . . and I contrasted them with the pallid copyist, and thought to myself, Ah, happiness courts the light, so we deem that misery there is none. These sad fancyings . . . led on to other and more special thoughts, concerning the eccentricities of Bartleby. Presentiments of strange discoveries hovered around me. The scrivener's pale form appeared to me laid out, among uncaring strangers, in its shivering winding-sheet (BS, 23).

"The bond of a common humanity," upon which the ideal of com-

6. In requiring the reader to approximate Bartleby's vantage point even as the events are recounted by his establishment-oriented employer, Melville has anticipated the sort of challenge that R. D. Laing has issued to traditional psychoanalysis. His approach is not to classify psychotic patients as examples of disease, but by approximating the point of view of the patient in his particular environmental circumstances, to show how apparently odd or irrelevant behavior can be meaningful and appropriate. Schizophrenia thus appears a psychological strategy devised to defend the victim's humanity in the midst of threatening circumstances, and even his most bizarre behavior can be seen as comprehensible response to his immediate situation. The parallel to Melville's story is quite remarkable as Laing seeks to anchor the explanation of psychotic symptoms in the social setting of the patient. See the "Preface" to the Pelican edition of *The Divided Self* (Middlesex, England: Penguin Books, 1965), 11.

munity and the concept of communion both depend, is not constant in the narrator's consciousness. The pressure of his Wall Street peers is still there, affecting him both before and after his move to new quarters. The new tenant who finds Bartleby is no more successful in getting him to work or to leave, and when he seeks out the narrator to question him about his former employee, the narrator admits to no personal knowledge of or responsibility for Bartleby. In fact he denies Bartleby three times publicly before returning to his old quarters in a final effort to oust him. Bartleby, however, shows no interest in any other possible employment and refuses the narrator's remarkably generous offer to take him into his own home.

He has seen something more in the offer than generosity and his refusal indicates his unwillingness to expose himself further to the kind of situation that has repeatedly victimized him. The situation has all the ingredients of what psychologists have come to call a *double-bind*: (1) two or more persons, one of whom can be designated the "victim"; (2) a repeated pattern that comes to be a habitual expectation in the victim's experience; (3) a negative injunction, such as the narrator's "if you do not go away from these premises . . . I shall feel bound—indeed, I *am* bound" followed by a threat of abandonment (BS, 41); (4) a secondary injunction conflicting with the first, communicated by either verbal or nonverbal means, and absolving the narrator from responsibility for whatever punishment follows, as in the narrator's offer to take Bartleby into his home, with the unspoken injunction that Bartleby will subsequently have to do his part; and (5) a further injunction prohibiting the victim from escaping, sealing him into the situation, as the symbolic walls and the narrator's reacting to Bartleby's immobility with "Stationary you shall be, then," seem to have done. Once an individual has come to perceive his relationships in double-bind patterns, almost any part of the expected sequence can be enough to precipitate the end result.[7] For Bartleby, who has learned to expect this kind of entrap-

---

7. The double-bind situation, first formulated by Gregory Bateson and his associates, is well summarized by R. D. Laing, *Self and Others* (London: Tavistock Publications, 1969), 125–31. In addition to the double-bind patterns that play such an important part in the stages of schizophrenia, Laing discerns another pattern (applicable to Bartleby) in the way people close to such a victim perceive his having gone through three basic phases from *good* to *bad* to *mad* (*The Divided Self*, 181–205).

ment, any attempt at communication invites catastrophe; existence becomes increasingly circumscribed, the walls more rigid, permanent, and inescapable.

In a scene that must be an ironic reversal of Christ driving the money-men from the Temple, Wall Street landlords and city authorities, with considerable difficulty, remove Bartleby from the Wall Street office, arrest him as a vagrant, and lock him in the Tombs. When the narrator visits him there, he can stimulate in Bartleby no will to live. Bartleby's last words to the narrator, who has tried to indicate what encouragement exists even in this environment, are, appropriately enough, "I know where I am," and indeed this place of total enclosure is not unfamiliar—the same encircling walls, the same repressive and punitive normality, and the same stony embodiment of antihuman institutions. The narrator imagines Bartleby spending his last days amid "murderers and thieves," tries unsuccessfully to provide him with food, and describes him, after he has died, as asleep "with kings and counselors" (BS, 46). The phraseology is extraordinarily portentous, yet somehow appropriate to "this forlornest of mankind."

Appended to the story is an unconfirmed rumor about Bartleby's previous employment as "a subordinate clerk in the Dead Letter Office at Washington" (BS, 46). Its position compels us to consider the paragraph even more carefully than the narrator does for its relevance to the preceding account. He sees it as a possible seed bed for Bartleby's negativism and a more certain source of his depression:

> Dead letters! does it not sound like dead men? Conceive a man by nature and misfortune prone to pallid hopelessness, can any business seem more fitted to heighten it than that of continually handling these dead letters, and assorting them for the flames? (BS, 46–47)

His question is not merely rhetorical, and to some extent he answers it himself. But the question is also a challenge to the reader who has been led through an account of Bartleby's last days in a somewhat stultifying law office in the heart of New York's financial district, where he labored in the service of a man who did "a snug business among rich men's bonds, and mortgages, and title-deeds." Thus part of the answer points to a society where the business of life is business and not life, and to the example of a man who chose the quietest alternative to such a desperate business.

The narrator's answer points to something else, too. Considering those undeliverable letters, he continues:

> For by the cart-load they are annually burned. Sometimes from out the folded paper the pale clerk takes a ring—the finger it was meant for, perhaps, moulders in the grave; a bank-note sent in swiftest charity—he whom it would relieve, nor eats nor hungers any more; pardon for those who died despairing; hope for those who died unhoping; good tidings for those who died stifled by unrelieved calamities. On errands of life, these letters speed to death.
> Ah, Bartleby! Ah, humanity! (BS, 47).

Undeniably, the narrator's words tend toward the sentimental and the melodramatic, but they are not banal. He has come a long way and has been drawn into a human problem for which there is no neat legal solution. In the only terms he could employ to express his tragic insight, he has again called our attention to the major areas of concern in the story—the frustration of timely communication, the barriers to productive human union, the utter despair of those who die still looking for answers, and the essential inhumanity of a society that treats these poignant records of human experience as so much waste for the incinerator. From his earlier perspective he could insist that while there is life there is hope, a way out of any disturbing situation. The sad, concluding sentences of the story, however, offer another view of the human condition: where there is life there is death, the most totally binding and inescapable aspect of existence.

The narrator had begun as a strong proponent of his own ethic of personal enrichment, a gospel of wealth for its own sake, and unexpectedly confronted a mysterious individual who, in an actual or an ironic sense, represented "the truth that would make men free" and who died in prison himself. But instead of merely recreating a basic pattern of Christian faith, Melville gives it compelling contemporary relevance by implying that the money worshiper's utilitarian and demeaning view of men as commodity or chattel is *deicidal* because it is essentially *homicidal*. It had cost Nippers and Turkey their full manhood, even before the "advent" of Bartleby. But paradoxically the lawyer–employer–master, who had been instrumental in stifling the human spirit and thereby denying God, is himself a slave to his Wall Street preconceptions. He seems to realize this at the end, but we do not know whether his insight will make him free. Like Emerson in his "Divinity School Address," Melville seems to be saying that any man can be his own Christ, not, however, in serving as his own savior, as Emerson insisted, but rather in realizing his own torment, abandonment, and martyrdom.

Despite the religious imagery in the story, there is little sense that death is Bartleby's liberation, somewhat more reason, perhaps, to believe in the narrator's redemption. He has had to serve as a not very willing or successful therapist in a relationship where the victim views his treatment as further persecution and where the narrator–therapist is forced to recognize in the victim an extreme example of what all men are heir to. Having lived as if he were already a prisoner, Bartleby precipitated a sort of self-fulfilling prophecy. Dying in the Halls of Justice, he confirms the metaphors by which he had lived—that the condition of life in human society is as circumscribed as that in a prison, and that a stony refusal is the most telling strategy against surrounding insensitivity.

R. D. Laing has used the term *petrification* to describe the kind of defensive network Bartleby employs. He suggests that an individual deprived of personal autonomy may fight back by negating the other person's autonomy, ignoring his feelings, and thereby depersonalizing him—as Bartleby does repeatedly, the last time being his answer to the narrator who has come to the Tombs, seen him, and called his name. Without turning around, Bartleby says, "I know you . . . and I want nothing to say to you" (BS, 43). According to Laing, such a contemptuous effort to turn the other person into a thing is a strategy of "nullifying any danger to himself by secretly totally disarming the enemy." Hence there is deep psychological trauma as well as social and economic threat in the circumstances which impel the narrator to refer to himself twice as "disarmed" and twice more as "unmanned." Beginning with Bartleby's first stony refusal, his circumstances illustrate Laing's reciprocal dynamic of petrification. The narrator describes his initial reaction in terms of stony transformation: "I was turned into a *pillar* of salt, standing at the head of my seated *column* of clerks" (my italics), but he simultaneously reveals his own earlier depersonalization of his clerks (BS, 14). Melville actually seems to have been using this imagery of petrification consciously, for not only is Bartleby early compared to a piece of statuary, he seems, when the narrator gives him money and orders him to leave, "like the last column of some ruined temple" (BS, 30). Laing's view, borne out by Melville's story, is that the petrification process "involves a vicious circle. The more one attempts to preserve one's autonomy and identity by nullifying the specific human individuality of the other, the more it is felt to be necessary to continue to do so, because with each denial of the other person's ontological status, one's own ontological security is decreased, the threat to the self from the other is potentiated and hence has to be even more desperately negated."[8]

Bartleby's stony behavior could thus be viewed as an attempt to forestall the threat of being turned into an inanimate thing by his employer, a defensive strategy to avoid being engulfed by the narrator's Wall Street whirlpool. To prevent his becoming an object and being drawn into his employer's world, Bartleby turns himself into a stubborn and steadfast stone. His function is far more limited than before; he is either an opaque immobility that puzzles and offends his employer or a reflector turning back the other's gaze. Frustrated by the fraudulent communication in which he has had to participate, he becomes a silence or an echo—the only communication one gets from a stone.

The narrator's last words express in part his realization of what Bartleby has exemplified and the general susceptibility of humanity to such a view. Not only has Bartleby been physically and psychologically crippled by the pattern of double-binds in his life, the narrator has also recognized his own involvement in the pattern, initially as master and ultimately as victim. Like the therapist who may be

---

8. Laing, *The Divided Self*, 46–52.

drawn into the psychosis of his patient or the lawyer who may participate vicariously in the criminality of his client, the narrator also recognizes that he has furthered the frequently unfair laws of the dominant society. In this sense of a shared fate he has become Bartleby's
double, and his account might even be suggesting the universal
applicability of such an appalling conclusion. At least he has
grasped the general lesson that Bartleby never fully articulated,
but we do not know whether he will act on any of its more immediate corollaries, such as the somber irony that there is as
much justice in the Tombs as there is equity in the Wall Street
law office.

There is no hint of a physical resurrection in the story; Bartleby
does not rise from the Tombs. But there is a possibility that the
narrator has accomplished in his record of mind, memory, and conscience the only immortality Bartleby was to have. Or to put it differently, Melville, in the artfully recreated conscience of his narrator, has ambiguously reaffirmed Bartleby's "cadaverous triumph"
and his ultimate "ascendency." In this sense the narrator's lament
for Bartleby and for humanity is prompted by his recognition that for
the greater number of persons now alive or yet to be born, Bartleby
can appear only an unredeemable fool, his contempt for the world
an unholy madness, his attempt at social insurrection an abortive
failure, and his resurrection out of the question. In Melville's dimly
lit theater of hope, life is too often a surrealistic allegory; and art,
which could reverse the conventional view of the world and invert
the more typical judgments of society, is our only feeble means of
redemption.

"I and My Chimney"

It is not likely at this stage that anyone will offer a radically new or
original interpretation of "I and My Chimney," but the story has important implications which have not been adequately explained and
a continuing relevance to the circumstances of American society
which warrants further exploration. At least two dozen critics have
turned their attention to this story, making it probably the third-

most-commented-upon story after "Bartleby" and "Benito Cereno."[9] The range of interpretations provides ample evidence of the schismatic character of American literary criticism and brings to mind the observation of James Fenimore Cooper's archetypical American, Aristabulus Bragg, regarding doctrinal and denominational differences, in Chapter X of *Home As Found*: "This is a free country . . . and freedom loves variety. 'Many Men, many minds.'" So one ought not be surprised to find that one reading emphasizes the autobiographical basis of the story, another the phallic byplay, and still others its covert recitation of the explorations of a leading nineteenth-century Egyptologist or its allegorical treatment of the national disagreement on the issue of slavery. Many minds, many meanings; and as in Melville's review of Hawthorne's *Mosses*, in dealing with the suggestive ambiguities of significant literature, we often succeed in defining ourselves.

The interpretation which seems closest to my own, at least initially, is that of Stuart Woodruff, which recognizes both private and public dimensions in the story. But instead of using the story to explicate Melville's "basic epistemology," as Woodruff does, I want to focus on the pattern of opposites and divisions which I feel constitute Melville's imaginative response to contradictions in his own circumstances and in American society at large. "I and My Chimney" offers a Pisgah view of American values, figuratively embodied in the domestic tensions that mark the marriage of mismatched mates.

The narrator of this story can be identified with the post-middle-aged narrator of several domestic tales, who gives his name as Will-

9. Full-scale inquiry into the meaning of the story was initiated by Merton M. Sealts, Jr., in *American Literature*, XIII (May, 1941), 142–51. Subsequent criticism of the story has been summarized by Sealts in "Melville's Chimney, Reexamined," in Ray B. Browne and Donald Pizer (eds.), *Themes and Directions in American Literature* (Lafayette, Ind: Purdue University Press, 1969), 80–102. Sealts understandably exhibits varying degrees of sympathy toward these latter interpretations—least sympathy of all toward the position he terms *revisionist*, illustrated by Stuart C. Woodruff in "Melville and His Chimney," *PMLA*, LXXV (June, 1960), 283–92. Woodruff's revisionist character apparently lies in the degree of difference between his argument that the story "may be considered a thoroughgoing symbolic expression of Melville's basic epistemology" (283) and what must be the "orthodox" interpretation—Sealts' argument that the chimney represents Melville's heart and soul, that the role of the wife in the story allegorizes the concern of Melville's own wife about the soundness of his mind, and that Scribe (the architect who examines the chimney) might be identified as Dr. Oliver Wendell Holmes, who might have examined Melville for something more than rheumatism and sciatica in 1855.

iam Ford in "Jimmy Rose." He is characteristically conservative and
well past the age when he might have welcomed competition and
conflict. He seems at least a chronological generation older—and I
think a psychological generation older, too—than Melville, even in
his post-*Pierre* slump. In "I and My Chimney" he is even more unabashedly conservative, readier to stress the emotional links he feels
toward Old World royalty and picturesque decay, and closer to that
age when a man thinks of a calm and comfortable retirement than in
the other stories. Thus he is a less readily identifiable spokesman for
Melville himself, or at most a very limited representation of Melville's point of view. But I do not mean to imply that he therefore
cannot be an effective means for articulating issues or problems that
concern Melville, but rather to stress that Melville did not necessarily stand in the same place as his narrator, even though he placed
that narrator in surroundings familiar to Melville himself. Surely
there can be differing perspectives even from the same piazza.

The first set of conjoined antagonisms suggested by the narrator's
musings on his chimney is that of church and state, as in his parallel-
ing the phrase which forms the title of the story with Cardinal Wolsey's "I and my King." Like Wolsey, who joined ecclesiastical and
political roles in a single career, the chimney combines both sacred
tradition and temporal substance and power. In one paragraph it is
described as "a huge, corpulent old Harry VIII" and steeple-like
with swallows' nests in it (IMC, 373). When guests come, the chimney and not the narrator "is, indeed, the true host" (IMC, 374).
Whalelike as it breaks through the roof, it seems modeled after older
architectural forms of sacred and temporal power such as "the pyramid of Cheops" (IMC, 377). Utilitarian modifications to the roof
which led to shortening the chimney by fifteen feet are likened to
"beheading my royal old chimney—a regicidal act" (IMC, 378).
Elsewhere it seems a "grand high altar . . . right worthy for the celebration of high mass before the Pope of Rome, and all his cardinals,"
or in a more pagan mood, "it has a druidical look" in the primeval
depths of the cellar (IMC, 382, 380). In a symbolic as well as in an
actual architectural sense, the chimney both dominates and extends
deeper than the house itself, and is appropriately associated with an
ancestor, Captain Julian Dacres, whose last name, as Merton Sealts

first indicated, is an anagram of *sacred*, but whose first name could suggest Julian the Apostate, who, after becoming emperor, abandoned Christianity.

But the house itself has some unusual features that are symbolically suggestive. It is not apparently one of those houses "which are strictly double houses—that is, where the hall is in the middle [and] the fireplaces . . . on opposite sides; so that while one member of the household is warming himself at a fire built into a recess of the north wall, say another member, the farmer's own brother, perhaps may be holding his feet to the blaze before a hearth in the south wall." Although the narrator's house, with its massive central chimney, is not so obviously a double or divided house, it nevertheless is a house with important divisions in it. Architecturally at least, the chimney serves to integrate the structure. Containing the flues from the several separate fireplaces, it forms "one federal stock in the middle of the house," in contrast to the more modern arrangement whereby each room with a fireplace "has its separate flue—separate throughout, from hearth to chimney-top" (IMC, 374–75). The arrangement of rooms, each serving as entry to another, is "like a philosophical system" (IMC, 389), and it thus becomes hard not to see some political analogy wherein separate flues suggest a states' rights doctrine contrasting with the stronger central tendencies of a federal system. This analogy, beginning with a description of domestic architecture and culminating with an account of irreconcilable differences within the domestic union of husband and wife, is strengthened by what follows in the story. It is a story of differences in domestic policy in virtually every sense of that phrase and of domestic strife that probably permeated the atmosphere of the United States in the 1850s as much as it did the Melville household itself.

I suspect that if the familiar quotation about "a house divided against itself" were less uniformly associated with Lincoln, it might already have been applied to Melville's story.[10] Surely Lincoln's source for the statement (Matthew 12:25) was no less available to

10. Since writing this section, I have read Laurie Lorant's discussion in "Herman Melville and Race" (Ph.D. dissertation, New York University, 1972), wherein she too uses the "house divided" phrase, views the chimney as suggestive of the integrity of the Union, and identifies it even more explicitly with the conservative character of the Constitution, especially in its tacit acceptance of slavery (154).

Melville. The context for the biblical statement, which Jesus addressed to the Scribes and Pharisees, suggests another characteristic of and source for Hiram Scribe, who so readily cooperates with the narrator's wife and who many, following Sealts' suggestion, have identified with Dr. Oliver Wendell Holmes in his dual role as writer and, on occasion perhaps, as physician to Herman Melville. Here is the basic quotation: "Every kingdom divided against itself is brought to desolation; and every city or house divided against itself shall not stand." Clearly, the analogy hinted at in the early paragraphs of Melville's story is more explicit in the biblical quotation, and the story in turn may be an even bleaker foreshadowing of irrepressible conflict than has been previously supposed.

I think Woodruff was correct in recognizing the degree to which the story may be considered a criticism of America's "infatuate juvenility" or "youthful incredulity"—both phrases used to describe the narrator's excessively dynamic, vital, and progressive wife (IMC, 386, 385). In her focus on youth and renewal she seems to believe in her own inexhaustible fertility, and thus constitutes a most appropriate Eve for an American Adam—a role for which the narrator is most decidedly unfit. The differences in attitude between these two are much more than the ordinary differences even among greatly mismatched couples. They seem, rather, like the cultural antagonism or the philosophical differences which could be present in any fairly open society but which were particularly poignant, Melville apparently felt, in mid–nineteenth-century America. In this sense, the chimney serves first as a means of discerning and ultimately as the means of separating or polarizing the attitudes which make this story of a house divided. The chimney, in short, becomes the touchstone for distinguishing what Emerson once called the party of "hope" from what he called the party of "memory," one oriented toward the future and the other toward the past.[11]

The narrator clearly belongs to the party of memory. Not only

11. R. W. B. Lewis employed these distinctions of "hope" and "memory" in *The American Adam* (Chicago: University of Chicago Press, 1955), having derived them from Emerson's 1867 retrospective appraisal of "Life and Letters in New England," but Melville could have had access to the same distinctions in the widely discussed 1841 lecture on "The Times," published in 1844, though there is no necessity to prove that he derived his polarity of outlooks from Emerson.

does he think better of Old World palaces, redolent of power and privilege, than he does of New World egalitarianism, where "any man can buy a square foot of land and plant a liberty-pole on it" (IMC, 375), his affinities are invariably with age and decay. His tastes run to "old cheese and old wine," and he avoids "young people, hot rolls, new books, and early potatoes." He confesses himself "very fond of my old claw-footed chair, and the old club-footed Deacon White" (IMC, 386). His reverential feeling for the monumental chimney, he realizes, has put him "into a sad rearward way altogether; . . . quite behind the age, too, as well as running behindhand in everything else" (IMC, 374). Resisting reform and skeptical of renewal, he fancies that which is rooted in legend and overgrown with the moss and ivy of antiquity. Shunning that which bears the stamp of progress, practicality, or even worse, profitability, he laments that all too often "the picturesque yields to the pocketesque" (IMC, 379).

His wife, on the other hand, is "a natural projector." Far too active for his sedentary ways, she is physically and intellectually alert to an extraordinary degree. With a passion for change and reform, she lies awake planning her future campaigns—her motto being: "Whatever is, is wrong; and what is more, must be altered; and what is still more, must be altered right away." In contrast to the narrator's taste for "old cheese," "old wine," and "old Montaigne," she relishes "all sorts of salads and spinaches . . . green cucumbers," and "new cider." The intellectual counterpart of her avidity for "the greening of America" is her interest in Swedenborgianism, spirit rapping, or any novel scheme that denies or ignores death. She lives, the narrator says, "in a continual future . . . ever full of expectations," planting new flower beds on the windswept north side of the house and setting out spindly elms whose shade she cannot live to see. But she apparently ignores the fact that her most conspicuous, if unintended, successes are due to the warmth and protection of the chimney, which causes her geraniums to bud in December and her eggs to hatch if stored too close to its radiating warmth. She "likes young company," follows the fashions in the latest magazines, reveres the dawn, seeks out new courses of study, "offers to ride young colts," and unlike Abraham's old wife, she would not scoff at the promise of bearing a child in her old age. In her attitudes she seems a generation younger than her husband. Her dislikes characterize her as vividly as do her likes, and the narrator cites her "spite against my elbowed old grape-vine, and my clubfooted old neighbor, and my claw-footed old chair, and above all . . . my high-manteled old chimney." Thus it is that the chimney becomes the pivot of the story, the means by which the opposing identities or life-styles of husband and wife assert themselves (IMC, 384–88).

Put most simply, the chimney is the past, a weighty compacted mass of history, an accretion of significant individuals, institutions, and traditions. It is as old as human society itself, mysterious in that its secrets cannot be fully fathomed, but important for what it suggests—particularly about the limited nature of human abilities and aspirations. It can be measured but the measurements give no adequate idea of its magnitude, a conception which can only "be got at by a sort of process in the higher mathematics, by a method somewhat akin to those whereby the surprising distances of fixed stars are computed." For the wife, who is in many ways a parodistic embodiment of the more optimistic beliefs about American possibilities, the chimney is an oppressive and frustrating impediment to her freedom of activity in her own house. She tells her husband that it is "like the English aristocracy" in the way it limits her freedom or blocks her progress, and her solution is simply and directly to eliminate it and thereby liberate herself (IMC, 381–82). He, of course, finds it a necessary psychological support for himself and an essential physical support for the house, and in this sense it takes on the conservative character and secular sacredness of the Constitution. Her intention is not to circumvent or minimize the past but to abolish it and thereby deny it; and in view of her husband's dependence on the past, her intention is the culmination of a series of emasculating strategies by which he finds himself "insensibly stripped by degrees of one masculine prerogative after another" (IMC, 387–88). He might fancy himself the head of the household, but his wife, who calls him Holofernes for his alleged tyranny, figuratively threatens him with decapitation if he does not capitulate.

Much more than Melville himself, the narrator seems to live by and for his authorities; and much more than Melville's wife or his

mother, I suspect, the wife in the story is a determined antiauthoritarian and exponent of the new. Hence, the cultural dimension of
the story seems to me of greater importance than the difficulties
within a particular family, the troubled union of husband and wife
being a fictional means of projecting these larger oppositions. In any
case, it is over the matter of authority and the role of the past that
the battle lines in the story are drawn.

Some readers have been led by Melville's repeated use of the
word *abolish* in his description of the wife's crusade against the
chimney to see the story as a covert comment on slavery. True, a
good part of the architectural arrangement suggests a political allegory concerned with the strains, inefficiencies, and uncertainties of a
federal democracy—as in the conservative narrator's criticism of the
house with its flow of rooms and overabundance of doors which confuse strangers and guests so that they are never quite sure of where
they are or whether the next door will lead them up, down, or out
(IMC, 389–90). But the issue of slavery can be made relevant to the
story only by insisting, as the story does not, that slavery is part of
the traditional order, part of the institutional mass of the chimney.
Of course, the idea of slavery is linked by subsequent historical circumstances to the "house divided" passage, so that we are moved by
associations unavailable to Melville when he wrote the story. My
feeling is that Melville is here concerned with an ideological split between the backward-looking and the future-oriented extremes in society, a division more basic than, though it can certainly be related
to, the division of national opinion on slavery. In associating the wife
with the idea of abolishing the chimney, Melville is trying to connect
her with the most radical and total species of reform. She is essentially an anarchist in her intent to abolish all authority, not only that
of church and state but that of her husband too. A ludicrously over-
drawn figure, she is an antinomian as well, this new woman, so im-
passioned in her quest for self-determination and emancipation from
the oppressive past.

The wife gains an ostensible ally with the appearance of Mr.
Scribe, the master mason and amateur architect, who is summoned
to ascertain the feasibility of abolishing the chimney, and here the
action in the story properly begins. After nearly twenty pages of pre-

liminary exposition, the narrator describes the pressures which finally forced him to take his stand, to guard his chimney as if it were a sacred citadel; and indeed the religious character and connotations of the chimney, as it is subjected to the examination of the greedy rationalist Mr. Scribe, dominate the rest of the story.[12]

Like the narrator and his wife, Scribe is a comic caricature, grossly inept even as he is convinced of the infallibility of his scientific methods of analysis. And like Poe's professional sleuth, the Prefect in "The Purloined Letter," Scribe is all too ready to attempt a quantitative analysis of what is clearly a complex qualitative problem. The narrator has said that the magnitude of the chimney could be apprehended only by a kind of "higher mathematics"; Scribe, with his rulers and probes, is merely a practitioner of simple arithmetic and a devotee of "the pocketesque."[13] To the narrator, as he shows Scribe the massive base of the chimney, "we seemed in the pyramids"— the mausoleum of gods as well as men and the kind of setting that to Melville, in story as well as journal, suggested the ancient origins of the idea of God.[14] Scribe sees only wasted space, and "after no small ciphering," he computes "how many thousand and odd valuable bricks" in the chimney represent the loss of "a considerable interest

12. W. B. Stein has interpreted the religious imagery of Melville's story, but with emphases different from my present reading, in "Melville's Chimney Chivy," *Emerson Society Quarterly*, No. 35 (1964), 63–65.

13. There is also a possibility that Melville might have been thinking of the very well-known French playwright Eugene Scribe (1791–1861). Known primarily as a craftsman whose well-made plays, sentimental tendencies, and bourgeois attitudes made him a prime example of middle-class efficiency and business values in the arts, Scribe's name has become synonymous with superficiality and artifice in the theater. Melville's hack architect shares many characteristics with this hack writer; in fact one of Scribe's better-known banalities, a play called *Verre d'Eau*, implicitly denigrates history by suggesting that the course of English politics was merely the result of petty details and momentary infatuations.

14. Melville had referred to the pyramids several times in his prior fiction, but the references most closely linked to the ideas of "I and My Chimney" date from his trip to Europe and the Middle East during 1856 and 1857, closely following the publication of his last short stories. Of these references the two most pertinent seem to me to be the following: (1) "I shudder at idea of ancient Egyptians. Terrible mixture of the cunning and awful. Moses learned in all the lore of Egyptians. The idea of Jehovah born here"; and (2) "As with the ocean, you learn as much of its vastness by the first five minutes glance as you would in a month, so with the pyramid. Its simplicity confounds you. Finding it vain to take in its vastness man has taken to sounding it and weighing its density; so with the pyramid, he measures the base, and computes the size of individual stones. It refuses to be studied or comprehended. It still looms in my imagination, dim and indefinite." Herman Melville, *Journal of a Visit to Europe and the Levant*, ed. Howard C. Horsford (Princeton: Princeton University Press, 1955), 118, 123.

upon a considerable principal." By Scribe's ciphering the chimney is merely the sum of its many parts, and in his judgment it could be quite profitably dispensed with. Its greatest value—its cash value— can be realized only through its destruction (IMC 391–93).

In his attack on the chimney, so carefully distinguished by its historical and mythical accretions of centuries, Scribe seems a parody of Enlightenment rationalism. His addition, subtraction, and multiplication, much as he relies on them, constitute a specious form of "higher mathematics." His name certainly suggests that Melville had in mind a kind of writer who in cultural terms filled the sort of role that Scribe fills as an architectural consultant in the story. The biblical connotations of self-serving hypocrisy in a semiofficial, quasi-clerical capacity are also important in understanding Hiram Scribe's meaning in the story. Then too, his function in serving the cause of antiauthoritarian modernism and reform must be considered. For these reasons I feel that the most readily available analogy in the mid–1850s and the one most consistent with the direction of Melville's story is that of the Higher Criticism, which sought a naturalistic explanation of the mysteries of Christianity and a scientific approach to the life of Christ. (Melville's denigration of Niebuhr and Strauss—"The deuce take their penetration and acumen"— mentioned in the discussion of "Jimmy Rose," is also pertinent here). Scribe's residence called New Petra reinforces this interpretation: it not only recalls that ancient city in the Holy Land, it also suggests the newer, more empirical basis for the forward-looking faith of America. Named for the rock which formed the foundation of the historical church, Scribe's house, however, is made of stucco and wood; yet the narrator tells us it is meant to advertise "his solidity as a master-mason." An ornamental monstrosity, "graced with four chimneys in the form of erect dragons spouting smoke," it seems also to suggest some new paganism (IMC, 395–96). Exemplifying his bad taste and dubious skill, the house advertises the fact that Scribe is a pious and pretentious fraud.

The opportunistic Hiram Scribe is clearly for hire. In apparent conspiracy with the narrator's wife, he sends a note stating that his careful measurements and subsequent calculations indicate the presence within the chimney of a concealed closet, quite possibly containing some extraordinary treasure. He concludes his note, quite irrelevantly, by asking "whether it is Christian-like knowingly to reside in a house, hidden in which is a secret closet" (IMC, 397). Scribe's Christianity would permit no mysteries, and the pressure is on the narrator from all sources to abandon the chimney. Determined to protect the chimney from destruction, even though the story of his dead kinsman Captain Dacres, an importer of orienda who built the house, lends some plausibility to the possibility of hidden treasure, the narrator refuses to probe its hidden mysteries.

His wife has not the grace to desist. She continues to talk of a secret closet, only to have her husband respond, with equal lack of grace, that it must be some "secret ash-hole" (IMC, 401). Since he cannot dissuade her from her campaign, the narrator gets his wife to agree to at least a temporary truce if Mr. Scribe, with all his instruments and measurements, cannot locate the secret closet and grace his reputation by exposing its presumed treasure. On this third examination of the chimney Scribe blunders more than ever in his calculations, and with his patience exhausted and his science defeated, he longs to try his crowbar on the chimney, brute force supplanting calm reason. Now having the upper hand, the narrator offers Scribe fifty dollars for his time and effort and persuades him also to sign a certificate affirming that his investigation found no structural weakness and no secret closet in the chimney. Pocketing only a tenth of what he hoped to gain, Scribe signs the paper, but the spirit of faction and dissension in the house continues. Wife and daughters keep up the battle for change, the narrator maintains his defense of what seems thoroughly traditional.

Their differences have, if anything, diverged even further, and no compromise is likely. The narrator has become obsessed with the idea that any threat to the chimney would be not only a threat to his well-being but an act of violence against his person as well. Warning his wife, who still goes on about the secret closet, that "infinite sad mischief has resulted from the profane bursting open of secret recesses," he invokes the myth of Momus, who complained that man should have been constructed with doors in his chest so that he could hold no secret thoughts. Implying that his wife is a faultfinder like Momus, he connects Momus' desire to break into man's breast, his wife's wish to break through the chimney wall, and the crime "of a church-robbing gossip and knave." But all this passes by his wife, who manages to confuse the reference to Momus with Moses and with mumps, for mumps seem to her part of the same category of ailments as her husband's biblical and mythological allusions or his need (and perhaps Melville's too) for privacy, mystery, and metaphor.

Having earlier stressed his agreement with the sentiments of Solomon (IMC, 396), the embattled narrator draws his final biblical reference from Ecclesiastes. His wife's hostility is leveled also at his companionable old clay pipe, a more vulnerable object than the chimney. Its vulnerability causes him to live "in continual dread lest, like the golden bowl, the pipes of me and my chimney shall yet be broken." Like the waters of life draining from the broken bowl, he feels that the end to this conflict will yet come from his wife's "terrible alacrity for improvement, which is a softer name for destruction" (IMC, 406). But he is determined not to make it easier for her by dropping his guard.

The mood at the end of the story is like that of a less than stable government threatened by a revolutionary coup. The narrator cites a series of narrow escapes from disaster: "a whole portfolio of plans and estimates" which he finds in a drawer; the presence of an outsider whom he recognizes as "a meddlesome architectural reformer . . . ever intent upon pulling down . . . old-fashioned houses"; "three savages" atop the roof attacking the chimney during his absence and nearly braining him with dropped bricks when he returns (IMC, 407). As a result, he fears to leave again and grows even more conservative in his stubborn determination not to yield in this standoff, actually a cold war over the fate of this irremediably divided household and over the nature of this uncertain union.

From the focus on a family immobilized and sundered by differences that no counselor can reconcile, the story has expanded to suggest the deeper implications of a "house divided against itself." With some partiality toward the much-abused but stubbornly resistant narrator (though not as much partiality as most critics have insisted on), Melville has dramatized the conflict between the pull of the past and a faith in the future within a kind of nucleus of the nation. These polar forces, as embodied in the repellant particles of husband and wife, have produced a stalemate, a condition where each is far more capable of reaction than of action and neither can shape his own destiny. In the broader cultural terms suggested by the story, the immediate future would have to be an enduring state of siege and defense, with the constant threat of violence and disruption hanging over this troubled union.

It would be overly trite and less than true to say that Melville in 1855 predicted the Civil War. Many less perceptive and more routine minds than his were far more pointed in their predictions. But I hope that it is somewhat less trite and a little more true to say that the immobilizing conflict which Melville detected in mid–nineteenth-century American society could not possibly be healed or purged by war, and has been perhaps even more visible in our time than in his. If one of his protagonists could be charged with immaturity, impracticality, and a lack of historical perspective that might encourage folly and lead to instability, there was still an intense vitality in her devotion to change and reform and her sometimes misplaced faith in progress. By his own estimate, the other protagonist is marked by maturity and conservatism, a man far more comfortable contemplating the securities of the past than the follies of youth or the uncertainties of the future. He has gained his solidity and stability but is largely insensitive to the challenge of change. Such oppositions are still capable of producing a house divided.

One of the more readable surveys of the issues which divided the United States in the late 1960s and threatened the stability of older, established values was Theodore Roszak's *The Making of a Counter Culture*. I find it interesting and highly appropriate that Roszak chose to preface his second chapter, which is a persuasive analysis of youthful opposition to an oppressive past and to the burden of a technocratic present, with a quotation which glosses Melville's story as effectively as it launches current inquiry:

> In the "today," in every "today," various generations coexist and the relations which are established between them, according to the different condition of their ages, represent the dynamic system of attractions and

repulsions, of agreement and controversy which at any given moment makes up the reality of historic life.[15]

In the "today" of his story, Melville tried to project the contemporary conflict of his day and succeeded in conveying to us a sense of that "controversy which . . . makes up the reality of historic life." In the deeper psychological or philosophical sense as well as in the more surface matters of taste, manners, and expression—in what current usage sums up as "life-style"—the husband and wife are a generation apart and widening the gap while sharing the house. Defending her values, she customarily addressed him as "old man," and insists, "It's I, young, I, that keep you from stagnating" (IMC, 387). She is so extreme in her beliefs and so apparently irrational in her procedures that most readers feel no more sympathy for her psychological or sociological position than for the more militant extremes of our present-day counterculture. More surprising, however, is the degree of sympathy expressed toward the male chauvinist prig who narrates the story.

Mindful of wrenching "I and My Chimney" out of its historical context, I still want to emphasize the currency of the conflict that ultimately constitutes Melville's subject—a conflict in the American mind or character capable of crippling or immobilizing society, psychomachia become sociomachia. More profound and less sensational than the myriad schizoid characteristics of Poe's "House of Usher," Melville's tale of a house divided forecasts the moral paralysis, occasional flare-ups, and ultimate ruin of a domestic cold war—a fertile field for the kind of confidence man who would ask us to trust him to bring us together again. I wonder whether the increasing interest in Melville's short fiction is not due more to the half-realized awareness that his themes strike deep into the collective American psyche (to a level that makes them recurrently contemporary) than to the remarkably innovative technical means he employed. But both theme and technique ultimately served the same purpose: to project the other side of our assumptions and hopes, to deflate our vaunted superiority to Europe, and to assert our partiality and imperfection in

15. The quotation from Jose Ortega y Gasset, *Man and Crisis*, trans. Mildred Adams (London: Allen & Unwin, 1959), 45, appears in Theodore Roszak, *The Making of a Counter Culture* (New York: Doubleday, 1969), 42.

what is from the start a fallen world of inevitable duplicity and recurrent deceptions.

For Melville these responsibilities constituted the unique province of the serious writer, compelling him simultaneously to serve as philosopher, theologian, cultural anthropologist, psychologist, redemptive icon-maker and icon-breaker. He was drawn to contemporary controversy and repelled by contemporary cant. In a society that boasted of individuality but held out its greatest rewards for conformity, that postulated freedom of speech and writing but condemned its own most estimable critics, Melville recognized the dangers and the possibilities. His strategy of going under to assert ideas contrary to the more reassuring surface of his narratives was a calculated gamble and could have led to his disgrace rather than mere neglect. His attempt to save those social and spiritual values that he felt were going under was the act of a troubled patriot and a cynical idealist. He lost in the short run, but after more than a half-century's eclipse, he may have won in the long run.

If he sacrificed the chance for immediate popularity and success forecast by *Typee* and *Omoo*, his earliest works of the 1840s (*Mardi* and *White-Jacket* more accurately forecasting what followed in the 1850s), he clearly broke new ground by devising the means which made him our first underground author. Even though he celebrated his discovery of Hawthorne as the unrecognized underground messiah of American letters, basing his praise on his own epiphanic response to Hawthorne's short fiction, Melville more completely grew into the role himself. From his review of Hawthorne's *Mosses* and the consequent correspondence of the early 1850s, Melville tried unsuccessfully to enlist Hawthorne in a kind of American *samizdat*, an underground literary community that valued private praise more than public acclaim, that developed covert means of communication to circumvent official ban, and that somewhat paradoxically hoped to gain acclaim by courting obscurity. His fifteen short stories, three subsequent novels, and much of his poetry developed in this context and survived the long years of neglect until the emergence of a readership sufficiently interested to become involved in arguing over what they mean.

Index

214